Jazz Notes

JAZZ NOTES

Interviews across the Generations

Sanford Josephson

PRAEGER
An Imprint of ABC-CLIO, LLC

A B C ☙ C L I O

Santa Barbara, California • Denver, Colorado • Oxford, England

Copyright © 2009 by Sanford Josephson

All rights reserved. No part of this publication may be reproduced, stored in a retrieval system, or transmitted, in any form or by any means, electronic, mechanical, photocopying, recording, or otherwise, except for the inclusion of brief quotations in a review, without prior permission in writing from the publisher.

Library of Congress Cataloging-in-Publication Data

Jazz notes : interviews across the generations / Sanford Josephson.
    p.cm.
    Includes bibliographical references and index.
    ISBN 978–0–313–35700–8 (hard copy : alk. paper) — ISBN 978-0-313-35701-5 (ebook : alk. paper)
1. Jazz musicians—Interviews. I. Title.
ML394.J67   2009
781.65092'273—dc22
[B]   2009009898

First published in 2009

13 12 11 10 9   1 2 3 4 5

This book is also available on the World Wide Web as an eBook.
Visit www.abc-clio.com for details.

ABC-CLIO, LLC
130 Cremona Drive, P.O. Box 1911
Santa Barbara, California 93116-1911

This book is printed on acid-free paper ∞

Manufactured in the United States of America

Includes material originally published in the following publications: *Indianapolis Star, Los Angeles Herald Examiner, American Way, Louisville Courier-Journal, Toledo Blade, ELECTRICity, New York Daily News, Cincinnati Enquirer, St. Louis Post-Dispatch,* and *The Trib.*

Dedications

"This is it. This is the big show ... The scene is steaming now, energy flowing throughout this musical atmosphere ... "
  From "The Cotton Club on Fire" by Dan Josephson

I would like to dedicate this book to my wife, Linda, and my two sons, Alex and Dan, all of whom gave me great encouragement as I embarked upon this project. Linda was both my strongest supporter and toughest critic, as she edited each chapter with her unwavering eye for detail. Alex retrieved his alto saxophone, which had languished in our attic for close to 15 years, and took it with him to his apartment in New York City to reprise the first jazz piece he had played on it, Miles Davis's "Freddy the Freeloader." The lyrical lines reprinted above are from an award-winning poem written by Dan when he was a high school freshman in 2001. He had been inspired by Ken Burns's jazz series on PBS.

This book is also dedicated to all those wonderful jazz musicians who have never received anything near the celebrity they deserve for an art form that is sadly underappreciated in the United States.

Contents

Preface ix

Acknowledgement xi

1 Seeing Stardust: "Hoagy" Carmichael 1
   *(Additional interviews with Hoagy B. Carmichael,
   Bill Charlap and Bob Wilber)*

2 The Joint Is Jumpin': Thomas "Fats" Waller 15
   (Additional interviews with Mark Shane and Aaron Diehl)

3 No Joke: Giuseppe "Joe" Venuti 23
   *(Additional interviews with Stan Kurtis, Andy Stein,
   Jonathan Russell, Aaron Weinstein and Paul Anastasio)*

4 One O'Clock Jump: William "Count" Basie 37
   *(Additional interviews with Butch Miles, T. S. Galloway,
   Howard Alden and Marvin Stamm)*

5 Melody Man: Jonah Jones 51
   (Additional interview with Warren Vache)

6 God Is in the House: Art Tatum 57
   *(Additional interviews with Barbara Carroll,
   Marian McPartland, Aaron Diehl and Mark Shane)*

7 Road Warriors: Earle Warren, Howard McGhee, 65
   and Milt Hinton
   *(Additional interviews with Phil Schaap, Joe Temperley,
   Noreen Grey Lienhard, Warren Vache and Derek Smith)*

8	The Happy Singer: Helen Humes *(Additional interviews with Norman Simmons and David Leonhardt)*	89
9	The Religion of Bebop: John Birks "Dizzy" Gillespie *(Additional interviews with Jeanie Bryson, John Lee and Cecil Bridgewater)*	95
10	Classical Jazz: George Shearing *(Additional interviews with Dick Hyman, Rio Clemente, Bill Mays and Marvin Stamm)*	103
11	Take Five: Dave Brubeck	111
12	Duke's Man: Norris Turney *(Additional interviews with Art Baron, Joe Temperley, Virginia Mayhew and Norman Simmons)*	117
13	Singing the Chords: Jon Hendricks *(Additional interviews with David Leonhardt, Janis Siegel)*	131
14	Traveling with King Louis: Arvell Shaw *(Additional interviews with David Ostwald, Ed Polcer, Bria Skonberg and Gregory Rivkin)*	141
15	Beyond the Big Bands: Gerry Mulligan *(Additional interviews with Bill Charlap, Bill Mays and Rich DeRosa)*	155
16	Musical Chameleon: Dick Hyman *(Additional interviews with Randy Sandke, Bill Charlap and Dan Levinson)*	163
17	Flying High: Maynard Ferguson *(Additional interviews with Don Sebesky, Randy Sandke, Denis DiBlasio, and Steve Schankman)*	173
18	Growing Up With Jazz: Stanley Cowell	181
19	Horn of Emotion: David Sanborn	187
20	Jazz Ambassador: Billy Taylor	193
Index		199

Preface

When I was a college student in the early 1960s at the University of Missouri, I attended concerts featuring the Dave Brubeck Quartet and Sarah Vaughan. Jazz was something I listened to occasionally, but it did not occupy any special place in my life.

Then, in September 1965, I accepted a job as a writer in the public information office of the Far Eastern Area headquarters of the American Red Cross, located on an army base, Camp Zama, about 45 minutes from Tokyo. In Japan, I saw Duke Ellington, Oscar Peterson, Ella Fitzgerald, Herbie Mann, and numerous other well-known jazz artists in concert and in clubs. More importantly, however, I frequented many jazz coffee houses and bars, in both Tokyo and outlying towns. At each of these coffee houses/bars, there were hundreds of record albums, and whatever record was currently playing was featured in a special spot of prominence. The venues had various names, but I do remember that two of them, in the Shinjuku section of Tokyo, were named the Village Gate and the Village Vanguard, after the famous jazz spots in New York's Greenwich Village.

By the time I returned to the United States in December 1967, I was an enthusiastic jazz fan at a time when jazz had hit rock bottom in this country. In January 1968, I moved to New York City to accept a reporting job with Fairchild Publications and was disappointed by the scarcity of places to hear the music.

I often went to a midtown eastside spot called The Apartment, where you could listen to the pianist Marian McPartland, or to the Top of the Gate on Bleecker Street in Greenwich Village, where you could listen to the pianists Bill Evans and Junior Mance or the vibraphonist Gary Burton for the price of a drink. I also listened to traditional jazz at Jimmy Ryan's on West 54th Street, and I remember traveling down to the East Village to see the bassist Charles Mingus at a daunting place called Slug's in the Far East.

Gradually, jazz began to experience a mild resurgence in New York, and in the 1970s I frequented clubs such as the Half Note on West 52_{nd} Street, Boomer's and Sweet Basil's in the Village, as well as the venerable Village Vanguard, which had survived the lean years and was (and is still) going strong. In my day job as editor of the *Daily News Record*, Fairchild's trade newspaper for the men's apparel and textile industries, I had met a publicist by the name of Peter Levinson. When a fledging new newspaper, *The Trib*, was launched in January 1978, Peter called me on behalf of one of his clients, trumpeter Maynard Ferguson. *The Trib*, he said, had agreed to interview Ferguson, who was appearing in concert and was hot at the time (he had recorded the theme from the movie, *Rocky*), but the paper hadn't assigned the story yet. He suggested I call the entertainment editor and offer to interview Ferguson and write the story. I did write a feature on Ferguson for *The Trib*, and that blossomed into a weekly jazz column for the paper, which lasted only three months. (I think I received one check, for $25.) But it gave me some clippings and enabled me to embark upon a modest freelance career writing about jazz musicians in the 1970s and 1980s. (Peter Levinson, who had amyotrophic lateral sclerosis, died in October 2008 at the age of 74 from injuries sustained in a fall in his Malibu, California, home).

This book is based on 18 articles that were published in various newspapers and magazines. In addition, there are two chapters that have never been published: "Road Warriors," which chronicles the hardships faced by three African-American musicians while traveling on the road in the 1930s, 1940s, and 1950s, and "Jazz Ambassador," which features pianist/composer Billy Taylor, who was interviewed in the original articles on Fats Waller and Art Tatum. All of the previously published articles, plus "Road Warriors," have been updated with new interviews—with the original artist if he/she is alive, and with others who may have encountered or been influenced by the initial subjects.

This book is clearly not meant to be a comprehensive work. Some wonderful jazz musicians are not included, and the selection of those interviewed has been somewhat random. But I hope it reflects my love of the music and the wonderful musicians—both famous and obscure —who create and perform it, often to smaller audiences than they deserve.

Acknowledgement

I would like to thank the concert and record producer and photographer, Hank O'Neal, for assisting me in the early days of this project. Hank, who is interviewed in the original article on Joe Venuti in "No Joke" (Chapter 3), gave me suggestions regarding the 'Update' interviews and provided me with a long list of phone numbers and e-mail addresses that would have otherwise been difficult, if not impossible, to find.

David Demsey, coordinator of jazz studies at William Paterson University in Wayne, New Jersey, was extremely helpful. Not only did he facilitate interviews with two of his faculty members, Cecil Bridgewater (on Dizzy Gillespie) and Rich DeRosa (on Gerry Mulligan), but he also helped me locate a link to the late trumpeter Howard McGhee—pianist, vocalist, and educator, Noreen Grey Lienhard, who reminisces about McGhee in "Road Warriors," (Chapter 7).

Author David Margolick, who had read my original article on Arvell Shaw, introduced me to David Ostwald, the tuba player/attorney who shares his considerable knowledge about and love of Louis Armstrong in "Traveling with King Louis," (Chapter 14).

Thanks also to Meghan Thornton and Zooey Tidall in the public relations department at Jazz at Lincoln Center for assistance in contacting some of the Center's artists.

I am also indebted to tenor saxophonist Virginia Mayhew, interviewed in Duke's Man: Norris Turney (Chapter 12). She helped me connect with other links to Duke Ellington and alto saxophonist Norris Turney: trombonist Art Baron, baritone saxophonist Joe Temperley, and pianist Norman Simmons.

Finally, although previously mentioned in the preface, I would like to again acknowledge and thank the late Peter Levinson, who was instrumental in helping advance my fledgling freelance writing career in the 1970s and 1980s.

CHAPTER 1

Seeing Stardust: "Hoagy" Carmichael

The Book Nook, an establishment on the Indiana University Bloomington campus in the 1920s, derived its name from its previous function as a purveyor of books. But by 1924 it had been transformed into a combination candy store and refreshment parlor that is now assured a spot in American musical history because Hoagland (Hoagy) Carmichael designated it the official birthplace of "Stardust."

"The first eight bars of 'Stardust' were whistled by me as I walked across the campus of Indiana University," Carmichael recalled in a 1979 interview. "I was on my way to bed, but I was intrigued with the melody, and I had the sense to know that I might forget it. So I went back to the college hangout I'd just left called the Book Nook and pounded on the door until Pete Costas, the proprietor, let me in so I could play the strain on the piano and see the chord structure to enable me to remember it. That was a wise move."

"Stardust," it is safe to say, has become one of the most popular songs of all time. Lyrics were added later by Mitchell Parish, and Hoagy Carmichael went on to become one of the most prolific American songwriters.

In June 1979, he was honored at a special Newport Jazz Festival concert at Carnegie Hall,"The Stardust Road: A Hoagy Carmichael Jubilee," and he agreed to be interviewed in his room at the Plaza Hotel. The 79-year-old singer-songwriter-musician spoke and moved about gingerly, and his memory admittedly often failed him. If he paused long enough, however, sipping Old Rarity Scotch and munching on Cracker Jacks, the recollections began to come back.

For instance, his first association with the blues occurred when he was growing up in Westside, Indianapolis. "There was a young man there who played the Jew's harp," he said. "We guys in our late teens would follow him around at night because he liked to play while he was walking along the street. It fascinated me, and by late 1918, I was playing some of those blues notes on the piano. By 1919, I was using some of the blues notes for dance music in Indianapolis. My bands at that time consisted of a big smiling Irishman playing drums and myself." Carmichael didn't remember the drummer's name. "I wish I could, but it was too far back," he admitted.

A little while later, Carmichael heard a record made by two black musicians, again anonymous, that left an enduring impression on him. "The beat they employed," he recalled, "was more pronounced than I'd heard before. It's impossible for me to explain the beat on paper, but I immediately started playing a tune on the piano. I not only played the melody note, but I used my middle finger to hit the grace notes in order to emphasize the beat. I called it 'sock time.' The effect was quite a departure from ragtime. This, plus blues, helped me enter the new Dixieland jazz era."

Carmichael used these new techniques while leading a dance band in Bloomington during his university days in the early 1920s. Then he met a tenor saxophonist by the name of George Johnson, "and he told me about the Friars Inn in Chicago and the way the band there was playing. The music was partly a takeoff from the music that the original Dixieland bands played and the music that some of the New Orleans boys played on the Mississippi riverboats."

Carmichael went to Chicago and heard the Friars Inn band, with Bix Beiderbecke on cornet, and King Oliver's band, with Louis Armstrong on trumpet. "They were great," he smiled. "At this point, what we call 'jazz' was born. It was easy for me to pick it up and add it to my own style of playing."

The natural temptation was to coax from Carmichael some comparison between Beiderbecke and Armstrong. He obliged, but not without hedging a bit. "Bix Beiderbecke's playing can't quite be compared in style to the playing of Louis Armstrong," he said. "They were both great, but it's impossible for me or practically anyone to explain why. You have to listen to one, then listen to the other, and then make up your own mind."

Carmichael had been destined to become a lawyer. He received his degree from Indiana and went to work for a Miami law firm, but the real turning point in his life came about nine months after his arrival in Florida. "Someone told me there was a new record out made by cornetist Red Nichols," he recalled, pausing to add that, "Red was a great exponent of jazz from the state of Indiana. I went to hear it at a record store across the street. It was a great record, and something told me I should get back into the music business and try to write more music. So I packed up and was off to the good old state of Indiana where I started my songwriting career."

That career produced an almost endless list of songs. In addition to "Stardust" were, among others, "Georgia On My Mind," "Rockin' Chair," "Lazybones," "Lazy River," "One Morning in May," "Heart and Soul," "Hong Kong Blues," "Small Fry," "In the Cool, Cool, Cool of the Evening," "Skylark," "The Nearness of You," and "Buttermilk Sky."

"People ask me if I have a favorite song," he said, "and I have to honestly tell them, no. The reason is that I find melodic phrases in many different songs that please me, and I hate to choose one song as a favorite, eliminating those bits and pieces."

When "Stardust" was first performed it was played at a fairly fast tempo; later it became a dreamy ballad. Although it has been recorded by countless musicians and singers, one of the most popular renditions was the record made in the 1930s by Artie Shaw and his band, believed to have sold more than 2 million copies in five years, according to David Ewen in *All the Years of American Popular Music* (Englewood Cliffs, NJ: Prentice-Hall, 1977).

Another of Carmichael's more celebrated hits is "Georgia on My Mind." It was written in 1930, his first composition after coming to New York, but it enjoyed a rebirth in 1960 when Ray Charles won a Grammy with it. It was revived again in 1978 when Willie Nelson included it on one of his albums, which was also titled "Stardust." In 2008, Nelson made a CD with jazz trumpeter Wynton Marsalis called "Two Men With the Blues." Its selections included both "Georgia on My Mind" and "Stardust." Carmichael acknowledged that "Georgia started from scratch and built very slowly into a solid piece."

The composer had strong opinions about vocalists. His favorites were Nat King Cole, Ray Charles, Mildred Bailey, Bing Crosby, and the Mills Brothers. Although Rudy Vallee had a hit recording of "Lazybones," Carmichael never liked him. As for Frank Sinatra, "He's good, but he's overrated. As to the people who have made a lasting impression with vocalization of my songs," he said, grinning, "I must say that with some of my more or less offbeat comedy or jazzy stuff, I think I'm the best."

Carmichael was only half serious about his own ability as a singer, but it was just this combination of folksiness and humor that propelled him into the national consciousness as a performer in the late 1940s and early '50s—first in the movies and later on radio and television.

His movie career began when "the wife of Howard Hawks sent me a telegram and asked me if I would play the part of Cricket in 'To Have and Have Not' with Humphrey Bogart and Lauren Bacall," Carmichael said. "I accepted and enjoyed the experience very much. Fortunately, one picture led to another, and I had a happy 10 years of moviemaking."

Carmichael's appearance on the screen also had an ebullient effect on the sale of his records. His success as the piano player, Cricket, and its afterglow were best characterized by a report that appeared in *Newsweek* on June 4, 1945:

> Carmichael was a deadpan sensation. With hair still falling over his forehead, he dispersed philosophy, played the piano, and sang 'Am I Blue' and his own 'Hong Kong Blues.'
>
> All this came as a shock to many admirers of 'Stardust,' who had thought Carmichael was retired—if not dead. Rushing out to the nearest record shops after the picture's release late last year, they began buying Carmichael.
>
> Since 'Hong Kong Blues' was incorporated in an earlier album, Decca pressed extras to try to meet a demand that, by last week, had reached 25,000 daily.

Carmichael followed "To Have and Have Not" by playing a singing taxi driver in "Johnny Angel," which starred George Raft. The most memorable films to him, however, were "Love Song" with Dana Andrews and Merle Oberon, and "Young Man With a Horn," a film based loosely on the life of Bix Beiderbecke. Adapted from the Dorothy Baker novel of the same name, it starred Kirk Douglas.

Although Carmichael has written more than his share of hits and professed no favoritism among his creations, he did seem to have a soft spot for his lesser-known compositions. Some of these, such as "Baltimore Oriole" and "I Walk With Music," were performed at the Carnegie Hall concert, prompting the composer to confess to the audience that "I heard so many songs I didn't think I wrote that I wanted to see if I was in the right hall."

At the time of the interview, Carmichael was splitting his time between two homes—one in Palm Springs and the other in West Hollywood. His place in the annals of American music, though, was a permanent one. Fellow songwriter, Alec Wilder, in his book, *American Popular Song, The Great Innovators, 1900–1950* (New York: Oxford University Press, 1972), said, "I think it is unquestionable that Hoagy Carmichael has proven himself to be the most talented, inventive, sophisticated and jazz-oriented of all the great craftsmen."

The meaning of Carmichael's music to musicians was best exemplified in comments made by George Masso, a trombonist who performed at the Carnegie Hall tribute. "When I first started to play, 'Stardust' was one of the tunes I played and liked," Masso said. "I played it as solo when I made my first public appearance. I've been playing it ever since."

(Adapted from an article that appeared in the *Indianapolis Star Magazine*, September 30, 1979.)

UPDATE

Hoagy Carmichael died of a heart attack at home in Rancho Mirage, California, in December 1981. He was buried in Bloomington, Indiana. His songs continue to be recorded by a seemingly endless list of pop vocalists, including Norah Jones, James Taylor, Barry Manilow, and Willie Nelson.

Numerous attempts to create and produce a Broadway show based on his music have so far failed. His music is preserved at Indiana University, however, where the Hoagy Carmichael Room has been established. It contains a collection of material that includes approximately 750 sound recordings, 30 films/videos, 520 scores/pieces of sheet music, 1,000 photographs, 1,000 newspaper clippings, and 300 pieces of correspondence.

Hoagy Bix Carmichael

"Dad always had this stuff rolling around in his head," said the musician's son, Hoagy Bix Carmichael. "He would always say, 'These songs are lying around on the keys. All you have to do is find them.'"

That comment by the senior Hoagy Carmichael is lodged in the memory of his son, who recalled that "Dad would stop the car occasionally to write down something. When you think back, he wrote very few songs on order. They used his songs in movies, but he didn't sit down like a Broadway musical guy and write 16 songs. He had 16 songs, but they were all different. There was no formula. That's *why* his songs are so different."

"It's wonderful when you think how he really stayed away from convention in many ways," he continued. "I don't know if you could name another performer who had his own television programs, his own radio shows, who wrote songs for himself, wrote songs for movies, sang the songs in the movies, and acted in the movies. He had a part in the TV series, 'Laramie' just because he wanted to be in a western."

Hoagy B., who has had a long career as a TV producer, primarily in public television, has made several attempts to mount a Broadway show based on his father's music, but "all the pieces have never come together. We're working on yet another idea," he said, with more of an air of resignation than optimism.

In a brief biography written for the Indiana University Digital Library, musical historian John Edward Hasse observed that "with rare exceptions, until Carmichael came along, songwriters were a separate group from singers." Hasse, curator of American music at the National Museum of American History at the Smithsonian Institute, characterized Carmichael as "something of a modern minstrel. (He) was one of the first singer-songwriters in the age of mass media. He paved the way for later such performing writers as Bob Dylan, Billy Joel, Bruce Springsteen, and Joni Mitchell."

Hoagy B. agrees with that assessment. "I guess that Irving Berlin sang a couple of his songs in movies, but Dad went out on the road and played all over the place and, often, just with himself on piano," he said. "It was all about singing his own material, only the way he could sing and play it. And he had quite a following. It was inevitable that other people were going to do it. The Billy Joels of the world were going to come along. But Dad did blaze that trail." In 2004, Jsp Records released a four-CD set entitled, "Hoagy Carmichael The First of the Singer Songwriters: Key Cuts 1924–1946."

Although he still does a lot of work relating to his father's music, Hoagy B.'s passion today is tap dancing. He is a member of the board of trustees of the American Tap Dance Foundation and is very involved in Tap City, a festival held every July at Symphony Space in New York City, during which hundreds of tap dancers gather from around the world to teach, study, perform, and collaborate.

His partner in promoting tap dance and emerging dancers is Pamela Koslow Hines, the widow of the extraordinary dancer-actor-singer, Gregory Hines. "Since I was a teenager, I always loved tap dancing," Carmichael said. "It's music played with your feet, not your hands. In addition to the festival, we have a lot of children's programs, and we have a preservation program. Greg gave us all of his films and tapes, and we have a touring company."

When asked whether there is another Gregory Hines on the horizon, Carmichael singled out a young tap dancer named Kendrick Jones, describing him as, "already one of the great tap dancers alive. Greg introduced him to me." Jones, who is originally from Michigan, is currently studying at New York University's Tisch School of the Arts. In May 2007, he was performing in a production of City Center's Encore! series entitled, "Stairway to Paradise." Michael Feingold, writing in *The Village Voice*, described him as a "hitherto unknown tap dancer (who) evoked Bill Robinson."

Of all the artists who interpret Carmichael's music today, his son prefers the jazz pianist Bill Charlap, who released a CD in 2002, entitled "Stardust: The Music of Hoagy Carmichael" (Blue Note), that included such guest artists as Tony Bennett, singing "I Get Along Without You Very Well," and the late Shirley Horn, singing "Stardust."

Coincidentally, when asked who he would *like* to see record his father's songs, Hoagy B. doesn't hesitate: "Tony Bennett. He could do it."

Bill Charlap

In the best popular songs, said jazz pianist Bill Charlap, "the lyrics drip off the notes ... or vice versa." That combination comes together perfectly, he believes, in the Carmichael song, "The Nearness of You," which would explain why it has been recorded by so many popular singers, ranging from Norah Jones to James Taylor to Maureen McGovern. "I think it's a very natural coupling of lyrics and melody in the sense that the lyric on its own doesn't have a lot of depth, but when you put it with that music, all of a sudden it has more layers to it," Charlap explained. "I think it is, in many ways, Hoagy's most natural 'songwriterly' lyrical utterance. That's one of the reasons people relate to it. It doesn't sound 'period,' and it will accept many different types of interpretations. There's a folkish quality to it."

There was also a folkish quality to Carmichael, although Charlap believes it was a cultivated persona: "I don't believe he really was an 'aw, shucks' guy. He was too smart to just be that simple." He *does* feel Carmichael helped lay the groundwork for today's singer-songwriters. "One of the things that's different in our world of popular song today is that the performer and composer are one and the same—it started with people like Carole King."

Unlike many of today's singer-songwriters, however, Carmichael's recordings, Charlap pointed out, were not necessarily the definitive interpretations of his songs. "I don't think there's a more definitive version of a Beatles song than the way the Beatles did it. The same is true for Stevie Wonder," he explained. "But there are probably better recordings of Hoagy's songs than his recordings. His singing isn't great singing any more than Fred Astaire's voice was an incredible voice. But it's a perfect interpretation theatrically."

The decision by Charlap to record an album of Carmichael's compositions in 2002 was timed to coincide with what would have been Carmichael's 100_{th} birthday. Carmichael, Charlap said, "was, in a sense, a very unique composer. He's something of a jazz man in that he was kind of a focal figure of white jazz in the '20s. Hoagy loved Beiderbecke. Beiderbecke was, in a sense, Carmichael's younger/older brother. And he was, in a way, the fountainhead of an entire movement of playing. He was a highly influential figure in terms of his melodic invention. Carmichael's music sounds as if he codified Bix improvisations into compositional ideas. If you listen to the verse of 'Stardust' played at the original tempo, it's essentially a written Beiderbecke chorus. However, when you get to the chorus, in my mind, that's Louis Armstrong, the *real* center of American music. Bix, for all his brilliance, is, compared to Armstrong, an offshoot."

If a Broadway show based on Carmichael's music were produced, Charlap believes "it would have to be a revue. Carmichael is not like (Richard) Rodgers, (Cole) Porter, (Jerome) Kern, and others. He wasn't a major theater composer. So, it wouldn't be a show with a book. That's not to say a good revue couldn't be launched, but it takes a very special talent to make something like that fly."

In producing the Carmichael album, "Stardust," Charlap was careful "not to make an album of all ballads or up-tempos. The tempos are almost always dictated by the lyric and the ability to sing the song. Even though I'm not singing them, I'm singing them in my mind. But I broke that rule with 'Jubilee.' I played it much faster than it was originally intended. I lost the original feeling of the song to achieve something else for the trio."

The album, says Charlap, was "by and large just a matter of a mixture of things you can't *not* do, like 'Stardust' and 'Skylark' and finding things that perhaps might be fresh to people's ears, like 'I Walk with Music.'" Horn's lingering, nine-minute-plus interpretation of 'Stardust,' Charlap acknowledged, might not have pleased "the purist faction. They might not have felt it was the 'Stardust' that they think Hoagy did. I think, of course, they're wrong because (Shirley Horn) was the extension of Billie Holiday in many ways. You couldn't get a more profound reading than what she did."

Bob Wilber

In the 1960s, soprano saxophonist-clarinetist Bob Wilber had recorded a successful three-set album of Irving Berlin tunes called "All By Myself" on the Monmouth-evergreen label. "The producers had been very pleased with this album," Wilber recalled, "so they asked me to pick another favorite composer and devote a record exclusively to his music."

"I picked Hoagy Carmichael because I thought he is a major composer and his relationship with jazz is such a strong one," he said. "He's an ideal composer to highlight on a jazz label, which Monmouth-evergreen was." The resulting album, "The Music of Hoagy Carmichael," was released in 1969 and was nominated for a Grammy Award.

Selecting the album's 14 tracks was a challenge. "First of all, I got the list from the ASCAP (American Society of Composers, Authors and Publishers) of all of his compositions because there were so many," said Wilber. "I had to pick and choose. The ones I finally ended up with were among my personal favorites. Some of them were big hits, of course, like 'Stardust' and 'Georgia on my Mind,' but others were rather obscure. One of the tunes I always loved was a tune called 'One Morning in May.' Hoagy told me that was one of his own favorites, although it was never a big hit."

"The Nearness of You" is treated as an instrumental on Wilber's album. "I thought of that as being a great soprano saxophone solo, so I did it that way," he said. There was, however, a need for some vocals. "The producers, Bill Borden and his partner, Steve Marvin, asked me what we were going to do about vocals because so many of these songs have marvelous lyrics." Wilber's response revived the career of Maxine Sullivan, a popular big band vocalist in the 1930s and 1940s. "I said, 'I think Maxine Sullivan would be perfect,' and they said, 'Maxine Sullivan, is she still singing?' I was working in New York at Eddie Condon's jazz club quite a lot in those days, and Maxine would come in, and she had a little pocket trumpet, and that's what she wanted to play. She didn't want to sing. We would always say, 'C'mon, Maxine, sing a song,' and she *would* sing, and she still sounded wonderful."

"Maxine had been devoting most of her time to community projects, but I knew that she could still sing. So they agreed, on my recommendation, to use her for some of the songs," Wilber continued. Sullivan, handling the material with the tender delicacy that had become her trademark, did five songs on the album: "Georgia On My Mind," "I Get Along Without You Very Well," "In the Cool, Cool, Cool of the Evening," "Rockin' Chair," and "Skylark."

"It really started a whole new career for her because this record got so much notice," said Wilber. "From that day on, she started working, and she worked right up to the day she died (in 1987, just short of her 76_{th} birthday). She became constantly in demand, not only in the United States but all over the world."

Wilber, at age 80, remains very active as a musician, arranger, and concert producer. In the spring of 2008, he was a judge at Jazz at Lincoln Center's "Essentially Ellington" contest that encourages high school jazz bands across the country to play the music of Duke Ellington. In the summer of 2008 he traveled across Europe with French vibraphonist Danny Doriz to present a 100_{th} birthday tribute to Lionel Hampton, and in May 2009 he was scheduled to present a 100_{th} birthday tribute to Benny Goodman in New York with the Lincoln Center Jazz Orchestra.

But it was a chance encounter in 1972 at the Broadmoor Hotel in Colorado Springs that perhaps had the greatest impact on Wilber's career. Dick Gibson, a jazz producer and fan, would hold an annual jazz party every Labor Day weekend in Colorado. "Dick's idea," Wilber remembers, "was that he wanted his audience to be saturated with jazz for three days and nights."

"Now, it was Monday afternoon of Labor Day weekend. By then, the crowd was getting a little exhausted because they'd been listening to jazz for hours and hours. So, Dick came up to Kenny Davern and I and said, 'You guys go out there and do something. I want to wake this audience up. Why don't you do something with two soprano saxes?' Kenny and I had sort of known each other, but we hadn't had a chance to play together. So, we very hurriedly put together an arrangement of Duke Ellington's 'The Mooch.' It was a very good little band—Dick Hyman on piano and either Milt Hinton or George Duvivier on bass. We went out there and started to play 'The Mooch,' and we finished up with the two sopranos playing way up at the top in thirds. We finished with this huge big sound, and the audience rose up on their feet—all 700 or 800 of them—and applauded. We couldn't believe it. We thought, 'We must have something special. We energized the whole audience.'"

"So, that was the start of 'Soprano Summit,'" Wilber said. "The next step was putting together a recording. We thought about who we wanted on the record. The two sopranos would, of course, double on clarinet. We had Dick Hyman on piano, George Duvivier on bass, Bobby Rosengarden on drums, and Bucky Pizzarelli on guitar. We picked a mixture of old songs—many of them going back to the '20s—and some newer songs. It did quite well, and we made a lot of albums."

Wilber and Davern recorded eight Soprano Summit albums. The first two were on the World Jazz label, and subsequent recordings were on Chiaroscuro, Jazzology, Concord, and Fat Cat's Jazz. In 1994, Chiarascuro reissued a two-disc set of the first two Summit Soprano recordings. The selections range from Wilber originals, such as "Chalumeau Blues" and "Grenadilla Stomp," to standards, such as "Everybody Loves My Baby" (Spencer Williams-Jack Palmer) and "Lover Come Back to Me" (Sigmund Romberg-Oscar Hammerstein II).

The unusual aspect of all this, Wilber pointed out, is that "Kenny and I were very different people. Somebody once described me as the thinker and Kenny as the inspirational guy. I would do the arranging, but everything was on the spur of the moment with him. It worked because we admired each other's talents so much. He was Dionysian, and I was Apollonian, but we both had a great love for the traditional jazz of Jelly Roll Morton, Louis Armstrong, Sidney Bechet, Pee Wee Russell—all those magic names from the '20s. But we also didn't want to copy old records. So, I was the arranger-composer, and Kenny, while he didn't arrange, had some great ideas for tunes. Whatever it was, we had this magic thing that when we played together, we always stayed out of each other's way."

"Sometimes I would play the lead on the soprano and Kenny would play the lead on the clarinet or on the other soprano," Wilber continued. "We used go from soprano to clarinet, from clarinet to soprano.

I played the little curved soprano and Kenny played the straight one. It was a unique group, and inevitably we began to experiment. I took up the alto, and Kenny took up the C melody saxophone. And we had some different sounds with those instruments."

Wilber's earliest recollection of music was as a three-year-old: "I heard 'Mood Indigo' by Duke Ellington. I still have a fondness for that original recording, which must have been done in 1931." Wilber was nominated for another Grammy for doing the soundtrack of the Francis Ford Coppola movie "Cotton Club." "The credits at the end of a movie go on forever, so I was able to use the whole three-minute original recording behind the credits. I got my beloved 'Mood Indigo' into the movie," he said.

The idea for the 2009 birthday tribute to Benny Goodman surfaced during a lunch Wilber had with the trumpeter Wynton Marsalis, who is the director of Jazz at Lincoln Center. "I said to Wynton, 'Benny Goodman was not only a great musician, he was a pioneer in giving work to black musicians at a time when blacks and whites didn't mix in the band. You were either a white band or a black band. Benny hired Teddy Wilson on piano; he hired Lionel Hampton on vibes; and later on, there was Charlie Christian on guitar. I think a tribute to Benny Goodman would be a great idea for a concert.' About a month later, I got a call from Wynton saying, 'I think we're going to do that tribute to Benny Goodman, and I want you to lead the band like you're Benny Goodman. I'm just going to sit back in the trumpet section.'" The Benny Goodman Centennial was held on May 28 to May 30 in the Rose Theater and featured the Jazz at Lincoln Center Orchestra.

"Benny Goodman was one of my first idols when I started to play the clarinet at age 13," said Wilber. "This was in the early 1940s, and music was all over the place. The clarinet was a major instrument in jazz in those days. The two major figures were Benny Goodman, who came up in 1935 and really introduced the swing era, and, later on, this young, handsome clarinet player named Artie Shaw, who had some big hits in the later '30s like 'Begin the Beguine.'"

"You either had to be a Benny Goodman fan or an Artie Shaw fan," he added. "There were heated arguments about who was the best. Benny was always my favorite between the two. He was a great inspiration to me in my formative years, and he continued to be an inspiration as I was developing in my profession. But Benny was a character. There were a lot of things that were part of his personality that could be difficult."

One of the problems in the early Goodman band was the popularity of drummer Gene Krupa. "Gene Krupa was this handsome young drummer who was a great visual act," Wilber said. "His hair would bounce all over the place. He was like a matinee idol for all these teenage girls, and he'd get tremendous applause whenever he took a drum break or a solo. Well, Benny didn't like that."

Another story involved a Goodman performance at the Paramount Theater. "A young vocalist who had just left Tommy Dorsey was on the bill with Benny's band, a guy named Frank Sinatra. To Benny," he pointed out, "a vocalist was somebody who sat on the stage and then, during the arrangement, would get up and sing one chorus of the tune and sit down. Well, Frank gets up, and Benny looks around and says, 'What's going on?' because these teenage girls were screaming and jumping up and down. Benny did not like to be out of the spotlight."

Wilber, though, appreciated Goodman's musicianship "because he was a superb clarinetist, a hot jazz player, and a great bandleader. He knew how to rehearse a band, and he knew how to pick musicians who would give him the best results. So I did many tributes to him in later years." One tribute, in particular, sticks in Wilber's mind. "He was 75 years old in 1984, and I noticed that nobody was paying any attention to his birthday. I got in touch with the New Jersey Jazz Society and suggested some kind of tribute to Benny. There was an opening on a Saturday night in August at a park out in New Jersey. Benny was going to be the guest of honor. The governor of New Jersey was going to fly in by helicopter to present Benny with an all-time musical award. But, typical Benny, he calls a week before the concert and cancels. We went ahead with the band to do the tribute, and his lawyer, who was also a clarinetist, was at the concert. He recorded the whole thing on a pocket recorder, and the next day I get a call. 'Hey, Bob, Benny here.' I said, 'Benny, we really missed you last night. Everything was great. The concert was a big success. There must have been 5,000 people there. They loved it. But you weren't there.' And he said, 'Well, Bob, I haven't been well, and I haven't played for about a year. I was afraid if I came, the public and the critics would try to get me up on stage to play.'"

"Well, Benny was a perfectionist; he wouldn't do anything that was second rate. So I could understand why he wouldn't come," said Wilber. "He listened to the tape, and he heard his classic songs like 'Sing Sing Sing' and 'Don't Be That Way.' And then he heard the roaring applause of the audience, and he said, 'They're applauding my music, but I wasn't there.' He started making plans to get back in shape. The inspiration was that he didn't want anyone else playing his music."

CHAPTER 2

The Joint Is Jumpin': Thomas "Fats" Waller

Sonny Greer, a veteran drummer who spent 27 years with the Duke Ellington Orchestra, swore that Fats Waller wrote "Ain't Misbehavin'" on the back of a menu from Jack Dempsey's restaurant on Broadway. "He sold it for $25," said Greer, "and Fats, Andy Razaf (Waller's lyricist), and I spent the money on Chinese food and a bottle of gin."

Whether or not Greer's account was accurate, it is symbolic of the enigma surrounding Thomas "Fats" Waller, a man who was both genius and clown and who went largely unappreciated by the general public until a production celebrating his music opened on Broadway in 1978. It is not entirely impossible that Waller could have written perhaps his most popular tune on the back of a menu in order to eat. Pianist Chuck Folds recalled that the guitarist Eddie Condon always called Waller "a last-minute guy." That, said Folds, was because "he had all this music bubbling inside of him."

To say that Waller is revered by contemporary jazz pianists would be an understatement, but thanks to the popularity of "Ain't Misbehavin,'", the Tony Award-winning Broadway musical, that approbation spread beyond his musical peers. Just as the movie, "The Sting," brought the brilliant ragtime composer, Scott Joplin, to the public's attention in the early 1970s, "Ain't Misbehavin'" reawakened the world to Fats Waller in the latter part of the decade.

During "Ain't Misbehavin's Broadway run, Luther Henderson, the musical supervisor who also played jazz piano, pointed out that "there are a lot of people who never heard of him, but somehow or other—just like Scott Joplin—they realized they've heard his music all their life. Nobody had to learn 'The Sting,' and nobody has to learn 'I'm

Gonna Sit Right Down and Write Myself a Letter' (a song Waller recorded but didn't write). It's part of the fabric of our culture."

Waller played a style of piano known as stride, which was the chronological successor to ragtime. The big difference between stride piano and Scott Joplin, said Henderson, was "that Fats is closer to a gutty beat rather than just having to do with the rhythm of things. Joplin was very classical—his rags had a lot of European influence. The difference is really a matter of degree. All of it is music to be happy to. It has a spirit and a joy about it. But stride is a little bit more diversified than the oompah-oompah of ragtime."

Folds believed the divergence between ragtime and stride was "basically a rhythmical difference. In both ragtime and stride piano, the key thing is the feeling. Stride became a looser thing. The essential vocabulary's the same except that ragtime is limited to simplistic harmonies—they're very nice, but they're limited, considering what came later," he explained. "By the time Fats Waller started recording for Victor in 1935 that was the beginning of the swing era, so Fats swung, whereas most ragtime doesn't by our standards." Pianist Dick Hyman, who has recorded the complete piano works of Scott Joplin, believes "there are points in the evolution of ragtime into stride when you simply can't decide which it is. Stride was kind of a cousin of ragtime. The left hand fingers were busier. It involved wider leaps, and the whole feeling of the music was swingier."

Waller, who was born in New York City, started playing piano professionally at age 15, usually as an accompanist for blues singers or on recording sessions with big bands. He was a protégé of the two other great stride pianists of the 1920s—James P. Johnson and Willie The Lion Smith. However, Waller took stride piano a step further, adding elements of felicity and grace that hadn't existed before.

"Ain't Misbehavin' " consisted of 22 musical scenes utilizing music either written by or performed by Waller. There was no attempt, however, at blatant mimicry. "Really perceptive people who come to see 'Ain't Misbehavin' will realize there is very little imitation per se of Fats Waller going on," Henderson said. "What is going on is an expression through us of the spirit of Fats Waller. I think we should be proud of having achieved that." It is precisely that spirit that has kept the Waller flame alive among respected members of the jazz fraternity even though he died in 1943.

Pianist and educator Dr. Billy Taylor wrote the dissertation for his doctorate in music education on the history of jazz piano. To him, seeing Waller was "a wild experience. Too many people have been interested in him as an entertainer. That makes it too easy for people to overlook the tremendous depth of his playing. The man was one of the all-time great jazz artists."

Hyman compared Waller to Louis Armstrong in that "the public thought he was a clown. He was an amusing entertainer, a personality of great charm. The public didn't understand that what was fundamental to all that was being a great musician. Even when Fats was being his most clownish on his records, you hear fine piano playing. 'Ain't Misbehavin' ' isn't only about his piano playing; it's about his charisma as an entertainer."

It would be difficult to find a jazz pianist who hasn't been touched in some way by Fats Waller. Taylor said Waller was "the first jazz influence I had. An uncle of mine in Washington, D.C., took me over to his house and played Fats Waller records for me. All I had heard up to that point were classical composers—Mozart, etc. This turned me around. Then Fats Waller came to town and played solo piano. That really blew me away. I went out and bought all the records I could afford."

Pianist Brooks Kerr, a protégé of Duke Ellington, said Waller "was really the first influence on me. RCA put out a two-record set in the mid '50s of transcriptions he made in 1935 and 1939. This was my initial exposure to him. Those two records got me started and launched me into the world of Fats Waller. It's a world I've reveled in and thrilled at ever since. Fats had a way of approaching the keyboard—he had a wrist and finger technique that would make all the notes within a chord sound like chimes. His left hand had a certain drive and a bounce that was all his own. He loped across the keyboard the way a champion horse does."

Waller's resurgence was helped by the release of the Broadway cast album by RCA in 1978, along with a complete Fats Waller series, produced by the record label's Red Seal division. Kerr took note of what he perceived as a "Fats Waller explosion. I was at a screening of jazz films at the New School for Social Research," he said. "The audience was 75 percent black and mostly under 30. The black kids clapped very perfunctorily for the giants—Duke (Ellington) and Louis (Armstrong)—because they figured they were people they were supposed to understand. Then they showed the Fats film, 'The Joint is Jumpin.' When that thing was over, there was a rush of applause, almost a standing ovation. With the intensity of the discovery, everybody just went 'wow!' They were just absolutely bowled over. It does my heart good to see a response as spontaneous and strong as that."

The show, "Ain't Misbehavin,' " was a nonstop entertainment executed charismatically by five very talented performers. They were backed by an onstage piano player, a role sometimes taken by Henderson, and a six-piece jazz band. Before opening on Broadway, the show had a trial run at an off-off Broadway site called the Manhattan Theatre Club.

To Henderson, who had been associated with a previous failed attempt to bring jazz to Broadway ("Dr. Jazz"), the attraction this time was "simply the music of Fats Waller. It was like ice cream and cake to me. What distinguishes Fats Waller is not only his stride technique but his ability to communicate through composition and performance. In this show there are no lyrics that are sung that aren't really reflective of Fats Waller's attitude on life. That is what sets him apart. He was a communicator par excellence." Henderson unabashedly acknowledged that "all of us who play piano have to come by Fats Waller." But two who are constantly cited as direct Waller descendants are Art Tatum and Count Basie.

Tatum, considered by many to be the greatest jazz pianist ever, went beyond stride, developing a facile, fleeting style that was uniquely his. According to Kerr, Tatum "called Fats his favorite all his life. People couldn't understand that, because Art had so much more facility. But Art wouldn't have developed the touch he had if it wasn't for Fats. Art Tatum worshipped Fats Waller."

Basie was considered an excellent stride pianist, although he didn't often display this facet of his musical skills. In fact, he would often make light of his own stride abilities, saying only that "I've tried a little of it. I'm not great at it." At the mention of Fats Waller, however, Basie broke into a grin, praise pouring from his mouth: "He's my man. He was just so fine. I'm very happy he's getting recognition. It's about time."

(Adapted from an article that appeared in the *Los Angeles Herald-Examiner*, July 9, 1978.)

UPDATE

Mark Shane

Mark Shane came to Fats Waller through Teddy Wilson. "Teddy had a tremendous influence on me, and I wanted to find out what Teddy was listening to," he said. "I knew it was Fats Waller and Earl Hines, but I started out with Waller, getting a good collection of his stuff. I found the essence of swing in Waller. And Waller led me back pre-Waller to James P. Johnson. I found a real kindred spirit in James P. Johnson."

All of which is somewhat odd because Shane, who grew up in Metuchen, New Jersey, was first exposed to jazz through a more modern player, Ahmad Jamahl. "When I was 13, a neighbor had records of the Ahmad Jamahl Trio with Israel Crosby on bass and Vernal Fournier on drums, and that just knocked me out," said Shane. "Ahmad is just an amazing player. That trio thought and breathed and played as one. I thought Israel Crosby was something descended from heaven, and then, later, I discovered that he had driven the Fletcher Henderson Band."

Shane met Bob Wilber in the 1980s, and when Wilbur asked Shane who he liked, Shane listed Hampton Hawes, Ahmad Jamahl, and Hank Jones. "He almost had a heart attack because what he needed to hear was Fats Waller and Teddy Wilson," Shane said. But after joining Wilber's band in the 1980s, Shane was exposed to "a lot of jazz I hadn't heard. We did a tour for the Smithsonian Jazz Repertory Ensemble. I had to play all this stuff—Jelly Roll Morton, James P. Johnson, Fats Waller, Teddy Wilson. It was a tough job because you had to play in everybody's style."

In 2008, Shane released a CD called "Fats Lives" (Amber Lake). He described it as "kind of a Fats Waller party on CD. There's one composition that's not Fats, but it's in the Fats spirit. I sing on a number of things. It's a fun album. Nothing I do is verbatim, but the feeling is there." Selections range from the predictable "Ain't Misbehavin'" and "Your Feet's Too Big" to "Lonesome Me" and "That Rhythm Man." The rest of the band includes saxophonist/clarinetist Dan Levinson, trumpeter Jon-Erik Kellso, bassist Brian Nalepka, and drummer Kevin Dorn.

"Fats was a tremendous entertainer, which kind of let him slide his art out to the people easier," Shane said. "Because he was such an attractive entertainer, he got to people through his humor, which was a great thing. If he'd have come on in a more standoffish way, he wouldn't have reached the people."

Shane finds a "delicacy" in Waller, and "yet, a very controlled and sure touch, a great touch. And I found something of Fats in Teddy, and I found something of Fats in Art Tatum. I'm sure they had a tremendous mutual respect. At the same time, I was attracted to one of Fats Waller's disciples, Count Basie. A lot of things center around Fats. Fats as a mentor and Fats as a student of James P. Johnson. And that also led me to listen to Duke Ellington's work as a pianist. Anyone who hasn't heard Fats Waller is missing a tremendous part of this puzzle. I say puzzle because we're all trying to get a mental picture of what went on. Fats and his disciples; Fats and his forebears. I guess he was kind of the center of the hub. You can't escape Fats's influence on the entirety of the American music scene—from jazz players to the average person on the street who just likes to tap his foot."

Shane began his career playing piano for dance bands in and around New York City. He also had an extended stay as the house pianist at the New York jazz club, Eddie Condon's. That, he said, was a great experience: "We had Roy Eldridge playing next door at Jimmy Ryan's. That was cool. I also played with Vic Dickenson there. Talk about being able to get a feeling from the old masters. The only way to get it now is from recordings."

Trumpeter Eldridge and trombonist Dickenson weren't the only horn players who inspired Shane. Other horn influences, he said, include tenor saxophonists Coleman Hawkins, Ben Webster, and Chu Berry and alto saxophonist Johnny Hodges. "All of these people affected my melodic concept. As a matter of fact, some of them I heard and was listening to before I ever got into seriously listening to some pianists." He continues to listen to and play with present-day saxophonists who "have a real mainstream classic sound, such as Scott Hamilton and Harry Allen." He also mentioned other tenor influences as early Lester Young, Herschel Evans, and Buddy Tate. "I always loved that big tenor sound. I have a student who's in a music school. I always tell him, 'You've got to get grease in your playing. Once you're into it, you've got it in your soul. It pours out of you."

Shane recalled a teacher he once had who gave him an important exercise, although he didn't follow it the way the teacher had intended. "He said, 'This is what I want you to do. I'll give you a Charlie Parker solo. Memorize the solo. Sing the solo. Come back to me next week; bring the recording; put the recording on; sing with the recording. If you miss, you've got to go back and do it again.' After two lessons, I said, 'Wait a minute. I don't even like Charlie Parker.' But he had taught me everything I needed to know. Just get into somebody and learn their style. Memorize some solos; memorize some phrases. For me, it was big tenors and piano players who were hooked into the mainstream of jazz."

Aaron Diehl

Fats Waller's left hand, said young pianist Aaron Diehl, "was a whole rhythm section by itself. So, he had the horn section in the right hand and the rhythm section in the left hand, and he brought it all together. The way it influenced me is the importance of the left hand and how it can really help in terms of keeping that rhythm going and alive. When you're playing jazz piano, especially by yourself, you've really got to have that rhythm; and it's got to feel good. Fats always made it feel good."

The 23-year-old Diehl grew up in Columbus, Ohio, and started playing classical piano when he was seven years old. He made the transition into jazz in his teenage years. He was greatly influenced by his high school band director, Todd Stoll, who happened to be a friend of trumpeter Wynton Marsalis, who is the artistic director of Jazz at Lincoln Center. When Diehl was in high school and part of the Columbus Youth Jazz Orchestra, Stoll invited Marsalis to come to Columbus and do a master class with the band.

"At that master class," Diehl recalled, "Wynton gave me his number and said, 'Call me sometime.' " As a result of that meeting, Diehl was invited to join the Wynton Marsalis Septet on its summer European tour in 2003. In 2002, as part of the Columbus Youth Jazz Orchestra, Diehl had been recognized as one of the outstanding soloists at Jazz at Lincoln Center's annual Essentially Ellington competition. A 2007 graduate of Juilliard who now lives in New York City, he released his first CD, "Mozart Jazz," on the Japanese Pony Canyon label in 2006. "The melodic material," he explained, "is from Mozart, but I adapted it into a jazz setting."

In August 2008, he performed at the Caramoor Festival in Katonah, New York, and in the fall of 2008 he was scheduled to appear at one of the Jack Kleinsinger Highlights in Jazz Concerts at the Tribeca Performing Arts Center in New York.

The 2003 tour with the Marsalis Septet was an enlightening experience, he said, "because it was very difficult keeping up with those guys. I was really left in the water, so to speak, to swim for myself. But all of them were very gracious and tried to help me out. They were very patient; I think I will really cherish that experience."

If he had to single out one living pianist who has had the greatest influence on him, Diehl said it would be the 90-year-old Hank Jones, who he described as "stately, noble, having just a great sound on the piano. He understands the complete tradition of jazz piano, and there is an extreme amount of elegance and taste in his playing."

CHAPTER 3

No Joke: Giuseppe "Joe" Venuti

"I once had a piano player who kept his foot on the loud pedal all the time. I asked him to please take his foot off the loud pedal because of the ringing of the piano. After 20 tunes, he finally took his foot off, and I nailed his shoe and his foot to the floor." That's a vintage Joe Venuti story, one of many related by the jazz violinist to Dick Cavett on his TV talk show in 1978. When Joe Venuti died on August 14, 1978, at the approximate age of 80, the world not only lost a virtuoso jazz violinist but one of the most adept practical jokers of all time.

No one really knew Joe Venuti's age because there were so many versions of when and where he was born. Most sources agree that he was actually born in 1898 in Italy. Zoot Sims, a tenor saxophonist with whom he often played and recorded in the 1970s, characterized Venuti as "the only guy I knew who lied about his age and made himself older because he thought it was more commercial." Bucky Pizzarelli, a guitarist and friend of Venuti's, thought 80 was the correct age, but he said Venuti "kept everybody guessing. Sometimes he'd give you a phony figure; then he'd give you another figure."

Giuseppe Venuti began his professional career around 1920, teaming with another Italian immigrant, Salvatore Massaro—later known as Eddie Lang—to form a popular violin-guitar duo. He recorded with many now-famous musicians in the 1920s, including Red Nichols, Bix Beiderbecke, and Hoagy Carmichael, and in 1929 he joined the celebrated Paul Whiteman orchestra.

It was during his tenure with Whiteman that Venuti's reputation as a prankster spread, and many of the Venuti stories so popular among musicians began in that era. Some of his most notorious stunts were performed at the expense of the brilliant but troubled cornetist Beiderbecke. One of those was recounted on the Cavett show. The Whiteman band was on a cross-country tour. It had given a concert in Omaha, "and then we had a heavy jaunt from there to Phoenix," Venuti recalled. "We had to cross the desert. That night the conductor came by and said, 'Boys, make sure all your windows are closed. We're coming to a heavy sandstorm.'"

"Bix had never been west of Davenport, Iowa. He had a stateroom, and he was drinking it up pretty good. In those days, they had two buckets of sand at each end of the car as fire extinguishers. So they had 64 buckets. We dumped the whole 64 buckets in Bix's compartment. When he got to the dining room the next morning, he said, 'You know boys, I been traveling this route all my life, but that's the heaviest sandstorm I've ever been through.'" In another Beiderbecke story, the cornetist, again under the influence of alcohol, fell asleep in an empty bathtub. Venuti filled the tub with water, added Jell-O, and waited for Beiderbecke to wake up, encased in purple gelatin.

Every musician had his own favorite Venuti anecdote. Pianist Jimmy Rowles had two pet stories—one about the bass players and another involving flour and a tuba. The bass player prank was probably Venuti's most celebrated and one he apparently pulled more than once. He would phone at least a dozen bassists and book them for an engagement, asking each one to meet him at 50_{th} Street and Broadway in New York or Hollywood and Vine in Los Angeles. Then, as all the bassists began congregating on one corner, a jubilant Venuti would be watching the scene from a hotel window. The flour-in-the-tuba prank occurred in the Whiteman band. Venuti dumped five pounds of flour into the tuba and, as he described it, "When Paul Whiteman came out to direct the band we looked like a bunch of snowmen."

Rowles also recalled the time Venuti was with "a young band he didn't like, so he just abandoned them. He just left them somewhere in Minnesota." Pizzarelli remembered an incident in the 1970s at Michael's Pub, a New York club where Venuti appeared regularly: "One night Joe had a lot of his relatives over from Italy, and they were all sitting around the table. The comedian Henny Youngman came over and started to tell a few jokes. Nobody laughed because nobody understood him. It was a typical Joe Venuti situation. After Youngman told three or four jokes, he looked up at Joe and said, 'Does anybody speak English here?' and Joe nonchalantly answered, 'No.'"

Another Pizzarelli favorite involved Teddy Wilson and occurred at Dick Gibson's Jazz Party, an annual jam session held in Colorado

Springs: "Teddy Wilson was sitting around late one night. We were all sitting in the room there. Teddy asked Joe to play some melody that he had heard him do once before. Joe played about eight measures, and Teddy dozed off. So Joe quietly went to bed, and the next morning when he woke up, Teddy was still sitting in the seat sleeping. So Joe took his violin out and played the end of the song as Teddy woke up."

For all his clowning, though, Venuti was deadly serious about his music, and he wouldn't tolerate inferior musicians. "He never kidded around playing the violin," said Gil Wiest, owner of Michael's Pub. "He was really a tiger about getting the right musicians. He'd really get upset when some booking agent slipped in some musician who wasn't up to snuff."

Hank O'Neal, an independent producer who recorded Venuti on seven albums for the Chiaroscuro label, said Venuti "would eat you alive if you performed badly. He would whack the music stand if someone made a mistake." However, he had one weakness musically. "Once in awhile he would call and say, 'C'mon, let's make a record. I got this great new guitar player and this great new bass player and this great new drummer.' They were always Italian. Joe had found an Italian trio, and he wanted to help them."

Bing Crosby told of a similar incident in his autobiography, *Call Me Lucky* (Simon and Schuster: 1953). It dealt with Venuti's desire to import a bass player from Italy for the band he was leading at the time. According to Crosby, "Joe went down to Ellis Island, fetched such a character back with him and put him in his band for opening night at Guinan's Playground." Everything apparently went well until the Italian bassist got hungry. When he couldn't get the waiter to bring him a steak, he asked Venuti what to do and, according to Crosby, Joe said, "The next time he comes near the bandstand, pick up your bass fiddle and hit him over the head with it." The bass player did as he was told, a riot ensued, and Guinan's Playground closed—never to reopen.

Venuti and Crosby had first developed a camaraderie when both were with the Whiteman band, and the friendship was to last well beyond those years. Venuti had broken up his own band during World War II because it was too difficult to find musicians. After the war, Crosby hired him for his radio show. "Joe was to Crosby what Phil Harris was to Jack Benny," said O'Neal. "He was comedy relief, and he always had a featured part. That relationship lasted until the mid-1950s, or whenever Crosby's radio show went off the air. Then Joe did what studio work he could find in Los Angeles; he also worked in Las Vegas. But by 1960–61, jazz had died, and people had just forgotten about him."

Venuti began to resurface in the late 1960s, making a triumphant appearance at the Newport Jazz Festival in 1968. "The most interesting thing," O'Neal said, "was how he was able to come back and play at such a ferocious level of intensity after going through a period when nobody really gave a damn about him.". Venuti was able to stage a comeback, in O'Neal's view, merely "because it just became fashionable to find old folks and pay attention to them again. But the main reason why it worked with Joe Venuti is that he didn't play like old folks. He could still blow you away."

Pizzarelli, when asked to characterize Venuti's style of playing, simply said: "You can't put a label on what Joe did. It was classical. It was jazz. It was everything. What Joe and Eddie Lang did was the basis for all the duets that came later—guitar duets, guitar-violin, guitar-piano. They were like a little band by themselves, but they were forever making up all kinds of tunes and ditties on other songs, well-known songs. Plus, they'd play their own songs. You know, when we did a Bix Beiderbecke revival in 1975, Joe knew all the parts by heart. He never even looked at the music."

Venuti first started appearing at Michael's Pub in 1973, the same year he recorded his first album for O'Neal at Chiaroscuro. "He was a superlative musician," said Wiest. "He used to run them all ragged. He could play so fast it looked as if his hands were standing still." Sims said Venuti "could play classics, anything. Everywhere he went, symphony players would come to watch him." Jascha Heifetz, the classical violinist, reportedly threw a party for the Whiteman band just so he could hear Venuti play. "He was great to record with," Sims continued. "He could lead without being offensive. He played so fast that I couldn't keep up with him."

Venuti lived an exuberant life. He had settled in Seattle in the 1970s, but, according to O'Neal, "he loved to come to New York, and he loved good Italian restaurants." Venuti, said Rowles, "always seemed like the indestructible man." Despite a bout with illness in 1970, it was a shock to his friends to see him finally surrender to failing health in early 1978. "The last time he was here was in April 1978," said Wiest, "and we were packed every single night. It was as if everybody knew this might be the last time they could see him. He couldn't stand up very long; he sat through most of the engagement—that was very unusual."

During that same visit to New York, O'Neal had a couple of recording projects planned. "For the first time since I've ever known him he was due down at the studio on a Saturday morning, and he called and said, 'I'm just too tired. This cold just won't go away.'"

Pizzarelli played in one of Venuti's last professional appearances. "It was at the Mondavi Winery in Napa Valley on June 25, 1978," he said. "It was just a rhythm section and Joe Venuti, and he sat down throughout the performance." O'Neal remembered that "the last night I talked to him was his last night at Michael's Pub. There was some pest there who was really bothering him, and Joe was downright polite to him. In the old days, Joe would have whacked him one."

(Adapted from an article that originally appeared in the *Los Angeles Herald Examiner*, November 26, 1978).

UPDATE

STAN KURTIS

Stan Kurtis only met Joe Venuti once—in 1978 at Michael's Pub. "I do recall him sitting," Kurtis said. "I remember him sitting off the bandstand in a little spot, so I talked to him. I told him, 'Joe, I'm interested in jazz.' He said, 'Come up to my hotel.' I took the information, but I guess I got busy freelancing. Unfortunately, I wasn't smart enough to take advantage of that experience. Maybe I was afraid he'd be too tough on me. But he was pretty friendly to me in that one little moment."

A classically trained violinist, Kurtis discovered Venuti almost by accident. "I had always done a lot research in acquiring sheet music, not so much popular sheet music, but arrangements for violin" he said. "My source was the Adelson Music House and a particular woman there named Diana Herman. Her knowledge of music was encyclopedic. She would pull out different things for me, and one day she offered me these orange-colored sheets. They were the original sheets of Joe Venuti transcriptions, and I bought a few of them. They sat on my shelf for a long time until a number of years later when I met the pianist Dick Hyman on a gig. He was conducting for Bobby Short at the Rainbow Room, and I was in the string session. It was the first time I had met Dick Hyman, and he told me he was going to be playing at Michael's Pub, so I went down to hear him, enjoyed his playing and wanted to play with him. I mentioned I had these charts of Venuti, and he said he thought there could be a project for an album."

The project took five years from beginning to end, but the result was "Runnin' Ragged, The Classic Hot Jazz Duets by Joe Venuti," released in 1987 on the Pro Jazz label. The album is out of print, but used copies are available on such Web sites as www.amazon.com and www.ebay.com.

The album was well received. P. E. McCorry III, writing in the January/February 1989 issue of *Horizon* magazine, said Kurtis and Hyman "translate Venuti's sizzling compositions into a brilliant, high-spirited disc. Smoking jazz classics like 'Black Satin,' 'Cheese and Crackers,' and 'Wild Cat' will fling even the most reserved listener right off the couch... Give 'Runnin' Ragged' a listen. There's nothing ragged about it."

When Kurtis and Hyman performed some of the selections live prior to the release of the album, Whitney Balliet, writing in the August 25, 1986, issue of *The New Yorker*, said, "Kurtis caught Venuti's sound and came close to his insuperable swing, and all that was missing was the guitar and the bass saxophone that Venuti used on some of his original recordings."

Kurtis graduated from The Juilliard School in New York in 1973, and, in order to earn a living, began playing club dates and society parties in orchestras fronted by such leaders as Peter Duchin and Lester Lanin. "I became aware of jazz to some extent," he recalled. "One of the gentlemen who really introduced me to playing jazz was Edward Finckel, a pianist and educator who had a summer chamber music camp in Vermont called Point Counterpoint. During my last year at Juilliard he had me come up to the summer camp and teach. He wrote variations on 'Willow Weep for Me' for me to play. That was really my first performance in the jazz style. We may have jammed on a couple of other things, but that's what got me interested in jazz."

Another influence was a Juilliard teacher named Hall Overton, a pianist-arranger known for arranging for Thelonius Monk's big band concerts in 1959 and 1963. "He played recordings of the jazz violinist Stuff Smith for us in class," Kurtis said. "When he played those recordings, he pointed out the qualities—how great his rhythm was. Then I jammed a little with Hall Overton on 'How High the Moon.' His basic advice to me was, 'Keep listening.' "

Kurtis, who is currently a member of the New York Pops Orchestra, has appeared with a variety of artists, ranging from classical to pop. His venues have varied from the Washington Chamber Symphony to the Broadway show orchestras for "Fiddler on the Roof" and "Beauty and the Beast" to accompanying such pop artists as Tony Bennett and Tom Jones. However, his two most celebrated achievements to date have probably been his "The Tango Project" album for Nonesuch Records and his violin solo in the tango scene of the movie, "Scent of a Woman." "The Tango Project" was Number 1 on the *Billboard* Magazine classical charts and was named "Record of the Year" in 1982 by *Stereo Review* magazine.

In his jazz performances, Kurtis has adopted the Venuti technique of playing four strings at once, wrapping his bow, upside down, around the violin. "When I play, there's a little bit of Venuti in there," he acknowledged. "His inflections were very clear. I listened to his early recordings in making 'Runnin' Ragged.' I didn't attempt to copy them note for note, but I got the ambiance of that era."

Andy Stein

Andy Stein didn't plan to carry on the legacy of Joe Venuti. He was a founding member of Commander Cody and His Lost Planet Airmen, playing baritone saxophone and violin and adding a swing flavor to what was essentially a country rock band. "We were out in Berkeley," he recalls. "Billy C., our leader, had a varied taste in music and first turned me onto old jazz in general. I was intrigued by the idea of swing violin, and a friend of mine, an amateur chamber player, gave me a Joe Venuti tape, so I got into Joe a little bit."

That was in the late 1960s. It wasn't until 1979 that Venuti resurfaced in Stein's consciousness. "I came back east to stay," Stein said, "and hooked up with Vince Giordano (bass saxophonist and banjoist who leads a band called the Nighthawks). I started getting serious about the Venuti arrangements and started copying them, which became preparation for a 1984 spring session that became part of my first album, 'Goin' Places' (Andy Stein Music). I was copying the arrangements and working them out with guys who could do that—Vince and guitarist Howard Alden. I think it was 1984 when I put together my first Andy Stein Hot Blue 5. Those cuts on that first album of mine with Dick Wellstood on piano and Vince and Howard and Chuck Wilson on alto or clarinet—that was a really slick swinging group."

But it was a 1985 gig with Alden that really propelled Stein to the forefront as a proponent of Venuti's music and style. "I started a duo Tuesday night thing with Howard at a little club called the Left Bank on Amsterdam and 81_{st} Street in New York. John S. Wilson of

The New York Times reviewed us. We thought we were doing Django Reinhardt and Stephane Grappelli, but he compared us to Joe Venuti and Eddie Lang."

"One of the most unusual, fascinating and, as it turns out, timeless jazz groups of the '20s and '30s was the violin and acoustic guitar duo of Joe Venuti and Eddie Lang," Wilson wrote, adding that, "This type of jazz duo has been taken up in its purest form by the violinist Andy Stein and the guitarist Howard Alden...And they are brilliant...Mr. Stein is dazzling in the dashing complexities that Venuti created on such tunes as 'Wild Cat' and 'Goin' Places,' " (*The New York Times*, February 28, 1985).

Alden disagreed slightly, claiming that he and Stein worked on *both* Venuti-Lang and Reinhardt-Grappelli interpretations. "Andy had put together a quartet that was intentionally trying to do some of the Venuti-Lang stuff, and we worked up several of the Venuti-Lang duets—things like 'Wild Cat' and 'Wild Dog,' " Alden said. "We did about two or three of those things regularly. We did a lot of that repertoire, and we did some Reinhardt-Grappelli stuff as well."

Although the Left Bank gig went on for about a year and a half, Alden left after eight months and was replaced by Frank Vignola. Alden also did some four- and five-piece concerts with Stein. "Once in awhile I'll revisit that stuff," Stein said. "The violinist Aaron Weinstein and I did a couple of those things on a cruise last year."

Wiest read the Wilson review and asked Stein to do a Joe Venuti tribute at Michael's Pub. Then, said Stein, "I got labeled as a Venuti guy. What the hell! I love the stuff. And I followed up 'Goin' Places' with another album, 'Doin' Things' (Andy Stein Music)." Since the early 1990s, Stein has been a regular on National Public Radio's "A Prairie Home Companion" show, playing violin and baritone saxophone. He is recognized as among the most eclectic of musicians—encompassing jazz, rock, tango, gypsy, country, and classical.

In fact, Stein maintained that Venuti was actually influenced by the classical composer, Claude Debussy. In January 1926, the classical violinist Jascha Heifetz had a hit record with his arrangement for violin and piano of a Debussy piano prelude called "The Girl with the Flaxen Hair." Venuti's "Doin' Things" was released in May 1926, which Stein believes was clearly affected by the Debussy piece. "Venuti continued to quote that piece for the rest of his life," Stein said. "On my record, I have a tune called 'Romantic Joe,' which is Venuti's successful attempt at writing a Debussy-like classical piece for violin and piano; and it's beautiful. That's Venuti writing classical music."

No Joke: Giuseppe "Joe" Venuti

Jonathan Russell

Trombonist Dan Barrett was taking a solo during a romantic ballad being sung by Becky Kilgore at the 2008 North Carolina Jazz Festival in Wilmington, North Carolina. Suddenly, a toy monkey dropped in front of him and started making a screaming noise.

According to Jonathan Russell, who had released the monkey, Barrett "started laughing, and then he started playing to the monkey through the trombone. Becky snatched it up and started singing to it. Dan was hysterical." Twelve-year-old Russell is undoubtedly the youngest descendant of Joe Venuti. Although also influenced by Leroy "Stuff" Smith and Stephane Grappelli, Russell admires Venuti's "ability to pretty much go anywhere on the violin and still make it sound good." Grappelli, he said, had "a sweeter tone. Joe Venuti had a rich tone and a bit of a bite. Stuff Smith was the opposite of Stephane Grappelli; he always had a bite. Venuti is somewhere in between Grappelli and Smith."

If it seems unusual for a 12-year-old to talk with such authority about legends of the jazz violin, it's because this 12-year-old has played with some of their contemporaries. On a January night in 2008 at Centenary College in Hackettstown, New Jersey, Russell appeared as a special guest with a trio that included the 82-year-old Pizzarelli and 86-year-old pianist John Bunch. The highlight of the concert was a moment when Bunch and bassist Phil Flanigan left the stage and Russell and Pizzarelli collaborated on a hauntingly uplifting version of the Johnny Green classic, "Body and Soul." Sitting on a sofa barefoot in his parents' Riverdale, New York, apartment, Russell acknowledged that "it's pretty cool to have a connection like that." Aware of the many Joe Venuti stories, Russell maintained that he only knows the story about the bass player prank in detail. During a break at the North Carolina Jazz Festival, he and his parents were walking around Wilmington when they spotted a magic store. "We were looking for something to buy for the people who took care of our pets when we noticed this monkey that made a screaming noise when you flung it," he said. The rest of the story unfolded in true Joe Venuti fashion.

Russell's mother, Eve Weiss, a classically trained guitarist, said that saxophonist Ken Peplowski "was willing to take the blame for the whole thing. But, of course, they knew it was Jonathan. What has been so wonderful for my husband, Jim, and I is to see all these musicians

Jonathan really reveres who have just kind of adopted him. They don't treat him like a kid; they treat him like just another musician. He and Bucky were interviewed the night of the jazz festival by a TV station there. They asked Jonathan, 'What's it like to play with an 82-year-old?', and Jonathan said, 'it's just like playing with anybody else.' Then they asked Bucky what it was like to play with a 12-year-old, and he said, 'He's a musician.'"

Russell was already taking violin lessons at the age of five when he heard a band playing "Bei Mir Bist Du Shein," the Yiddish classic made into a hit by the Andrews Singers. He began improvising on it during a lesson, and according to his mother, his violin teacher said, "I'm calling Andy." "Andy" was Andy Stein.

Stein, said Weiss, "is a great character. He has lots of personality, a great sense of humor, and he's a great teacher also. Added Russell: "He always shouts at me, 'Why did you play that note; that note's not any good; make it flatter.' It's all about the intonation to him. That's what he nails me on all the time." Stein, explained Weiss, "has taught Jonathan style and attitude; he hasn't taught him jazz the way they do it in the conservatories. He has never taught him modes or scales, but he works on phrasing with him."

"At one of his camps, for most of the classes he didn't have us reading different tunes; he just had us listening to different artists," said Russell. Stein, Weiss agreed, "is really of the tradition of listening and that's how you're going to learn."

Jazz came to the violin, Russell said, because "in Storyville in New Orleans the noise was too loud for the neighbors from the wind and horn instruments, so they just put a violin in there instead." Lester Young, Coleman Hawkins, and Stan Getz are his favorite saxophonists. He said he doesn't really listen to trumpet much, but "I *do* listen to Louis Armstrong." Another influence has been veteran cornetist and trumpeter Ed Polcer, who once played with Benny Goodman and owned Eddie Condon's jazz club in New York, where he led the house band in the 1970s and 1980s.

"Ed has been Jonathan's mentor," said Weiss. "Jonathan has been playing with bands since he was six years old—all different styles and abilities. A lot of these guys that Jonathan has been playing with, such as Ed and drummer Joe Ascione, all started at a young age, and they were out gigging by the time they were 12 or 13. So I feel like Jonathan is in good company, and I think they kind of feel an empathy with him because they see themselves when they were young." It is that kind of experience, she believes, that turned Jonathan into a jazz musician."

Aaron Weinstein

In 1998, thirteen-year-old Aaron Weinstein had been messing around with jazz on the violin, but he had never taken any formal music lessons. He was rummaging through his parents' music collection in their home in the Chicago suburb of Wilmette and came across a cassette tape of Joe Venuti that happened to be in one of the drawers. Weinstein played it, and it literally changed his life. "It was the first jazz recording I heard," he recalled. "It was a live concert played in Italy around '77. 'Sweet Georgia Brown' was the first tune on the record. This was my first exposure to jazz violin and to jazz—it just happened to be through a violin player. The way Venuti played—he had such authority that every note he produced struck me as the absolutely definitive note to have been played at each given moment. He was really playing jazz on the violin. Venuti was genuinely using that swing vocabulary—the same type of swing language that Benny Goodman played on the clarinet. That's one of the things that made Venuti great. He was able to successfully synthesize the jazz vocabulary into a 'violinistically' accessible language."

Weinstein was born in 1985; Venuti died in 1978, "so we kind of missed each other," he said. But Venuti was the inspiration for what has become a flourishing jazz violin career. *Downbeat* Magazine has called Weinstein a "rising star," and Nat Hentoff, writing in *The Wall Street Journal*, said his playing heralded "the rebirth of hot jazz violin."

After first hearing Venuti, Weinstein said he "became obsessed. I went back and got all his earlier recordings. And, along the way, I was able to check out the other music that was going on at the time." Venuti, said Weinstein, is, "my hero. I can't say enough good things about him. He swings as much as any jazz musician, regardless of instrument. The way I see it, Venuti was the first violinist to really get it."

"I had the pleasure of spending some time with the great violinist, Paul Anastasio, who was one of Venuti's students for a time," Weinstein continued. "Paul told me that Venuti had this technique he would call the capo. He would use his first finger as if it were a guitar capo. In other words, he was playing a lot with closed positioning—and that was his approach to playing in all those flat keys."

According to the Web site, www.fiddlingaround.com, this technique was "groundbreaking; Venuti had a sharp, bright tone, excellent intonation and an ability to play in any key, anywhere on the violin. He developed what has become known as the 'violin capo' technique, using his first finger as the root and fifth of whatever key he was playing in."

Weinstein went on to attend and graduate from the Berklee College of Music in Boston on a four-year scholarship. His early exposure to Venuti, though, was, in his opinion, the best education he could have received. "Many of my peers at Berklee were first exposed to jazz through the music of John Coltrane or Charlie Parker," he said. "Unfortunately, it seemed like some treated it as a chore to have to go back in time and study anything that was around before bebop."

"Coltrane," he added, "was a protégé of Charlie Parker, who came out of Lester Young, who came out of Frankie Trumbauer, who was a contemporary of Joe Venuti. If someone is attempting to play modern jazz but is unfamiliar with the roots of the music, I can't imagine that anything worthwhile will result. Doing that would be like trying to speak intelligently about a book without reading it."

Weinstein listens and learns from all instruments. "Learning jazz from listening only to violinists is musically equivalent to asking only Republicans about politics—both provide merely one point of view. Jazz is not instrument-specific," he said.

Asked about saxophonists he likes, he replied, "I love Lester Young, and Bud Freeman is also a guy I like a lot. The musicians I gravitate toward all tend to be melodic players. Each of my favorite players seems to have a few extraordinary and distinctive musical elements that make each of them so attractive to my ears—maybe they have a unique harmonic sense or they swing really hard or they have a special way of phrasing or utilizing dynamics. That's how I learned the most, from listening to these guys who really play."

The night he was interviewed, in January 2008, Weinstein was playing at the Bickford Theater in Morristown, New Jersey, with one of those "guys who can really play"—guitarist Pizzarelli, who, as indicated earlier, often played with Venuti. "I love how Bucky plays, but I also love playing *with* him," Weinstein said. "He's a guitar player, and I'm a violin player, but I can learn so much from him because Bucky is one of the great masters of this music, and I value my time with him."

Earlier that day Weinstein had recorded a new CD with Pizzarelli for Arbors Records. "It's Bucky's record," he said. "Dick Lieb wrote tremendous string arrangements. It's just beautiful music—it's that mentality of respecting the melody. It's Bucky, bassist Jerry Bruno, and I'm with a string quartet—two violinists, a cellist, and viola." The CD, titled "So Hard to Forget," was released in early 2009.

Weinstein is aware of all the Venuti stories, and even related a couple of them himself. But he is concerned that "with any larger-than-life character, the stories sometimes overshadow his importance as a musician. That should never be understated."

PAUL ANASTASIO

Growing up in Seattle, Paul Anastasio started playing the violin in 1962 at age nine, but he really wasn't interested in jazz. His passion was fiddle music. "I had a chance to go see Joe Venuti, and I passed it up," he recalled. "A violinist, Paul Shelasky, suggested I join him to see Venuti in the bar of the Olympic Hotel. I was probably 20, and very likely wouldn't have been able to get into the bar anyway. Later, I was kicking myself because, even if I hadn't been able to get into the bar, maybe I could have at least listened from outside. About three years later I read in the *Seattle Times* that Joe was appearing for two or three weeks at a place called the Pioneer Banque restaurant in Seattle's historic Pioneer Square district. Up to that time, the only jazz violinist I had heard was Stephane Grappelli, and I was mostly into western swing and fiddle music."

"The first night I heard Venuti," he continued, "I introduced myself to him, and he invited me to bring my violin down the next night. When I played, he would make up names: 'This is John Phillips from Paducah, Kentucky' or 'He just won a big fiddle contest in Roswell, New Mexico.' It was toward the end of his run, around Christmas time in 1976 when I asked him, 'Would it be possible for me to take some lessons from you?' He said, 'Sure, kid.' Other violinists had made the same request of Joe, only to be told, brusquely, that, 'I don't teach.' He lived with a couple, Helen and Bill Fischer, and Helen had told me, 'He likes you.' "

"Maybe it was my Italian surname, but he had me over to the house," Anastasio remembered. "It was less than 20 lessons over two years. He would tell me to pay attention to the classical composers, such as Rodolphe Kreutzer, Paganini, and Bach. He told me there was a lot of jazz in Bach, that, in fact, people used to hand Bach musical themes that he would improvise. He'd run me through some of his pieces, such as 'Wild Cat' and 'Wild Dog,' and then he actually loaned me some sheet music so I could make copies. He would sit down at the piano and have me do the violin parts. The most important thing he did was to change my grip on the bow from the Franco-Belgian grip to the Russian grip. It allowed me to draw a bigger sound out of the music. It was a very minor change, but it made a tremendous difference. He always told me, 'When you're playing, make sure it's you. If you make a mistake, make it a good one.' He gave me a lot of confidence. Looking back, it was not so much the lessons, per se; it was listening to him from about six feet away."

Anastasio currently plays with a western swing band called Jangles. In addition, he is working on developing a new thermoplastic chin rest insert because, he said, "chin rests have no relation to a player's jaw." He continues to study Joe Venuti's recordings because "you can find little hidden corners of his technique. He showed me how to get all the way up the neck. He could play anything." But, virtuosity notwithstanding, Anastasio's lingering image of Venuti is very simple: "Joe was the quintessential guy sitting next to you on a barstool."

CHAPTER 4
One O'Clock Jump: William "Count" Basie

The year was 1957, and the Count Basie Orchestra was in England without any written music. Singer Joe Williams recalled that the music was "lost in transit," but saxophonist-flutist Frank Wess remembered it differently.

"Basie didn't want to carry the music because it was heavy," Wess recalled. "He said, 'You all don't look at the music anyway, so I'm not going to spend all that money.' So we went to England with no music; we'd memorized everything. We did the whole tour without music, and that really knocked them out. And then we were invited back for a command performance that same year."

William "Count" Basie died in April 1984 at the age of 79, but his memory lives on not only through his music but also through the recollections of those musicians who were fortunate enough to have been a part of a musical aggregation that stayed together for nearly half a century. A special bond seemed to unite alumni of the band regardless of where their individual careers took them. "When we see each other our arms fly around each other," said Williams. "We hug. Everybody that was in that band feels it was really a special thing." Williams was with the Basie band from 1954 to 1961. He left the band because he "wanted to sing other things than the things I was working on. Mr. Basie and I talked about it. He agreed that it was time for me to leave."

Williams first met Basie in Chicago in 1942. "A friend of mine was the manager of the Regal Theatre," he recalled. "He said, 'Joe, I need someone on that back door to make sure people don't steal from the musicians and also to make sure the backstage area is secure. Would you be my stage doorman?' I said, 'Sure.' I wasn't doing anything.

At that time, the Basie band would come in and play for a week. Jimmie Lunceford's orchestra would come in and play for a week. Others who would come in were Andy Kirk, Ella Fitzgerald with Chick Webb, Duke Ellington, (and) Cab Calloway. I had a chance to meet all of them." Williams also got a chance to sing with Fats Waller at the organ. "He called me onstage. I said, 'I got to watch the door.' He said, 'Come on out here and sing.' I told somebody to watch the door. I walked out onstage and sang three songs with him."

Although he worked briefly with Basie in 1950 at the Brass Rail in Chicago, Williams really broke in with the band four years later. "I was singing at the Cotton Club," he explained, "I went over to the Trianon Ballroom to tell them how great they sounded, and they asked me to sing with them. I did two numbers, and I split. Later, some fellow came by and told me Basie wanted to see me. I went down to his hotel, and we talked. He said to me, 'Why don't you come with me and see what people all over the country think of your work?' The week before Christmas he sent me a money order by telegram, and I left Christmas morning and flew into New York. The day after Christmas, we left and started a southern tour."

Wess was with Basie from 1953 to 1964, but he initially was reluctant to join the band. He first heard from Basie in 1949. "I was in Washington, D.C.," he recalled. "I was in school studying flute. He called me to join the band, and I told him I was busy doing something. Sorry. So, he kept calling. When I finished school I talked to him, and we finally got together."

His initial reluctance was due to the constant traveling band members endured. "I wasn't planning on going on the road," he explained, "but there's one thing Basie said that influenced me. He said, 'I can give you more exposure than you've ever had.' I thought about that for a little while and decided maybe that's what I need."

Wess later recruited another key member of the band, trumpeter Thad Jones. In the early 1950s, Jones was on the road with the Detroit-based Jimmy Tyler band. He recalled that Wess "was working in the front bar of the Club Harlem in Atlantic City, where I was working with Tyler. We got to be very good friends, but he left to join Basie, and I left to go back to Detroit. I was sort of contemplating my future; I was thinking about going to New York, easing into the city and finding out what I could come up with, when I got a call from Frank, who said, 'How would you like to join Basie's band?' It took me exactly a half a second to say yes. That association lasted almost 10 years, and my whole life from that moment on was full of musical adventures."

When Williams first encountered Count Basie in Chicago, trumpeter Wilbur "Buck" Clayton was nearing the end of his stint with the band. As a teenager in Parsons, Kansas, in the late 1920s, Clayton would take the train to Kansas City practically every weekend to hear the music flowing from the local clubs. "I was too young to go into the clubs," Clayton said, "but I used to stand outside and listen to 'Lips' Page play through an open window."

Almost a decade later, Clayton replaced Oran "Hot Lips" Page as a trumpeter in Count Basie's band. Traveling from Los Angeles to New York City to join a band led by singer Willie Bryant, Clayton stopped in Kansas City to visit his mother. While there, he happened to hear the Basie band, which had just lost Page. "They needed a trumpet player," he recalled, "and Basie asked me if I'd join, and I said, 'Yeah, I'll go.' I had never heard a band swing like that one." Clayton stayed with Basie from 1936 to 1943, playing trumpet and writing many of the band arrangements. Some of his best-known arrangements for Basie included "Down for Double," "Red Bank Boogie," and "7_{th} Avenue Express." Basie, Clayton said, made him a better arranger. "Basie couldn't write music," he explained, "but he and I would sit down to the piano, and he'd say, 'Buck, I want the brass to do this,' and I'd write what he'd hum to me. And he'd say, 'I want the saxophones to do this,' and I learned a lot. That's what made him great. He knew a hell of a lot—in his own style."

Jones said the experience of playing with Basie taught him the meaning of the word "ensemble." "You can listen to soloists all day long, but a soloist can perform with any group," he explained. "When you hear a band play ensemble, you immediately form a picture, and you hear what the band truly is. You understand the personality of it and the power. You understand how the power can be unleashed. That band has always been the number one band for ensemble playing. Each tune had its own balance. If you take it too much to one side, you lose the real force of it. Basie was the master at balancing and finding out the tempo at which a tune should be played. And he gauged it in many different ways. He would take the meter of the band. He would just look around, and he could sense how we felt. And the first number that he played would be an indication of how he perceived this. It was incredible. He was never wrong. The tempos that he set would be just perfect for the way we felt."

Basie's psychic sense worked in other ways, too. Wess claimed Basie "always had a head game going. If he sensed that you'd been drinking or you didn't feel like working or something like that, he'd have you running to the mike to do solos. He'd work you to death. But if he thought you wanted to play, he might not call you to play until the last set of the night. But it worked both ways. If I really felt like I wanted to play, I'd come in and say, 'Boy, my head's killing me. Anybody got an aspirin?' I'd let him hear me say that, and if he thought I felt bad, he'd call on me. A lot of times you wouldn't think Basie was in charge because he never said nothing. But if somebody did something wrong, you'd hear from him. He'd just say enough to let you know he was aware."

Williams used to argue with Basie over what song arrangements to buy. "After fighting over something, we presented it, and the public loved it," he recalled. "I'd look at him as if to say, 'Why did you make me go through that?' He'd look at me as if to say, 'What did you learn from that, young man?' But he cared about me. He'd say to me, 'I'm getting ready to take about a month or two off to save some money,' and I'd say, 'I'm all right.' And he'd say, 'OK, I just wanted to make sure.'"

Recalling a stretch he had with a bad throat, Williams continued working because "I learned quite early in the business to be able to sing over whatever handicap I might have. I said to Basie, 'Jesus, my throat is awful.' He didn't say anything for a little while. He kept playing, and finally he turned and looked at me and said, 'Don't tell me, kid. I play piano.'"

Williams had a big hit, "Every Day I Have the Blues," the first year he was with Basie. After leaving Basie, he branched out from singing mainly blues to developing a reputation as an interpreter of pop ballads as well. His subsequent appearances in clubs and concerts throughout the world contained a mixture of both styles.

In the 1980s, Wess had a varied schedule. He co-led the Two Franks quintet with tenor saxophonist Frank Foster, and he also played tenor sax and flute in the New York Jazz Quartet, led by pianist Sir Roland Hanna. In addition, Wess played lead alto saxophonist with the Toshiko Akiyoshi big band and with Dameronia, a group dedicated to keeping alive the music of pianist-composer Tadd Dameron. In 2007, at age 85, Wess received the American Jazz Masters Fellowship award from the National Endowment for the Arts.

In 1984, Jones had assumed the leadership of the Count Basie Orchestra. When Jones smiled, the broadness of his grin seemed to envelop his massive frame—and the opportunity to head the Count Basie Orchestra at that stage in his career had him smiling often. "I feel just so fortunate to be a part of it," he said. "I feel truly blessed. It isn't anything you could accept lightly. You have to understand that it requires a full commitment."

Clayton did little actual playing during the latter years of his life because dental problems affected his embouchure (the way the lips and tongue are applied to the mouthpiece of a horn), but he was still active arranging. He arranged several numbers for a special "Tribute to Count Basie" concert held at Carnegie Hall in 1985 as part of the Kool Jazz Festival in New York City, and he also wrote some arrangements in 1983 for a Basie Alumni Band that toured several foreign countries. As he looked back on a career that stretched over 50 years, the high point clearly was the seven-year span he spent with Basie. "I'm very fortunate," he said, "to have lived through that experience."

The pleasant recollections, though, were tainted by some painful experiences related to traveling on the road. Civil rights was not even a phrase in those days. "We couldn't stay in certain hotels, and we couldn't even go into certain restaurants," Clayton recalled. "We had to send somebody in to get a bunch of sandwiches and coffee and stuff. I'm fortunate that I saw those days because these kids now don't know what happened. They don't know how it really was."

Sipping won ton soup with a glass of red wine at the China Song, a musician hangout on Broadway in New York City, Clayton maintained that there still was more good than bad derived from all the traveling. "We went to Hollywood and made many pictures, and we played at the San Francisco World's Fair, but we used to eat in the bus and live in the bus," he said. "Many times I've eaten hamburgers for Thanksgiving dinner, and I was glad to get it."

(Adapted from an article that appeared in *American Way* Magazine, September 16, 1986.)

UPDATE

Both Buck Clayton and Joe Williams died at the age of 80, Clayton in 1991 and Williams in 1999. Sadly, Thad Jones became ill shortly after taking over the Basie band and died from cancer in April 1986 at the age of 53. Eighty-seven-year-old Frank Wess is still actively performing and recording but declined to be re-interviewed.

BUTCH MILES

In his early days with the Count Basie band in the mid-1970s, drummer Butch Miles was befriended by Joe Williams, who had left the Basie band but still kept in touch with the leader. Miles recalled that "Joe used to ask Basie how I was doing by saying, 'Is it soup yet?' Basie would say, 'No. Not yet,'." "Joe told me that, finally, after I'd been with the band for maybe a year, he asked the question and Basie just smiled and said, 'It's soup.' That's when I knew that I finally was a lifetime member of the Basie family."

Miles initially joined Basie in 1975, leaving in 1979 to join the Dave Brubeck Quartet. Then he rejoined the Basie Orchestra in 1997, remaining for 10 years. An exciting, swinging drummer in the Buddy Rich tradition, Miles's drumming has often been described as heart-stopping, dazzling, and overpowering. "Just working every night with the greatest band on earth was a heart-stopper by itself," Miles said. "Basie literally made my name and my career and passed on tips to me, like the use of space for impact instead of 10,000 notes and to get my nose out of the chart and use my ears to *hear* the music instead of *read* the music. To this day, I try to make sense of the music I play; and I teach my students the same thing. Basie also taught me when to get out of the way and support a soloist and when to jump in and take command. That might have been the most important thing I ever learned."

Miles moved to Austin, Texas, in 2001 so his wife could accept a job offer there. He continues to travel extensively, "albeit a bit less than I did with the Chief." He also teaches at Texas State University in San Marcos, which is about halfway between Austin and San Antonio. "We just finished the first Butch Miles Jazz Rhythm Section Band Camp," he says, "and I feel it was quite successful."

Frank Wess's nickname was "Magic," Miles said. "He deserves it. All you have to do is listen to him play and you know why. I was greatly honored to ask him to be my special guest star on my last CD, 'Straight On Til Morning' (Nagel-Heyer: 2003), and he agreed. It's just a privilege to work with that brilliant man."

Miles never met Thad Jones, but he concurred with Jones's description of the Basie band as the epitome of ensemble playing. "In Basie's early band the arrangements were built around great soloists like Sweets (trumpeter Harry "Sweets" Edison), Prez (tenor saxophonist Lester Young), and Buck and on and on," Miles explained. "The later bands were built around great arrangers like Quincy Jones, Neal Hefti, Sammy Nestico, Ernie Wilkins, and on and on. Plus, the band had a way of phrasing that no other band could copy. Any high school or college band can play those charts—and do—but nobody swung 'em half as hard or phrased them half as musically as we did. That's ensemble playing and ensemble quality."

"Basie would sit at the piano and arrange an 'un-Basie'-like tune until we were jumping from letter A to letter F," Miles explained. We would repeat C three times, take the coda, and Basie would add his signature plink-plank-plunk, and suddenly the tune would make sense."

As for the mind games mentioned by Wess and Williams, Miles has his own story. "When I wanted to leave the band in '79, I gave Basie my notice. It was a month's notice, not the standard two weeks. The following day Basie asked me to extend that for two weeks in order to make a TV show until he could get another drummer on such short notice. Short notice, my ass—let the games begin. I was pretty young and unversed in Basie's subtleties. I agreed, and the next day Basie asked me to hold off until we finished our European tour at the end of September. Well, this went on for about four or five days until I had agreed to stay until the end of the year."

"I was supposed to be joining the Brubeck Quartet at the beginning of August," Miles continued, "but that sure didn't look like it was going to happen. Then, the light went on in my head, and I got hip to Basie's scene. I came back the following day and gave him one-week's notice. The finale to the story is that Basie agreed to let me leave at the end of the month, and we were right back at the original starting point. I did leave at the end of July, and Duffy Jackson was on the band bus and in my seat almost before I had vacated the premises. Short notice? Hah! That was Basie having some fun with me."

Miles is quick to acknowledge Buddy Rich's influence on him. "What drummer wasn't influenced by Buddy?" Miles asked. "Rich was Basie's favorite drummer, and the respect was mutual. Buddy could be on a rant and raving about anything that he hated, but as soon as Basie walked into the room Buddy became a kind and gentle person. I actually saw that happen."

Although there are too many memories to count, Miles singled out two Basie performances as special: a command performance in London and doing Broadway at the Uris (now Gershwin) Theater with Frank Sinatra and Ella Fitzgerald.

T. S. GALLOWAY

Trombonist T. S. Galloway received his B.A. in music from Roosevelt University in Chicago, but "I got my BS from Basie," he said.

Galloway was 22 years old when he joined the Basie band in 1968. "I'll tell you what Basie did to me one evening," he recalled. "He called me on the bus, and it was just me and him. I had been partying pretty heavily, and Basie said, 'You know, kid, slow down a little bit. All you really need is a croaker sack and a piece of chicken.' And then he said nothing else. Some of the other guys in the band asked, 'What did Basie say to you?' I said, 'Basie told me to kind of slow down on the partying, and all I needed was a croaker sack and a piece of chicken. What's a croaker sack?' They told me it was one of those sacks a bum or panhandler carries—a kerchief on a stick. You put a piece of chicken in it, and you're set. Basie was quite a character."

Three years earlier, the 19-year-old Galloway was working in Chicago with a band led by another trombonist, Harlan Floyd. Galloway said Floyd didn't want to leave Chicago, but Basie convinced him to go out with the band to replace the legendary trombonist, Al Grey. When Floyd left the Basie band, Basie hired Galloway. "Grover Mitchell was playing lead bone, and Bill Hughes, Richard Boone, and myself were the trombone section," Galloway remembered. The rest of the band also consisted of veteran musicians who "kind of helped raise me because I had never been out of Chicago. I hadn't even been on a plane." Playing with the Basie band inspired him to become the musician he is today. "It was so inspirational from a lot of standpoints," he explained. "It was also a life lesson to me because, coming out of the ghettos of Chicago and only being 22 and never having been anywhere, I found myself in London with the Basie band, playing for Princess Margaret. It was a wonderful experience for me and impacted me for the rest of my life. Once you've been in that band, it's almost like a fraternity."

Like Jones and Miles, Galloway said one of the main musical lessons he learned from playing in the Basie band was "what an ensemble was about. I remember we were in San Francisco, and the power went out on the block. We did two sets by candlelight; no music. No one in the band had made an effort to memorize the music; it just happened. I was surprised; it was all there in my head."

Galloway only stayed with Basie for two years, but the experience and reputation helped him get other gigs. "I did a three-year stint in the house band at the Schubert Theater in Chicago, and then I went to South Africa with a big band led by pianist Kirk Lightsey," he said. "We went over there with trumpeter Blue Mitchell and tenor saxophonist Harold Land without any music. So, we were trying to write music when we got there. This was my first chance to be an arranger.

They played my chart, and Harold Land looked up at me and said, 'You know, I really like avant-garde. Now, if you can put us all in the same key, I think we might have something.'"

Galloway, who now teaches jazz trombone, composing, and arranging at North Central College in Naperville, Illinois, said he tells young arrangers, "If it doesn't sound right the first time, just keep going because it gets better."

In 1980, Galloway received his degree from Roosevelt, and in 1981, he received a call from tenor saxophonist Patience Higgins, with whom he had toured in the orchestra for the Fats Waller-inspired musical, "Ain't Misbehavin'." "He said they were taking the show, 'Bubbling Brown Sugar," to Europe, but I had to be in New York in 36 hours." That tour led to a 27-year stay in Europe and residence in Amsterdam, interrupted only by a two-year stint teaching at North Texas State University in 1986.

Galloway became associated with a show called "A Night at the Cotton Club" while living in the Netherlands. "It was supposed to run for four months, but it ended up running for three and a half years," he recalled. "When we had the first meeting, they said they were getting the music from New York, but all New York sent were lead sheets. The producer came in and said, 'We have a company of 10 dancers, five principles, and an eight-piece band. Does anyone here know how to arrange?' I raised my hand. I ended up going with the show and conducting the orchestra on London's West End. The next musical I was involved with was 'Josephine,' the story of Josephine Baker, and then we did 'Bubbling Brown Sugar' again. It was originally arranged for a 16-piece band in New York, but the Dutch didn't have any money, so I rearranged it for five horns and a rhythm section."

In the late 1990s, Galloway began writing for the Chicago Jazz Institute, which had given him commissions to do original works. Eventually, he wrote some charts for a Chicago-based vocalist named Janice Borla, whose husband, drummer Jack Mouse, is coordinator of the Jazz Studies Program at North Central College and who recruited Galloway for the faculty there. In the summer of 2008, Galloway was commissioned to write an original composition to be played by trombonist Julian Priester at the Chicago Jazz Festival. Everything he's accomplished, Galloway attributed to "having been with Basie. I'm always grateful to him for having embraced a young kid. He called me, 'the original new boy.' He said, 'We've never had anyone this green in the band.'"

HOWARD ALDEN

Some of the first jazz records guitarist Howard Alden heard while growing up in Newport Beach, California, were Count Basie records. "I came across a collection of his 1930s Decca sides," Alden recalled. "I also saw him on a television special and was immediately drawn to the spirit and feel of the music."

Ironically, a member of the Basie band would be instrumental years later in furthering Alden's career. "I had come to New York to play with the pianist Joe Bushkin," he said. "I had a long engagement at the Carlyle Hotel with his quartet in January and February of 1983. After that gig ended, I had nothing booked in the near future. I went down to Eddie Condon's to sit in with some guys who were playing there. Cornetist Dick Sudhalter was leading the band, and George Duvivier was on bass. George said, 'Come on over here. Someone at the bar wants to meet you.' It was Joe Williams, and he said, 'Young man, my name's Joe Williams. What are you doing tomorrow night and for the next three weeks?' "

"He was opening the next night at Marty's, a club on the upper east side, with a trio, bass, and drums and on the spot he just asked me to join him. It was a thrill," Alden continued, "but he was so relaxed about the whole thing. And he was so easygoing on the bandstand that he made everybody feel at ease. I remember, about the second or third night, he turned to me and asked, 'Do you know the verse to 'Little Girl Blue?' I said I did, and he said, 'Okay, you and me play the verse, and then we'll go into the chorus.' I said, 'Okay, what key?' and he said, 'It doesn't matter. I sing in all 13 of them.' So, I just hit a chord, and he was right there. It was right in tune—no problems with range, no problem with the notes. From my brief experience with singers I had learned that, normally, it had to be just right or else the range was off."

For awhile after that, Williams, who usually played with a trio, would add Alden on guitar when he played in New York. Some people, Alden said, "are great musicians, but they tend to make people feel uptight. Joe always brought out the best in people. He was easygoing, but he was always in control. It was really a delight to play with him." Alden met Wess about the same time he met Williams and would see him from time to time on different gigs. In 1994, when Alden decided to do an album consisting of the music of the late pianist Bill Evans ("Your Story—The Music of Bill Evans," Concord Jazz), he asked Wess to participate. He knew Wess played flute as well as tenor saxophone and felt "he would lend his relaxed, assured sound to it, and it worked out very well."

Through the years, Alden has appeared with legends such as Woody Herman and Dizzy Gillespie and contemporaries such as tenor saxophonists Scott Hamilton and Ken Peplowski. In 1999, his guitar playing could be heard on the soundtrack of the Woody Allen movie, "Sweet and Lowdown," for which actor Sean Penn received an Academy Award nomination for his portrayal of a fictional jazz guitarist. Alden not only performed the music but he also coached Penn in how to look like a real guitarist.

"He was an amazingly serious student," Alden recalled. "He had never touched the guitar before. When I first got the call, I thought it was just going to be two or three days recording the music. Then the producer asked me if I'd spend some time coaching Sean on how to play the guitar. I would go out to the area of San Francisco where he lived for two days at a time, maybe three or four months before they started shooting the film. I got a guitar in his hands right away, and we spent a couple of weeks in Italy while he was filming another movie, and any time he had a spare moment, like during a lunch break, he'd spend some time on the guitar. I just tried to get him to do physical things, just holding the guitar with his fingers."

"I remember one night, four or five weeks after he'd started, we had a major breakthrough when I taught him to play eight bars to the melody of 'I'll See You in My Dreams' by sheer imitation of just plucking it out. I left him that night, and I called him the next day to find out what time I should come on the set. He said, 'Well, I think I have to take the day off. After you left last night, I played that thing you showed me over and over for six hours. So, my fingers are a little sore.' He was really obsessed with learning how to do it. He far exceeded Woody Allen's expectations. He picked up on a lot of body language and mannerisms by watching me. When my wife saw the movie, she said, 'Oh, he's doing you, the way your eyebrows go up and down.'"

The guitarist portrayed by Penn, Emmett Ray, was a composite. He worshipped Django Reinhardt, was a pool shark like Jelly Roll Morton, and was obsessed with trains like Duke Ellington. "It was a fun six months," said Alden. "I'd spend the day on the set, and whenever he was ready to work on the guitar, I'd be there to work with him."

Marvin Stamm

Trumpeter Marvin Stamm began playing with the Thad Jones-Mel Lewis band in late 1966, shortly after arriving in New York City from Memphis. To him, Jones was a real role model. "I've never seen anyone lead a band like Thad did," Stamm said. "Just waving his hands and the way he conducted the band, he could turn the band on. He could turn a 212-degree boil into a 500-degree sunstroke. He was absolutely amazing."

Stamm said Jones's conducting skills were matched by his composing and performing abilities: "His writing, to this day, is absolutely as original as anyone. He took all of the elements that came from Duke Ellington and modern composers. Whether he knew anything about Stravinsky or Shostakovich or any of those people, I can't tell you. But he had sounds in his ears, and he wrote things that other people would not even think about writing—putting it in a mainstream framework so that it fit the band as a jazz orchestration. His writing, his tunes, his orchestrations for the band were absolutely amazing. Thad was a genius."

As a musician, "things came out of the front of that horn that nobody else would even think of," Stamm continued. "He was so above and beyond anyone else in what he would play and how he would play it. The band had great soloists, but everybody waited for Thad to play. Thad featured everybody, but when he picked up that horn and played, he wiped everybody out."

For the 69-year-old Stamm, the Thad Jones-Mel Lewis Band was the springboard for his New York career. "I arrived in New York the last week of November in 1966. A week after I arrived, I had a phone call from the musicians' answering service asking if I could substitute for Jimmy Nottingham, who was one of the four trumpet players in the orchestra." As a result of that audition, Stamm became the "swing man" in the trumpet section, subbing for whomever had to take off on a particular Monday night when the band performed at the Village Vanguard. "It gave me an opportunity to be heard by a very important segment of the music and jazz community in New York," Stamm said. People who would come to hear the band at that time, Stamm recalled, included musician-composers such as Quincy Jones, Oliver Nelson, and Gary McFarland and composers such as Patrick Williams and Jack Cortner.

"Because at least one of the trumpet players was gone almost every Monday night, I got to play every chair," Stamm remembered. "This gave me a lot of notice from people wanting to know, 'Who's this new guy?' Also, Thad and Mel were very generous in letting people know about me. So I ended up working with Patrick Williams and even Quincy Jones and Oliver Nelson my first two or three years in the city."

Musically, Stamm already had considerable experience for a 26-year-old. While attending North Texas State University in Denton, Texas, he played with some of the top musicians in the Dallas-Ft. Worth area. He spent two years with the Stan Kenton band, almost two years in Reno doing show work, and a year with Woody Herman. But he found the Jones-Lewis band to "always be an inspiration. It gave me more exposure than anything else could have given me at that time." After about a year as "swing man," one of the trumpeters, Bill Berry, moved to California to work on *The Merv Griffin Show*, and Stamm became a permanent member of the band.

Stamm first picked up a trumpet when he was 12 years old. "Not even knowing I was trying to improvise, I copied off my brother's jazz record collection," he said. Early influences were Harry "Sweets" Edison and Charlie Shavers. Later on, he was impacted by Tim Hagans, a trumpeter who played with Kenton in the 1970s and is artistic director of the Swedish Norrbotten Big Band. Stamm also cited Randy Brecker as one of the finest jazz trumpet players in the world today. "All those sounds are in my head," Stamm explained. "You absorb it all, and what comes out is your own voice, but it's a compilation of everything I've experienced."

Today, Stamm tours with his regular jazz quartet, consisting of Bill Mays on piano, Rufus Reid on bass, and drummer Ed Soph, and with the Inventions Trio, a jazz-chamber group with Mays and cellist Alisa Horn. He said he could tick off a long list of "wonderful trumpet players who are on their way up to do a lot of really good things. I think many of them are marvelous technicians. They have all of the ideas and all of the licks down. They're monstrous players of the trumpet."

Sometimes, however, "they miss the subtleties of taking all of that and making music," Stamm said. "I don't hear many of these players ever play something warm and soft. I seldom hear a ballad played with just a beautiful sound. To me, much of it sounds like a trumpet player playing. I'm not much interested in hearing a trumpet player or a trombone player or a saxophone player playing their instrument. I want to hear them play music. When you listen to the people who are my heroes—Dizzy Gillespie, Clifford Brown, Kenny Dorham,

Miles Davis, Charlie Shavers, Roy Eldridge, Louis Armstrong—that's what these guys do."

Which brings him back to the Thad Jones-Mel Lewis and Count Basie bands: "Thad wanted the band to sound like an ensemble, but it wasn't perfection—like when you hear a really fine university band rehearsing something to death. It had the ensemble of the Basie band, but there was also the allowance for the individual sounds of the players. I feel that Basie's band, even though it had great soloists, was really about the ensemble. Thad's band was as much about the soloists as the ensemble."

CHAPTER 5
Melody Man: Jonah Jones

One afternoon in the mid-1940s, two jazz trumpeters, Jonah Jones and Charlie Shavers, were discussing the pros and cons of bebop, a musical development involving complicated melodic, harmonic, and rhythmic patterns. "Me and Charlie Shavers," Jones said, "were on the street talking about this new music, and Charlie says, 'I don't want to play no chord that nobody don't know about but me. I want somebody else to enjoy it, too.' " That conversation was to remain the core of Jones's musical philosophy. Jones wasn't necessarily interested in breaking new musical ground. He simply wanted to make people happy. "I just think that's what music's all about," he said, without pretense, "to entertain people and get some kicks out of it yourself."

In the late 1950s, Jones had two hit singles, "Baubles, Bangles and Beads" and "On the Street Where You Live." He won a Grammy Award in 1959 for the album, "I Dig Chicks" (Capitol Records/out of print), and he gathered acclaim and instant recognition via guest appearances on the award-winning Fred Astaire television specials.

Though his recording activity had slowed considerably in the 1970s, his live performances continued to attract a steady, ardent audience. In November 1979, he was brought back for a second extended engagement at the French Quarter in New York's Sheraton Centre Hotel, and he played regularly at many of the music rooms of the Hyatt Hotel chain, including those in New Orleans, Atlanta, and Chicago. At the time of this interview, he was planning to perform in his hometown of Louisville around Kentucky Derby time in May 1980.

Jones played pretty much the way he had since the height of his popularity in the 1950s. Most of his selections were recognizable, many of them tunes from Broadway shows. He leaned heavily on the melody, veering away just enough to give it an authentic jazz flavor. He played his horn both muted and open, varying back and forth between soft stabbing and hard blowing. And occasionally he sang.

What he played depended on the requests. "A lot of these people have my records," he explained. "I just kept my same style that I had in the Embers (a New York club at which he played regularly in the late 1950s and early 1960s). My audience knows they're going to get some melody along with the jazz. You've got to remember that everybody's not a musician." A typical Jones set included jazz standards, such as "Basin Street Blues," "Way Down Yonder in New Orleans," and "How High the Moon," and a couple of show tunes, such as "Just in Time ("Bells are Ringing") and "Too Close for Comfort" ("Mr. Wonderful").

Jones, who had lived in New York's Greenwich Village since 1959, learned to play alto horn and then trumpet with the Booker T. Washington Community Center band in Louisville. He first left home in 1919 to play aboard the Island Queen, a Mississippi riverboat traveling from Cincinnati to New Orleans. Although he played with several big bands, his past could be divided roughly into three periods: New York's 52_{nd} Street in the 1930s, Cab Calloway's band in the 1940s and early 1950s, and the Embers in the 1950s and early 1960s.

On 52_{nd} Street, Jones played at a club called the Onyx with a band led by the legendary violinist Leroy "Stuff" Smith. The street, he recalled, was great in the 1930s. "A lot of guys that talk about it now only know about it in the '40s," he said. "It was nothing in the '40s; it turned into a half-girlie place. But in the '30s all the clubs were right next door to each other. We were in the Onyx, and we met a lot of people there. Johnny Mercer and all those guys would come in. Mercer would wait for us to play the blues in B-flat. Then he'd get up and sing and make up his own words to it. Everybody in the place was a musician. There were studio men from NBC and CBS. Carl Kress, part-owner of the Onyx, was a guitar player. And when big bands like Glen Gray and Benny Goodman came back in town, they'd be there the first night."

At the Onyx, Jones built something of a reputation as a clown. He would wear different hats, and he and Smith perfected a humorous song-and-dance number, "Truckin'," which usually brought down the house. It was with Calloway's band, however, that Jones's abilities as a prankster reached their zenith. His prop was the spitball. "We'd be rolling up these spitballs all the time and putting them in our derbies, and then we'd shoot them. Many times Cab would come out on stage. He'd see all that paper, and he never said anything, so we thought it was all right," said Jones. "Well, one night in Hartford, Connecticut, he started arguing. 'You guys are acting like a bunch of kids,' he said. Then he jumped on Dizzy [Gillespie] right away. They started arguing, and then he fired Dizzy." (Legend has it that Jones actually threw the spitball that got Dizzy fired.)

"Cab put up with a lot of foolishness though," Jones added. "He'd be out there singing a beautiful ballad, and we'd be clowning around in the back. We'd do things like take two mutes and hold the point of one over the trombone player's head and make like we were driving it into his head with the other one. The audience would laugh; Cab would look around. 'What the hell is going on back there?' he'd ask. I stayed with him 11 years."

Though Jones had his greatest successes at the Embers, his beginning there was inauspicious. "In 1955, my agent got me a one-nighter on the regular band's night off," he remembered. "Then Ralph Watkins, the owner, asked, 'How'd you like to have a week?' We went in there to play for a week and stayed 12 weeks. In the meantime, my agent negotiated a five-year contract at 20 weeks a year."

Located in midtown New York, the Embers attracted an after-theater crowd, and that is why Jones played a lot of show tunes. "They liked to hear those songs and the treatment we gave them," he said. "One of the favorites was 'Till There Was You' from 'The Music Man.' That was a slow ballad, but we'd pick up the tempo and swing it." It was another show tune—"On the Street Where You Live" from "My Fair Lady"—that gave Jones his first hit record, and that recording was even more accidental than his chance booking at the Embers.

"You never know in this type of business," he mused. "I scuffled around all those years, recording. Then, all at once, I come in and this guy says, 'Hey Jonah. We got about 20 minutes to go before we finish this album.' He suggested 'On the Street Where You Live.' I said I didn't know the chords to it, but he said just to play it like I played it at the Embers and put a little shuffle beat behind it. I had never played with a shuffle beat before in my life. We did it and forgot all about it. Then we were playing in London, Ontario, one night, and some people came in and said, 'Play your hit record.' I said, 'Which one is that?' And they said, 'On the Street Where You Live.' I turned around to the guys in the band and asked, 'Did we make that?' None of them could remember. We played it, and they said, 'Well, that's all right, but it isn't like you play it on the record.'"

"The next day," Jones continued, "first thing, I went down to a record store and asked, 'Have you got a record here by Jonah Jones, 'On the Street Where You Live?' They said they had it, so I took it into the booth to listen to it. It all came back to me, so I went and got the guys. We made that record in 20 minutes. All the numbers we spent a lot of time on, had arrangements for, didn't do anything. But 'On the Street Where You Live'—boom! When we got back to the States it was playing everywhere. That was in 1957. We followed that up with an album called 'Swingin' on Broadway' (Capitol Records/out of print), which had another hit, 'Baubles, Bangles and Beads' from 'Kismet'."

It was one of Jones's albums of show tunes that caught the ear of Fred Astaire. "He told me, 'I got hold of one of your muted jazz albums, and I found myself playing it everyday. There was always somebody calling me to do a TV special. One day I was listening to the album, and the Chrysler people called me and asked me if I'd like to do a show yet. I said I would if they got the people I wanted.'" One of the "people" was Jonah Jones. The appearances on the Astaire special and his popularity at the Embers resulted in stories in both *Time* and *Newsweek* in 1959. In the *Newsweek* article (November 23, 1959), Astaire was asked to comment on Jones's playing. "He has a particularly fresh note," the dancer said, "a crisp kind of thing, a cool sound I like. His muted stuff is his specialty, but he can blow great wide open, too. He's a delightful guy."

Though Jones clearly developed his own unmistakable style, he was admittedly indebted to Louis Armstrong. "He was my idol," Jones said. "I was inspired by him—I never tried to play exactly like him; that is not only impossible, but as you grow up you learn you aren't supposed to be copying people note for note. Once when I was playing at the London House in Chicago, he dropped in. People wanted him to sing 'Hello Dolly.' So he sang it, and I played it. That was a great thrill for me."

Jones originally wanted to play the trombone, but his arms were too short, so he settled first for the alto horn and then the trumpet. "I was smart enough to know the alto horn didn't carry any melody, but I settled for that. I would have settled for anything; I wanted to get into that band (at the Booker T. Washington Community Center in Louisville) so badly. But I'm still a frustrated trombone player. When I see one I still pick it up. I know one number on it: 'Tin Roof Blues.'"

(Adapted from an article that appeared in *The (Louisville) Courier-Journal*, December 16, 1979.)

UPDATE

Jonah Jones died in 2000 at the age of 91 in New York City. One of his last live appearances, according to www.musicanguide.com, was in 1999 when he participated in a benefit for the Jazz Foundation of America at New York's Blue Note jazz club. In addition to "I Dig Chicks," some of Jones's other notable albums are "Back on the Street," recorded with pianist Earl "Fatha" Hines (Chiaroscuro Records: 1995) and "Jumpin with Jonah" (Capitol Records: 2000).

In 2008, Mosaic Records reissued "Jonah Jones at the Embers," consisting of 11 favorites from his Embers appearances, including three Cole Porter songs ("It's All Right With Me," "From This Moment On," and "All of You"), "Basin Street Blues," and "Tin Roof Blues." Mosaic's Michael Cuscuna said the album was reissued because it was a major 1950s jazz album that was not available on CD, adding that the audience for it is generally 1940s to 1960s fans of mainstream jazz.

The original liner notes, written by Ben Kemper in 1956, pointed out that "Jonah Jones and his trumpet have been a phenomenon on the New York music scene this past season at the famed jazz emporium, the Embers, where he and his group have been featured for a record-breaking run ... Offering his own specialized brand of relaxed and swinging show music, Dixieland standards and jump tunes, Jonah has proved to have an exceptional appeal for all types of Embers addicts."

An addendum, written in 2007 by Scott Wenzel for the reissue, pointed out that, "a trademark of his sound on these classic albums was Jonah's use of mutes, which was brought about during his initial engagement at New York's Embers Club. The club wanted their music soft and demanded that Jones use mutes, which at first was not what he had hoped to project with his quartet. But the sound caught on, carving out a new style to which he was known to use as many as seven different mutes."

WARREN VACHE

Jonah Jones, says trumpeter Warren Vache, was a "big sweetheart. I would see him at brass conferences, and he would always come over, and we'd have a drink. For a guy with all that history behind him—and as good a trumpet player as Jonah was—he didn't have the sort of ego you'd associate with stardom. He would seem more humble than he had to be."

Vache has a private theory about Jones. "I think throwing that spitball changed Jonah's life," he said. "Dizzy got fired because of it, and Jonah never really opened his mouth and told anybody about it until 20 or 30 years later. I think he felt guilty about it most of his life. Nobody talked about it, but it was Jonah who threw the spitball."

In Vache's opinion, Jones was "a wonderful jazz player. In his early records, he played stuff that was astounding. He made a conscious decision to use the bucket mute when that 'Baubles, Bangles and Beads' stuff came out. He had some commercial hits. He sold records and was in demand for a number of years. The hit records weren't necessarily the way Jonah wanted to play, but they were hits, and that meant he had to play like those records. It's the jazzman's conundrum—I'm popular, it must mean I'm selling out."

The anecdote about Jones's conversation with Charlie Shavers resonated with Vache. "You mentioned a guy I'm still learning things from. Charlie Shavers was an astounding musician."

CHAPTER 6

God Is in the House: Art Tatum

Acting like gunslingers in the Old West, some musicians occasionally squared off against Art Tatum. "When people were ignorant enough to challenge him, he would pull out all his technique," Dick Hyman said. "He would drink a beer with his right hand and play piano with his left hand in the key of B and still demolish his opponent."

The sensible pianists, though, learned from Tatum. Hyman played opposite him at Greenwich Village's Cafe Society in the late 1940s and found the experience "breathtaking." Roland Hanna first heard Tatum in 1942 on a radio program called "Piano Playhouse" and said, "He played the piano the way I felt I wanted to play."

As a 10-year-old, Billy Taylor was initially exposed to Tatum on a record called, "The Shout." "It just blew me away," he recalled. "There were chords running all over the place. I said, 'Who is that?' or 'Who are they?' It sounded like four hands instead of two." In his native Poland, Adam Makowicz listened to Tatum over Voice of America. "The first time I heard Art I knew what great music it was," he said. "There was a technique, chords I never heard before. I didn't understand jazz well at that time, but I knew this was great music."

Tatum was born in Toledo, Ohio, on October 13, 1910, to parents who had traveled to Ohio from North Carolina. There were cataracts in both of his eyes at birth, a defect that left Tatum blind in one eye and, after several operations, with only slight vision in the other. He studied piano, guitar, and violin at the Toledo School of Music and also attended a school for the blind in Columbus, Ohio. Originally determined to be a classical pianist, he supposedly changed his mind after hearing Fats Waller on the radio.

There is some irony in that story because, years later, Waller, while playing in a club, learned that Tatum was in the audience. As the story goes, Waller stopped, stood up, and said, "I play piano, but God is in the house tonight." At age 17, Tatum had become a staff pianist at Toledo radio station, WSPD, and four years later he reached New York as an accompanist for singer Adelaide Hall. In 1933, he made his first solo recording and then began to develop a reputation as a solo pianist, playing mostly on New York's 52_{nd} Street and in Chicago. In 1938, he performed in London.

By 1943, Tatum had formed a trio with bassist Leroy "Slam" Stewart and guitarist Tiny Grimes that enjoyed great popularity. Playing with Tatum, Stewart said, was "one of the greatest experiences in my life, one of my greatest thrills. I learned a lot just trying to do the best I could to back him up in the proper way. A couple of times he automatically changed keys into one of those strange keys we usually didn't play in. I was just thankful I was able to follow him."

Despite the trio's success, it was Tatum's skill as a soloist that elevated him to the level of virtuosity for which he is revered by other pianists. Unlike Waller, who helped popularize stride piano, Tatum's style fell into no particular musical school. "He wrapped up all of the styles that preceded him and pointed the way to those who followed him," Taylor said. "He is still one of the most important influences on solo piano playing. There has been a trend toward solo playing, and if you listen to any of the players, you hear things which are Tatum-esque." Taylor believed Tatum made such an impact on anyone seriously interested in playing jazz piano that, consciously or unconsciously, they are using some of the vocabulary he developed.

That impact was evident in the comments of John Lewis, pianist and musical director of the Modern Jazz Quartet. Lewis pointed out that not very much of his own playing was directly influenced by Tatum, but he added that there are "all kinds of indirect, subconscious things. I have great admiration for him." Veteran pianist Hank Jones pointed out that "every jazz pianist has been influenced by Art in a positive way. I know pianists who have transcribed his solos. They might be able to play his solos note for note, but they couldn't capture his feel, his conception, his inventiveness."

Hanna, who grew up in Detroit, remembered that "Art Tatum was there an awful lot. There was a place called Freddie Ganniard's where Willie Hawkins used to play. Willie Hawkins was a blind pianist, and one of his best friends was Art Tatum. In my opinion, he was the only guy who could really make Art Tatum play, and they used to have piano sessions late at night. When Art was in town, he'd go see Willie Hawkins, and he'd end up staying and playing until 4 or 5 o'clock in the morning. I used to go there when I was a kid—about 15 or 16 years old—and listen." Tatum was renowned for his after-hours piano-playing marathons. Jones recalled a time in Buffalo: "I was playing at a place called the Anchor Bar, and Art Tatum was at McVan's. After McVan's closed, Art would go to another place and play until 12 the next day."

With the exception of Erroll Garner, Hanna said Tatum was his "major influence. Other people didn't play the piano the way I wanted to. Some were too light; some didn't have harmonic invention. Hardly any had as much melodic invention as Art Tatum. He had the kind of technique I thought one should have—equal and in many ways far better than most European classical players. Also, his sound was individual."

Another pianist crediting both Tatum and Garner as major influences was Makowicz, who emigrated to the United States in the 1970s. "I like them equally, but it was easier to imitate Erroll Garner than Art," he said. "You could copy Tatum's techniques, but it would be an awful lot of work. And it would be ridiculous to do it because Tatum was the master already. Why would you want to repeat something you cannot do in the same quality? Art Tatum was the master of that style."

Describing the Tatum "style" in words is no easy task, but Hyman stressed that it was not just his technique. "It was what he did with it, how he expanded on a song and used it for his own improvisation. He didn't depart from the song, he was always playing it—sometimes tongue in cheek in a very sly, humorous way."

Taylor talked of Tatum's use of "themes and variation. If you listen to his records and hear just minor variations in themes, you realize just how creative he was—a minor manipulation of a melodic fragment. It's just really phenomenal. Because of his technical ability, most people didn't realize what a great harmonic contribution he made. One has to listen to some of the pieces he played out of tempo to get a sense of the clusters and the very contemporary harmonic devices." Added Hyman: "If you hear too much Tatum in one dose, it can be a little too much of a wonderful thing. You have to concentrate on a few things at a time. It's a self-discovery."

Tatum, who died in 1956 from uremia, was a private person. In fact, many believe that playing the piano was his personal and professional life all wrapped into one. "He was a very gentle, supportive person," said Taylor. "And he seemed to respond to people he considered talented." Taylor got to know Tatum quite well in the 1940s while playing at the Three Deuces on New York's 52_{nd} Street with the Ben Webster Quartet, which alternated with Tatum's trio. "He was very secure in his own talent and cared a great deal about others," Taylor recalled. "He taught me to be open to all kinds of pianists and to listen carefully to what everybody did."

Hyman remembered that Tatum liked to hear other pianists, even ones who weren't particularly distinguished or talented. "People would ask how someone so limited could interest him, and he would say, 'Everyone has a story to tell.' " Particularly savoring the memory of an interview Tatum once gave to Willis Conover of Voice of America, Hyman recalled that "Conover kept pressing him about his favorite pianists. Art wasn't about to slight anyone, so he said, 'There's a new kid in town. Have you heard Dick Hyman?' "

One of the last times Hanna saw Tatum was in Rochester, New York, when Hanna was at the Eastman School of Music. "He was playing at a place near to where I was, so I went around to hear him and went up and said hello. Even to his last days, he played primarily in nightclubs, unfortunately." That fact was also lamented by Hyman, who said Tatum "should have been a concert artist, but there wasn't a general market for it then, so he played mostly in funky clubs."

Because he didn't play often enough in the proper setting, many jazz musicians have felt Tatum did not receive the recognition in general music circles that he deserved. "He was appreciated during his lifetime by people like Vladmir Horowitz and George Gershwin," Taylor said. "They recognized his genius and celebrated it, but since his death he has not been romanticized. There has not been the documentation there should have been."

One exception, Taylor said, was the remarkable group of records that Norman Granz made just prior to Tatum's death. A concert promoter whose Jazz at the Philharmonic tours widely exposed the music both in the United States and abroad, Granz recorded 13 albums of Tatum "Solo Masterpieces" on the Pablo record label. There were nine additional albums featuring Tatum in a group setting with other musicians, including vibraharpist Lionel Hampton, drummer Buddy Rich, and trumpeter Harry "Sweets" Edison. Time-Life Records also put together a Tatum collection, Taylor added, and "although I would question some of the choices on the record, the documentation that accompanies it is excellent."

Makowicz felt that a lot of people didn't understand what Tatum was doing in the 1950s. "They appreciated and admired his style and technique and everything, but often they didn't know exactly what he was doing," Makowicz said. "It wasn't swing like James P. Johnson and Fats Waller. He broke rhythm. It seems for some people that he loses the rhythm. They cannot tap along like with Johnson. With Tatum, you had to listen very carefully to what he was doing. You have to have some knowledge about his music to appreciate how great he was."

Tatum's greatest legacy, in Hyman's opinion, was his "romantic harmony. With all the sophistication that has come to jazz, that sort of romantic harmony of his has never been taken any further. Nobody has ever come close to him. He is so revered by my generation of pianists and by all the younger pianists who have in contact with him. They run out of superlatives." The most important thing, added Taylor, was that "everything he did was on the very highest level of artistry. I never heard him play anything that wasn't very elegant and on a very high musical level. Even a throwaway—blues with a singer in an after-hours place—it was not only unique and personal, but he'd give that just as much careful attention as he would a record." (Adapted from an article that first appeared in the Sunday magazine of the *Toledo Blade*, October 9, 1983.)

UPDATE

Barbara Carroll and Marian McPartland

In the 1950s, Barbara Carroll was playing at the Embers on New York's East Side, while Marian McPartland was holding court at the Hickory House on West 52_{nd} Street. Both have great respect for each other, both were influenced by Art Tatum, and both helped pave the way for the acceptance of female jazz musicians other than vocalists.

McPartland believes the most important aspect of Tatum's playing was his harmonic ideas. "I certainly couldn't attain that kind of technique, but I tried," she said. "When I was in my 20s I was playing at a place in Washington, D.C., called Olivia's Patio, and I saw Art Tatum there. I was very nervous, but I decided he had come to hear me, and I wanted to play as well as I could. He complimented me on my playing, and we became friends. In New York, I would go to the Embers to hear him play, and sometimes my husband, Jimmy (jazz cornetist Jimmy McPartland) and I would go to hear him in other cities when we were on the road."

Tatum's technique, according to Carroll, "was so staggering, his comprehension, his harmonic sense so fabulous, that I don't think there's anyone who's playing jazz piano today who hasn't been influenced by Art Tatum. When I first heard him I was a kid, and I was totally overwhelmed; I still am every time I hear him."

Carroll never aspired to play like Tatum—"That would have been impossible," she said. She did get to meet him at the Embers, however, which she describes as "an Eastside jazz club. It was kind of a little more posh, with good food, as opposed to a lot of the jazz clubs that were small, intimate, dark, and didn't have any food. Anyway, it was a great place. I was lucky enough to have been booked there. They always had two attractions at once. Lo and behold, when we got there for rehearsal, I was told that the other act was Art Tatum. I restrained myself from running out on 54_{th} Street into the traffic. Anyway, it was such an experience because my trio would play and then he would go on. He was so wonderful to me, so encouraging. And having the opportunity to listen to him every night was stunning."

McPartland, because she traveled with her husband's group early in her career, had relatively few problems being accepted by male jazz musicians, but Carroll often had to resort to subterfuge. "It was hard to establish yourself because you were prejudged," she explained. "You were known as a 'chick' piano player. I remember when I first came to New York from Boston and I didn't know anyone here with the exception of one pianist, George Marshall, who I had known in Boston. He tried to help me get work. If someone called him for a job, say on a Saturday night for a club date or a wedding or bar mitzvah, and he couldn't do it, he would recommend me. But he couldn't tell them I was a girl because they wouldn't hire me. So, he'd say, 'I can't do it, but I have a friend, Bobby Carroll, who's good and can do the gig,' never mentioning he or she. So, at 8 o'clock on Saturday night, Bobby Carroll would appear, and the bandleader would probably fall off the bandstand. 'Who are you?' he'd ask, and I'd say, 'Well, I'm your pianist for this evening.' It would be too late to send me home, so they'd have to let me play; that's an example of the kind of prejudice there was."

The Hickory House, where McPartland played with her trio from 1952 to 1960, was known as a club that other musicians would frequent. One of McPartland's earliest influences, Duke Ellington, was a regular. "Ellington and I were very friendly, and he would agree to come up and play with the trio once in awhile," she remembered.

"By the same token, when I was going to hear him at Birdland or some other club, he would always invite me to join him."

Carroll's first influence was Nat Cole. "I think most people do not realize that, at the beginning of his career, he was *only* a jazz musician," she said. "He didn't start singing until later. He began singing, I think, because he had his trio, and they were just playing instrumentally in some club in California, and people would come in and say, 'Hey, don't you know the words to that song?' I guess he *did* know the words, and he started singing. That's what happened to me many years later." Today, Carroll has become a fixture at Sunday brunch at New York's legendary Algonquin Hotel, and she mixes in vocals with her playing. In 1986, when she was appearing regularly in Bemelmans Bar at New York's Carlyle Hotel, John Wilson of *The New York Times* described her singing as having "an ability to be simple, gentle and emotionally moving (May 11, 1986)."

Since 1979, McPartland has hosted "Piano Jazz" on National Public Radio, a program that consists of an hour of chatting and playing with other musicians. Guests through the years have included Oscar Peterson, Dave Brubeck, and Tony Bennett, among many others. In 1990, "Piano Jazz" reunited McPartland's trio from the Hickory House, which included bassist Bill Crow and drummer Joe Morello.

Aaron Diehl

Art Tatum was one of the first pianists Aaron Diehl listened to when his interest in jazz began. "One of the striking things about Tatum's playing," said Diehl, "is not just his facility—although that's the most obvious element. But what's also very impressive to me is his touch. I think that's the icing on the cake in regard to his playing. He had the technique, the facility, of course; he had the harmony—his understanding of harmony was enormous. But what really brought those elements together was the sound that he got out of the piano. The first time I heard Tatum, I was probably around 14 or 15. I was certainly in awe because there was so much going on at once. The more I listened, the more I heard the lyricism of Tatum. Once you got past the runs and all the fills and everything, you heard just how lyrical he could be."

"It's hard for any jazz musician not to take something from Tatum," he continued. "Harmonic vocabulary is one thing—things that you can do with jazz standards, re-harmonizing the melody.

When I'm playing, I'm always conscious of how I'm sounding and what kind of sound I'm producing out of the piano, the way you voice a chord. You could play the same chord twice, and it could almost sound like a completely different chord based on the way you voiced it, the way you actually executed the note. I think Tatum was definitely conscious of that all the time. I could just tell by how he played certain things; all of his stuff felt great. He would play at those very brisk tempos, but he would be relaxed and make it feel like it's easy when he was going at a neck-breaking pace."

Mark Shane

Although Mark Shane's primary influence was Teddy Wilson, he acknowledged "when it really comes down to playing solo piano, it's Art Tatum. I don't just mean the flamboyance of his technical execution. Even without that, I find Tatum's time just to be so rock solid. And his left hand is an extension of Fats Waller and James P. Johnson and just in the right groove. He used harmonies that, to my mind, better articulated what the composer had in mind than the composer himself did. So, I pay a lot of attention to Art Tatum. I know my limitations, though. Everyone takes from Tatum what they are capable of taking. His left hand and his time are to me such a worthwhile study."

Shane can't help, however, comparing Tatum with his personal hero, Teddy Wilson. Wilson was a pure jazz pianist, he said, and "while Tatum could play incredible jazz, sometimes his technique got in the way of the pure jazz expression. I know people will roast me over the coals for saying that, but that's just the way I feel," said Shane. "I worship Tatum; his articulations are unbelievable. And I have plenty of examples of Tatum playing the most unbelievable jazz effortlessly. But he didn't stick to that. Teddy did. Every time Teddy played, it was pure jazz."

CHAPTER 7
Road Warriors: Earle Warren, Howard McGhee, and Milt Hinton

EARLE WARREN

"We used to call him white folks. On a train, the conductor would make him go into the white coach. But it had its good points. When we were on a bus, sometimes we could send him into a restaurant to get the food." That was the singer Helen Humes reminiscing about traveling with the Count Basie band in the 1930s and about Earle Warren, a light-skinned African-American alto saxophonist who could pass for white.

In the 1980s, Warren spent most of his time in Europe, partly to escape a deteriorating marriage and partly to be rid of—once and for all—the carping that still followed him, stinging criticism by many of his peers for pretending to be something he wasn't. "They used to call me names even though I would go get them sandwiches and give them things," he said in a 1984 interview during a break at the West End Cafe in upper Manhattan. "I get it from people yet. They like to call me 'white folks' and 'cracker' and other corny-assed names, which they never outlived themselves."

Warren wasn't proud of his deception, but it was, he said, a matter of necessity. "I had an ulcerated stomach," he recalled, "and a lot of cities didn't offer decent food or nothing for colored people. The restaurants we could go to were greasy restaurants; or if we went to a place where they had a wall where it said 'colored on one side and white on the other,' it was still greasy and funky. They didn't give a damn how they served you. I went through all of that for about two years."

Then he decided to take advantage of his light skin. "I would get a decent night's rest and some decent food, and this was sort of repulsive to those other guys." The alternative, though, was worse. "It was hard to find places to stay. We had to stay in some pretty bad places. We'd pull in at one of the roadhouses, and maybe they'd let you go by the back door. They'd hand the food out the door in a box. You'd go ahead and sit in the bus, get a soda and be happy to go on to the next gig."

Born into a musical family in Springfield, Ohio, Warren recalled that, "My father, mother, and older sister played piano. I studied piano. I only started playing the saxophone after I got a C melody for Christmas. I used to go and have lessons with a man who had been in New York long before with Lloyd Scott's band." (Lloyd Scott, a drummer, and his brother, Cecil, a tenor saxophonist, had a band in the 1920s called Scott's Symphonic Syncopators. The Scott brothers were also from Springfield.)

Warren progressed rapidly on the alto saxophone. "I had a good ear. I knew the scales and everything, and I knew how to reach chord changes. I was playing ukelele, too. Everything fell into shape. In those days many bands used to come to my home. That's when I met Eddie Barefield (clarinetist), Jack Washington (baritone saxophonist), and Ben Webster (tenor saxophonist). Then I went on to Columbus and Cleveland."

As a young saxophone player, Warren had no particular idol. "I had no principal person I set my sights on," he said. "If I took a few excerpts from guys I was listening to, it was just melodically because I played almost as well as they did. They were only three or four years older than me. How do I play now? It's just individual thoughts and the way I think the instrument should sound."

In 1936, Warren was leading his own 17-piece band in Cincinnati when Count Basie arrived for one special weekend. "I said to myself, 'I don't know how the hell I'm going to get a chance to hear this band,' What happened was that Al Sears (a tenor saxophonist who also led his own band) asked me if I could work for him that weekend. My big band was playing down the street, and I had different intermissions. I'd play about 40 minutes and take off 20. During the 20, I would run down and work with Al Sears' band."

The featured attraction where the Sears band was playing was Count Basie, so "the guys from Basie's band were sitting around listening to me play," he said. The next day, a Sunday, Warren went back to the club to play the matinee performance with the Sears band, and at intermission, Herschel Evans (a tenor saxophonist with Basie), asked Warren if he would be interested in joining Basie's band.

He wasn't that impressed, telling Evans, "Truthfully, I really don't know much about your band. I heard it in '36 in Sandusky—on the radio out of the Reno Club in Kansas City. I enjoyed it very much, but I couldn't find any roots to it. All I found was some good unadulterated swing. It was worth listening to each night, though, for the solos and the rhythm." Two weeks later, however, Warren received a wire from Basie asking him to join them, and he did, meeting the band in Pittsburgh. "The rest," he said, "is history."

Warren became the lead alto saxophonist and occasional singer. According to *The Encyclopedia of Jazz* (Bonanza Books: New York), he was an "excellent section leader and virtual director of the band for Basie." He left Basie in 1945, rejoining him twice in the late 1940s before leaving the band for good in the early 1950s.

Warren freelanced through most of the 1950s and early 1960s, surfacing in a variety of roles—as musical director of the Apollo Theatre in Harlem and the Howard Theatre in Washington, D.C., as saxophonist and musical director for pianist Eddie Heywood, as MC for musical shows staged in New York by radio personality Alan Freed, and as musical director for rhythm and blues groups such as the Platters and Drifters.

In 1959, he toured Europe with Buck Clayton, who led a group of Basie All-Stars, and was impressed with the "warm receptions," a memory that influenced his permanent move across the Atlantic in 1979. The standard line about European audiences, he said, was "they like to see dark-skinned musicians. Guys used to tell me, 'Man, you can't make it over there because you're too light.' They always said such things to me."

UPDATE

Earle Warren died in 1994 at the age of 79 from complications caused by a stroke and kidney failure. He was living at Hope House Manor, a nursing home in Springfield, Ohio. In his obituary in *The New York Times* (June 7, 1994), Peter Watrous described him as "an important element in the Basie band's brilliance. As the lead alto saxophonist, he led the saxophone section, making sure it swung with authority."

Recordings by Warren are difficult to find, but two that are still barely in circulation are "The Count's Men" (Muse: 1985) and "Buck Clayton Jam Session, Vol. 2" (Chiaroscuro: 1975).

Phil Schaap

Jazz historian Phil Schaap was a teenager when he met Earle Warren. "I became a fan of the original Basie bands," he recalls, "and began producing jazz events." Schaap worked with Warren for 20 years as a producer for The Countsmen. "In '72, we started like a house of fire. We placed 10_{th} in the *Downbeat* poll, tied with Dave Brubeck and Ornette Coleman. We never equaled that," he said.

Schaap, who is a radio host on WKCR, the station of Columbia University, and curator at Jazz at Lincoln Center, said Warren didn't get a lot of thanks for pretending to be white and helping out his fellow musicians, but that he overcame it. More importantly, Schaap said, "He was a very good lead alto player. When the saxophonists in the Basie band soloed, they sounded like themselves; when they played behind him, they sounded like an ensemble."

He was also a good singer. "In the '30s, he had Perry Como-like pipes. His big hit was '9:20 Special,' and he was still getting royalties when he was in the old-age home in Springfield." While Warren was living at Hope House Manor, Schaap said, "The Basie band came through Springfield, and the Basie players left the bandstand and went over to his wheelchair. Tony Bennett came through two weeks later and made a bigger fuss."

Joe Temperley

Baritone saxophonist Joe Temperley's most enduring memory of Earle Warren was during the recording of the "Buck Clayton Jam Session." "Earle was playing a solo, and he was so enraptured with the rhythm section that he stopped playing and said, 'I'm dreaming. I'm dreaming,'" Temperley remembered. "It was a great band. The rhythm section was Earl 'Fatha' Hines on piano, Milt Hinton on bass, and Gus Johnson on drums. The other saxophonists were Zoot Sims and Budd Johnson, with Doc Cheatham on trumpet and Urbie Green on trombone." In the album's liner notes, producer Hank O'Neal pointed out that the recording was "a bona fide all-star session. As one would expect, such a roster of old-school talent does not disappoint, and a rotating solo spotlight allows every player the chance to stretch out."

HOWARD MCGHEE

Howard McGhee sat sipping a Coke in the bar of New York's Mayflower Hotel during the busy cocktail hour between 5:30 and 7:00 PM. A waitress passed by, paging a "Mr. Applebaum." "She knows it isn't me," McGhee exclaimed, a slight look of bemusement in his eyes. There was no apparent bitterness in his voice or on his weather-beaten face, but a trace of pain would have been understandable. It was 1983, and he was the only black person in the room. Nobody so much as lifted an eyebrow, but McGhee, a jazz trumpeter who was at the top of his trade in the late 1940s, could remember when people did take notice... when he had trouble finding a place to sleep because of the color of his skin.

Born in 1918 in Tulsa, Oklahoma, McGhee moved to Detroit with his parents when he was two years old. His grandmother remained in Oklahoma, however, and "she'd send for me every year to come down there and spend the summer with her. I used to see those guys digging ditches by my grandmother's house, and I figured right then—that wasn't for me."

McGhee heard Louis Armstrong play "Basin Street Blues" on the radio when he was 11 years old, and the experience had a profound influence on him. "I had been playing clarinet in the school band," he recalled, "and when I heard Louis on the radio, I said, 'That's what I like.' I had heard the sound of the trumpet before, but Louis really changed my mind about the whole situation." By the time McGhee was 13, he managed to get a job in Oklahoma City playing with a quartet, "at one of these drive-ins where people would come in and ask you to play a number. We really didn't make no big money; if you came out with $1.50 or $2, maybe that was a hot night. But that's how I got started."

As he gained confidence, he began playing with local bands in and around Detroit. "I was working at the Club Congo in 1941, when Lionel Hampton came in town to play a dance," he said. "His band had a night off, so they came down to the club. Hamp liked what I was doing and asked me to join his band. So I said, 'Why not?' You can't tell how long a job in a nightclub's going to stay."

McGhee remained with Hampton only two months. "It was a step up, I thought, but it really wasn't," he said. "The money he was paying, I'd have been better off staying where I was. I couldn't make it on the road financially, so I went back to Detroit."

He then received a telegram from Andy Kirk, a bandleader whose group, the Clouds of Joy, had risen to prominence in 1936 on the strength of a hit record, "Until the Real Thing Comes Along." "Some cat had told him in New York that I was a good trumpet player," McGhee said, "and he wanted me to join him in St. Louis. He told me what the bread would be, and that was like a $7 raise over what Hamp had been paying. I joined him in St. Louis at the Tune Town Ballroom."

McGhee stayed with Kirk about a year, achieving some celebrity during that time with a recording of his own called "McGhee Special." He left as the result of a chance encounter with Andy Gibson, a black arranger with an all-white band led by saxophonist Charlie Barnet. "Andy Gibson heard me play, and he told Charlie I was a good trumpet player, and that he'd like to write for me. So Charlie said, 'Okay, bring him on over then.' So I went over and talked to him and went to work for Charlie."

Being the only black member of an all-white band left its mark on McGhee. It opened his eyes to a world that was crueler than he ever could have imagined. He tried to gloss over some of the anguish he experienced, but the hurt still managed to break through. "They had a colored guy in there before me—Peanuts Holland (also a trumpeter), but when they hired me I was the only colored guy in the band. I really didn't know too much about traveling with a white band. I knew it was a little different; I didn't know it was that much different."

The "difference" manifested itself when the band checked into hotels. Usually the band's manager would make special arrangements to accommodate McGhee, but sometimes the manager would forget that one of the band members was black.

"One time we were up in Worcester, Massachusetts. Now, it ain't prejudiced up there, you know," he said, his voice reflecting a slight tinge of mockery. "I went to the hotel expecting to get a room like everybody else, but they said I had no reservation, and I couldn't stay there. We were going to be there four days, and I figured I had to have a place to sleep. Everybody else was checked into the hotel, so that was kind of a heavy blow, you know what I mean? It was a drag for me to have to walk all night looking for someplace to sleep."

The first thing McGhee did was ask a cab driver if any colored people lived in town: "He said, 'Yeah, there's one or two live around here somewhere.' He started scratching his head and all that kind of stuff. So I said, 'You know where they are?' And he said, 'Well, we might find them, but I don't know where they live exactly. I'll just have to keep asking around until I find them.' Finally, he got the right information and took me. That's the only way I could find a place to sleep. What else could I do? I didn't know nobody in Worcester. I don't think they had but about two colored families there."

McGhee didn't get to sleep until late that night, and the next day he didn't show up at rehearsal. "When Charlie asked me what happened, I said, 'Man, you don't look out for me. I didn't have no reservation here. I had to stay out all night trying to find a place to sleep.' Charlie got mad and fired his manager. Charlie was a nice guy as far as nice guys go."

Barnet, in fact, was one of the earliest white musicians to integrate his band with black performers. In addition to Holland and McGhee, he hired vocalist Lena Horne, trombonist Trummy Young, and bassist Oscar Pettiford—all in the early 1940s.

"I had a ball with Charlie," McGhee said, "even though some of the situations weren't too nice. We didn't have problems in some cities that were mixed. In Chicago, we could stay wherever we wanted, but in these small towns where they didn't know what was happening, they'd say, 'What's he doing here anyway?' They'd get kind of funny. I had some problems eating, too, on the road. I had to send one of the guys in to get something for me."

In 1943, Barnet decided to take a six-month hiatus, and McGhee went back with Andy Kirk. "Andy was such a nice cat," he recalled. "He didn't mind me coming back. But I did a lot of things for Andy. I could write and arrange. I remember we played in Texas somewhere, and they wanted to hear 'Deep in the Heart of Texas.' Andy got the sheet music that afternoon, and we rode the bus until we got where we were going. When we got there, he asked if I could write it out for that night. I did a swing arrangement. We did real good with it that night; the people loved it. From then on, Andy said I could write anything I wanted to. That was another income, so I started writing arrangements. Whenever anybody else would be shootin' dice or whatever else they'd be doing, I'd be writing arrangements so I could get some extra money. I'd get about $35 an arrangement—and I was making $25 or $27 a week."

Traveling on the road was "a bitch. It was hard work, but it didn't bother me too much because I liked seeing different towns," McGhee said. "I'd never seen America, but I never did like the South. I went down there once with Andy. The first time I played down there, some lady was sitting right by the bandstand, and every time I'd hit a high note, she'd squeal. I had a lot of high notes to hit, and her man kept looking at me. Every time I'd hit a high note, he'd frown, and she'd squeal. I said to myself, 'Gee, what am I doing down here in this territory?' It was somewhere in Louisiana. They were mean down there. Thank goodness we got out of town early that night."

McGhee left Kirk in 1944 to join Georgie Auld, a white saxophonist who had taken over Artie Shaw's band in 1940. Auld had a racially mixed band. "Georgie was all right," said McGhee. "At least he wasn't prejudiced. We got along good together."

After a brief stint with Count Basie the same year, McGhee met Coleman Hawkins, and that changed the direction of the music he was playing. "I was in New York, and I ran into Oscar Pettiford (the bassist), and he took me down to Coleman Hawkins. "That was good," he recalled. "He was playing a lot of music then. He was playing more than I knew because he had been playing with Monk (pianist Thelonius Monk), and Monk was one of the founders of the bebop school. We played in New York on 52_{nd} Street, two weeks in Buffalo, a week in Chicago, and then went to California. And that's where we really got into it because they didn't have nobody out there playing that type of music. And so, accidentally, they liked what we were doing. They recorded us out there; we made lots of records."

While he was playing with Hawkins, McGhee met Norman Granz, a white music impresario who originated the concept of presenting a jam session on the concert stage—an idea that blossomed into his now-famous Jazz at the Philharmonic concert tours.

"We ran into Norman Granz when he came down to the Long Branch, where we were playing, to hire Hawk for a concert," McGhee recalled. "After he heard me play, he asked, 'Would you want to make the gig, too?' I said, 'Why not?' Luckily, he recorded that particular concert, although I didn't know nothing about it. I was walking down the street one day, and I heard me playing, and I said, 'Gee, that sounds like me. Who is that guy?' So I went into the record store, and they told me it was a new album by Jazz at the Philharmonic. Norman had come all the way to New York and put it out and didn't say nothing to nobody. So I went to the union, and they said, 'The only thing we can do is make him pay you for the recording.' I called Norman and asked him what he was doing putting the record out without permission, but I wasn't wise enough to go to an attorney. Norman went on to earn a fortune on it. He sent me a check for $70 for my solo on 'How High the Moon.' " (Although musicians were not always fond of Granz's business dealings with them, he was the first jazz promoter to insist on nondiscrimination clauses in all contracts.)

The mid to late 1940s were undeniably the peak of McGhee's career, although he was still active in the 1980s, playing occasional gigs and concerts. In 1949, he finished first in the trumpet category in *Downbeat* magazine's Readers' Poll. According to the *Encyclopedia of Jazz* (Bonanza Books: New York), he was "one of the most recorded artists of the bop era. His solos showed a commendable flow of ideas, perhaps with fewer surprises and less humor than Gillespie, but swinging constantly."

In the 1950s, McGhee toured Korea during the war and played regularly for five years at a club called Christy's in Framingham, Massachusetts. In the 1960s, he tried briefly to keep a big band going and appeared with small groups in a number of New York-area clubs.

McGhee had gotten hooked on drugs in the 1950s. The addiction—to heroin and cocaine—lasted eight years, from 1951 to 1959, and he later gave lectures about its evils. He finally convinced himself to stop "because I blew all my money," he said. "It finally hit home." However, later—in the 1960s—drugs were replaced by alcohol. "I didn't really care about it," he said, "but everyone else was drinking, so I did." He quit in 1969.

The difficult social conditions for black musicians in the 1940s and 1950s caused many of them to become expatriates, moving to Europe where their music was appreciated and where they were treated as equals. McGhee, though, never seriously considered such a move because "in the first place, I couldn't speak their tongue. I gotta be able to talk with somebody," he explained. "Hawk went over there, and he came back talkin' French and all that shit; but I didn't see me doin' that."

Instead, he stayed in the United States and tolerated the discrimination that was inescapable. "I'm not sorry I had to go through that stage because it taught me a lot that I never would have considered before," he said. "I went through some of the most prejudiced places in America—like North Dakota and South Dakota, for instance."

But some of his memories were sweet—particularly those of New York and its famous *52nd* Street. "New York was probably the best experience a cat could have," he said. "Fifty-second Street was about the nicest thing that could have happened to New York because they had a whole lot of clubs, and they had a whole lot of musicians working there. Bird would be in one joint, and Dizzy would be in another joint, and Prez would be in another joint, and Billie Holiday would be in another. It was a pleasure just to walk from one club to another."

UPDATE

Howard McGhee died in 1987 at Mount Sinai Hospital in New York at the age of 69. Robert Palmer, writing in *The New York Times* (July 18, 1987), said McGhee "had the big, brassy tone and expansive melodic imagination of the great swing-era trumpeters. But his rhythmic fluidity and advanced harmonic thinking helped him become one of the first important big-band soloists to master bebop's intricacies." Among his available CDs are "Maggie's Back in Town" (Ojc: original release in 1961) and "Together Again" with tenor saxophonist Teddy Edwards (Ojc: original release in 1961).

NOREEN GREY LIENHARD

Pianist/vocalist Noreen Grey Lienhard remembers when she first met Howard McGhee in the early 1980s. "With Howard, the music always came first," she said. "It wasn't about me being a woman, or if you're white or black or this age or that age. It didn't make any difference to him. He had endured so much discrimination during his life that I think he thought, 'I'm not going to do this to anybody, ever.' I was so excited to get the opportunity to play with him. There was a point where I guess I passed the test. He said, 'Okay, you know what you're doing.' He was always so gracious and so kind and always gave his band members space to play. And he was always so encouraging."

Lienhard and her ex-husband, bassist Earl Sauls (she was then known as Noreen Sauls), played often with McGhee at the Jazz Vespers at Saint Peter's Church in New York City. "Some of the selections were from the hymnals, so guys would get the hymnal out, and if they didn't know the song, they would be reading it," she recalled. "One time, the song 'What Child Is This?' didn't go too well. Someone was sitting in, and they kind of got the form mixed up, skipped a line or something, and Howard turns around and looks at me and says, 'What child was *that?*' He just came up with this funny stuff."

Another time, she said, "We were in Florida playing a gig, and somebody was sitting in. I don't remember who it was, but we're playing a tune and we're soloing. So, it's this guy's turn to play, and he's kind of getting warmed up and inching into the solo, and Howard looks at him and says, 'Do something. Do something.' He didn't realize how funny he was."

Lienhard came to New York in 1977 after receiving her Bachelor of Music Education (BME) degree from the University of Wisconsin at Eau Claire. She recalled playing at a club called Far and Away in Cliffside Park, New Jersey. "The guy who owned the place liked to get bigger-name people on the weekends, but money being what it was, he would hire the guy and say, 'I will provide you with a rhythm section,'" Lienhard said. "I got to play with a lot of people as a result of that, and if they were happy with what happened, the next time they would say, 'Can you get those same people?' And it would branch out to other types of jobs."

She met McGhee while playing at a club in Paramus, New Jersey, called Emerson's with Joe Morello (drummer with the Dave Brubeck Quartet in the 1950s and 1960s) whom she had met at a percussion workshop in Eau Claire. McGhee also played at Emerson's with a pianist named Jim Roberts. A couple of years later, Lienhard became part of McGhee's band.

"Earl and I were really part of his last band," she said. "We really had wonderful musical experiences with him. You knew he was frustrated because all the stuff didn't come out the way he wanted it to. The drugs and alcohol that had been a big part of his existence definitely took its toll. His physical body just couldn't execute what was in his head anymore. And then his health just started failing."

Lienhard said the late Rev. John Gensel, who headed the "jazz ministry' at Saint Peter's Church, talked about Howard being "shoulder to shoulder with Dizzy Gillespie." "If you said that to the average person who knows something about music, they'd say, 'I don't even know who this guy is. What are you talking about?' His career didn't manifest itself the way that Dizzy's did," she said. "But could he have? Absolutely. He was a very special person. I wish he'd been in better health. His body just broke down."

Lienhard and her current husband, bassist Nate Lienhard, both teach music in the Caldwell-West Caldwell School District in New Jersey. They also co-lead a jazz group, Grey Lienhard Jazz. She is the author of several books featuring jazz piano arrangements, published by Ekay Music, and is a contributing editor/arranger to "Piano and Keyboard Stylist" and "Sheet Music" magazines.

Her relationship with Morello, she said, paid off in one of her classes at the Grover Cleveland Middle School in Caldwell. "I had my kids doing a project," she recalled, "and one of my little guys who's a drummer in the band chose something from a big band that Joe had for awhile. It was called 'Drumorello.' I hadn't talked to Joe in awhile, but I called him on the phone and said, 'This sixth grader chose your video, and we're watching it. If I put you on speakerphone, will you talk to the kids?' He spoke to the kids, and then I put Zach, the drummer, on. He had his practice pad and his sticks, so I said, 'Zach, come up and play something for Joe.' You should have seen the look on the kid's face. I said, 'Joe, you got any advice for my kid?' He said, 'Keep practicing, kid.' You have to grab those moments when you can."

MILT HINTON

During its heyday in the late 1930s and early 1940s, the Cab Calloway Orchestra would literally live on a train for three months of every year. Because it was difficult for black musicians to find decent hotel rooms, Calloway would lease a Pullman and, according to bassist Milt Hinton, drive from town to town and park the Pullman on the side of the tracks. "We'd play the town and come on back and go to sleep," Hinton said. "The next morning the train would come along and pick us up and take us to the next place. We'd take three months to play all the theaters, starting at Newark and going on to Philadelphia, Pittsburgh, Detroit, Youngstown, Akron, Chicago, Milwaukee—right straight west to California."

Once the band was finished in California, it would work its way back to New York, playing one-nighters. On that leg of the trip, however, it wasn't always possible to secure a Pullman. "Trains didn't come through all these places, so Calloway would hire a Greyhound bus," Hinton said. "We'd get into these small towns in the South, and there would be no place for us to stay. We would get there just in time to go to the dance hall and play."

But Hinton's wife, Mona—the only woman who traveled with the band—would usually find a solution. "Mona would go through the town and meet some nice black lady—she's got that amiable way about her. And she'd say, 'I'm married to one of the musicians who's playing at the dance tonight, and the fellows don't have any place to stay. Can you help me find some rooms in the neighborhood?' The lady would say yes and get on the phone. Then my wife would say, 'Look, if I go to the store and get about six or eight chickens, and if I give you $5, will you help me cook 'em? And I'll make some potato salad because the boys haven't had a thing to eat.' When intermission came, Mona would have two or three ladies with her with a basketful of chicken and ham and potato salad. And she'd have a list—'Now, Bob, you're staying over at Miss Jones's house, and, Charlie, you're over here at Miss Smith's house.' And she'd have this whole list made out. And this is how we survived the one-nighters in the South."

Even when the band had the Pullman, there were problems. Hinton remembered one particularly frightening time in Longview, Texas. "They had found oil in this town," Hinton said. "It was oozing up out of the ground. The white folks had sold this land to the 'niggers' for 50 cents an acre because it was making their cows sick. Then somebody came through and discovered all this oil, and, overnight, everybody's rich—the white folks and the black folks. A guy's getting $10,000 a month for the right to drill on his land, and he never had enough to eat before."

Some of the newly rich white citizens of Longview had decided to have a dance, "and we came down in our Pullman," Hinton continued. "We had to take cabs from the Pullman way the hell out in the country to a dance pavilion out in a park. It's dark as hell out there. Here we are, and we're playing, and they're drunk. The more we played, the hotter the music got and the more they drank. Thank God our road manager was a white Texan—Jack Boyd was his name. The piano player's sitting right by the side of the bandstand, and there's a white girl sitting there, and she's with her boyfriend, and she says to the piano player, 'Hey, boy, have a drink!' And he says, 'No thanks. I don't care for it.' Then, she says, 'What's the matter, you're too good to take a drink from me?' So then he takes a drink, and her boyfriend says, 'Hey, are you drinking out of my girl's glass?' So then he starts an argument."

Meanwhile, "they had a rule in the town that if you hit a 'nigger,' you could pay $300, and it was all over. So, everybody's lining up by the bandstand to hit Cab Calloway. Jack Boyd went and spoke to the manager—the guy who was giving the dance. The manager says, 'Well, I'll try to save you niggers if I can.' Jack had noticed there was a basement—just one hole in the floor under the bandstand, no back door or anything. He says, 'At intermission, you guys go downstairs.' There's no way out except right up the steps again. We're down there, and then they started. We heard whompin' and stompin' and bottles breaking. Well, after they didn't see us, they got drunk and fought amongst themselves. And they fought until they knocked themselves out. We stayed down there for an hour and a half until they cleared out the place. Then Jack Boyd sent for the cars to come and take us back to our Pullman."

As 73-year-old Milt Hinton sat in his office in midtown Manhattan in 1985, the fact that such incidents ever occurred seemed difficult to believe. But there were other memories, even more unpleasant, from his early childhood in Vicksburg, Mississippi. When he was around five or six years old he remembers standing under a tree and looking up to see "a black man wrapped like a piece of bacon around a drum of gasoline. People were shooting at him. He'd been long dead because they drug him all through town for some accusation. These people all around were shooting at his carcass."

"In Mississippi, when you lynched a 'nigger,' you cut the tree down and painted the stump red," Hinton explained. "When I came by on the way to school the next morning, the red paint was still dripping from the stump of this tree. I really didn't comprehend what was going on, but, later, since I've been grown, I've read newspaper accounts and books about these lynchings, and I look back and say, 'Wow! I saw this thing.'"

To African-Americans like Hinton, escape lay to the north. In 1910, the year he was born, his family began migrating to Chicago. It wasn't easy, however. They had to sneak out of Mississippi because "you couldn't just leave, especially the men," said Hinton. "They didn't mind the women and children, but they didn't want to lose the labor." Chicago, he recalled, looked like paradise. "It was the center of the United States, with all the hotels and the big stockyards and the railroads. And for the first time since slavery, black people were beginning to get some decent jobs."

The Hinton family migration, starting with adult men, took seven years. "My uncles migrated there first, then my mother and my mother's sisters. They got up enough money to buy furniture and get a nice apartment and furnish it properly. Then they sent for the old folks and the children," he said. To a seven-year-old from Mississippi, Chicago was great: "We had a nice apartment; everybody was working; we had food; I could go to a good school. People had an opportunity to see that their children got a break."

Hinton began taking music lessons while still in elementary school. "My mother was a schoolteacher and a pianist. She was Nat Cole's piano teacher, but it is very difficult to teach your own children," he said. "She wanted me to be a musician, so she farmed me out to a violin teacher named Professor James Johnson. He inspired and taught me."

Another inspiration was a woman he simply remembered as Mrs. Malone. She presented concerts—"violin concertos and other classical things"—on Sundays in a mansion she owned on South Parkway (later changed to Martin Luther King Drive). That street, recalled Hinton, was originally called Grand Boulevard and housed all the grand mansions owned by people like the Swifts (of Swift Packing). Later, as black people began to move into the community, these people made their exodus, and the houses stayed vacant until some wealthy black people acquired enough money to buy them," he recalled. Mrs. Malone had accumulated her wealth by "concocting something to straighten black people's hair."

Hinton attended Wendell Phillips High School on Chicago's south side, which he described it as having been "99 and 44/100ths percent black. The only white students were the children of merchants who owned stores in the neighborhood. While a student at Wendell Phillips (his classmates included Nat Cole and Lionel Hampton), Hinton helped out at his uncles' cleaning and pressing store, which was actually "a shill place for bootleg whisky, which was sold by Al Capone. Every Friday he would come in this long limousine with bulletproof glass and sell us a case of bonded whiskey. He'd say, 'Buy this alcohol from me for $12 a gallon and sell it for $18.' He'd already paid all the police off."

It was Hinton's duty to undo the seal and pour the whiskey into a tub: "Then, we'd pour alcohol in there," he said. "We'd take that one case of whiskey and make three cases, put the seal back on it, and sell it for $5 a pint, and people thought they had bonded whiskey. If anyone wanted their clothes pressed, we had a Hoffman pressing machine in there which I had to keep hot. I knew how to press a suit, and I got to keep the 25 cents we charged. But if they wanted something cleaned, it was my duty to tell them, 'the cleaner just left, and we won't be able to get it to you for two weeks.' Of course, people would go someplace else."

Capone owned a nightclub in Chicago called the Cotton Club (patterned after the more famous one in New York, which featured all-black entertainment). "He hired a band headed by Walter Bonds, a young man from Mississippi. Well, all the guys in my high school got jobs playing there, and they were making $75 a week, which was astronomical, but I didn't," he explained, "because I was playing violin and they didn't use violins in the band.".

At the same time, another potential source of music-related income for 19-year-old Hinton abruptly disappeared. "This was 1929," he recalled, "and in 1927, Al Jolson had made the first talking movie. All the theaters had been using violins, but because of talking movies, all the violin players lost their jobs overnight. There I was just preparing to come into this great market, and the soundies came in, and I'm completely out of work. I was delivering newspapers—271 papers every morning—and I got $9.75 a week. A friend of mine was working at Al Capone's Cotton Club, and he bought a Ford car with disc wheels. He would get home about 4:30 in the morning when I'm starting out with my papers. I'd be on South Parkway, and I'd see him coming, and I'd try to hide."

Hinton's solution was to learn the bass. "It was also a string instrument—the 4ths just become 5ths. I was able to convert quickly, and I played with orchestras around school until I got onto it," he said. "Then people began to give me jobs. My first job was with a trumpet player named Hugh Swift. I guess all the bass players must have died one night, and somebody recommended me. I made $19, which was absolutely unheard of. Every now and then this guy would call me, and I would have to stay up to do this job. My mother said, 'You've got to decide which you're going to be. You can't get up at 4:30 in the morning and come home at 4.' Picking music was one of the biggest decisions of my life. I didn't know if the music was going to hold up, and I was sure of my lunch money and carfare from the newspaper job."

By the early 1930s, Hinton had hooked up with Eddie South, a violinist who had been touring Europe with his own combo. "Eddie South had made a great name playing Hungarian songs and gypsy music. He was called the 'dark angel of the violin.' An agent in Chicago got him to agree to come back to the United States," Hinton said. "That was 1931 or 1932. They promised him they were going to build a big society orchestra around him. They promised him the Palmer House and the Edgewater Beach hotels. They got a violin player in Chicago who had been a friend of Eddie's to organize a big orchestra, and we were rehearsing until Eddie got back. The agent signed us all up to contracts for $75 a week, 40 weeks a year. We had three or four violins and trombones, and we were playing beautiful songs 'Dancing on the Ceiling'—cocktail music.

"Eddie came back, and he was just ecstatic," he added. "We continued to rehearse, and then the powers that be said, 'No, we can't do this. The time isn't right (for a black orchestra to play at places like the Palmer House and Edgewater Beach). So this agent said, 'The only thing to do is, we'll just have to pay these guys. We'll give them $300 apiece to buy their contracts back.' He bought everybody's contract back except mine. When they got to me, he said, 'Look, Eddie, don't give the bass player anything. We can use him. We'll give him

$75 a week, and we can go into one of the small clubs on the north side and add the bass player to your group.' Eddie had a clarinet player, a guitar player, and a drummer, so I made the fifth piece. We went into a club that Al Capone had opened on the north side called the Club Rubaiyat. I don't think it seated 100, but it was just ideal for Eddie. The people liked to hear a classical violin player who played some jazz. We played 'American in Paris' and 'Rhapsody in Blue.' We had a mishmash of a repertoire."

If Chicago had seemed like paradise to seven-year-old Milt Hinton in 1917, it was a musical heaven in the early 1930s. "Ben Pollard's band was right across the street. Ben Berney's band was at the College Inn. Benny Goodman and Jack Teagarden were with Ben Pollard, and they used to come over to hear us play," he said. "In 1933, when the Democratic Convention was held at the Congress Hotel, they put us in the lobby. That was the convention where Franklin Delano Roosevelt was nominated for President."

Exclusion from the fancier Chicago hotel rooms was not the only humiliation faced by Eddie South in the early 1930s. He had been recommended by Joe Venuti to be an accompanist for Bea Palmer, a singer with the Paul Whiteman band, which Venuti was leaving. "Well, there was no way Eddie South could play in Paul Whiteman's band," said Hinton. "Bea Palmer threatened not to go on, so they put up a screen. She stood in front of the screen, and Eddie stood behind the screen and played."

Venuti, meanwhile, was on the road playing what was known as the country club circuit. "He was very successful," Hinton recalled, "and they'd ask him, 'Joe, is there anybody else we can get who plays like this?' And he'd say, 'Get Eddie South.' Consequently, we got the job playing the country clubs."

In 1936, as South headed back to Europe, where he would eventually enjoy his greatest success playing with guitarist Django Reinhardt and violinist Stephane Grappelli, Hinton hooked up with a band led by Zutty Singleton. Singleton, said Hinton, was "a great drummer from New Orleans. He had played in Louis Armstrong's Hot Five, and now he had his own band at the Three Deuces at State and Lake streets. A lot of the musicians in Chicago were New Orleans guys. I was from Mississippi, which my grandmother always said was 'hollerin' distance,' so they tolerated me."

While Hinton was playing with Singleton at the Three Deuces, Calloway was on his way back from California after making a movie with Al Jolson called "The Singin' Kid." Calloway's bass player had decided to stay out in California, so he returned east short a bassist. His trombone player was a friend of Hinton's, and he suggested Calloway stop in at the Three Deuces to hear Hinton play. Calloway hired Hinton, a job that lasted 16 years. "Cab," he said, "really wasn't a musician, but he could hire great musicians because he was paying good money. When there was a vacancy, he would depend on the musicians to decide on the replacement. He was a great showman, a great disciplinarian, and a generous man. He paid us $100 a week, and, man, that was a lot of money in 1936. The average person on the street was making $25-$30 a week."

Calloway's band endured until 1951, and when it finally broke up Hinton found himself out of work. "I came to New York, and I didn't know anybody." He remembered standing on Broadway between 49th and 50th streets and running into Jackie Gleason. "I knew Gleason in Jersey when he couldn't get arrested," he said. "He was telling jokes in these little joints, and nobody was laughing. The musicians were getting tips, so we'd buy him drinks. Now he's at CBS, and he's a big man. He was with his manager, and he saw me walkin' down the street. He said, 'You guys were so nice to me I want to put you in my band. We're recording tomorrow.'" In the 1950s, Gleason recorded a series of mood music albums with cornetist Bobby Hackett under the "Music for Lovers Only" title.

"He told his manager, 'I want Milton on the bass,' and his manager looked at him like he was crazy. He said, 'Jackie, we *got* a bass player.' Jackie said, 'I don't care; I want him.' As a result, I did all the 'Honeymooners' TV shows. Everybody saw me on the Gleason dates, so I got Andre Kostelanetz dates and Percy Faith dates and CBS work. It just mushroomed like that."

Hinton was one of the few blacks at that time doing studio work, but he never experienced problems fitting in. It was never the musicians who were responsible for barring blacks, he pointed out, "it was the powers that be, the public, society. (Trombonist) Jack Teagarden could come to see *us*, but we couldn't go to see *him*. In Miami, if a black guy was caught on the beach after midnight, he had to have a note in his pocket that said, 'This boy works for me, and I'm Mr. so-and-so, and I live down the street, etc.' Dizzy Gillespie and I got put in jail one night. We had stopped at a club to hear some white guys from New York playin'. We knew we couldn't go in the club, so we stood in the back behind the club on the side by the door. The musicians knew we were out there, but the police came along and locked us up."

In the 1980s, Hinton was as busy as he wanted to be. He taught a jazz workshop at Baruch College in New York City. He played concerts, clubs, and record dates in both the United States and abroad, and he presented jazz clinics at schools. He was known in music circles as "the judge," a nickname he acquired in the 1950s. "After I got with Gleason, for 10 or 15 years I made two or three record dates every day," he recalled. "Everybody told stories about themselves during a record date, and I told a story about Vicksburg when I was a kid. This one guy used to get drunk every Saturday night, and he was a drag to the community because Sunday morning he'd be lying in the street, and people would be going to church. So people went to the police department and said, 'Look. He's gonna get drunk whatever you do. Just pick him up and put him away. Some of the ladies will put food down for him. Leave him stay up there until Sunday so he won't be seen on the streets—it looks bad. Then let him out on Monday.' So every Monday he'd sober up and walk into court, and he thought he was in for something, and he'd say, 'Good morning, judge.' And the judge would say, 'Case dismissed. Get outta here.' It was a funny story the way I told it at the time. Cab Calloway had been a stickler for punctuality, so I was always the first guy there for a record date. I'd have my instrument out and be all set and have my coffee. I never wanted to be rushed into anything. One day, the conductor came in and said, 'Well, the judge is here. Good morning, judge.' And it just stuck."

UPDATE

Milt Hinton died in 2000 at the age of 90. In addition to his considerable talent as a bassist, Hinton was a prolific and talented photographer, taking his camera with him practically everywhere. In February and March 2008, Baruch College presented an exhibit called "Playing the Changes: The Jazz Photographs of Milt Hinton." The exhibit, in the college's Mishkin Gallery, was shown in connection with the publication of "Playing the Changes: Milt Hinton's Life in Stories and Photographs" by David Berger and Holly Maxon (Vanderbilt University Press: 2008). The 40 photographs on display included Cab Calloway with a group of children in Providence, Rhode Island (1938), alto saxophonist Johnny Hodges at Beefsteak Charlie's restaurant/bar in New York (1960), and Dizzy Gillespie at the Grande Parade du Jazz festival in Nice, France (1981).

Available CDs with Hinton performing include "The Second Time Around" with vibraharpist Red Norvo and Kenny Davern (Progressive Records: original release 1975) and the previously mentioned "Buck Clayton Jam Sessions" with Earle Warren.

Warren Vache

Cornetist/trumpeter Warren Vache led a small group playing at a reception held at Baruch College for the Hinton photo exhibit on February 7, 2008. Vache, who played often with Hinton, particularly liked a whole series of photos Hinton had taken at Beefsteak Charlie's, a hangout for jazz musicians in the 1950s and early 1960s. "You look at those guys, and it seems like they're having such a good time," Vache said. "You can see this love for everybody; they're having a ball, laughing. You look at the bar, and there's not a Chardonnay glass or a beer glass to be seen. It's all 15-cent shot glasses, water back."

Vache, now 57, was in his twenties and early thirties when he played with Hinton. "Mona called me one of her kids," he recalled. The Hinton group included pianist Ralph Sutton, drummer Gus Johnson, and, sometimes Davern, in addition to Vache. "When we'd go on long trips, such as to a ski resort in Taos, New Mexico, and Mona would go out shopping, and she'd always come back with something for the musicians. It might have cost 50 cents or a dollar, but she'd always come back with something," Vache said. "As dumb as I was and all the mistakes I'd make, Milt was so tolerant and willing to help. If you asked him a question, he'd take the time and answer it. There was always this willingness to share both his life and his personality. He was just the most open and caring human being. I really miss the sort of relationship I had with older musicians when I was young. I don't know if I'm doing my bit to keep up that end. I try."

The camaraderie that existed among musicians 30 years ago, in Vache's opinion, doesn't seem to exist now. He remembers a bar called Jim & Andy's on West 48_{th} Street. "Every musician hung out there," he said. "I would finish working at Eddie Condon's at 3 o'clock in the morning, and I'd go over there and knock on the door. The door would be locked, but they'd open it, and every musician was in there." That camaraderie manifested itself in other ways as well. Two other contemporaries of Hinton who were influential in Vache's life and career were trombonist Vic Dickenson and trumpeter

Roy Eldridge. "Both Vic and Roy thought enough of me not to pull their punches.," Vache said.

Recalling one night when he was playing with Dickenson, Vache said, "I was playing 78 different notes. Vic put the trombone in my ear and very softly played the melody. I had a choice. I could be angry or I could learn from that. Later, when we talked, he said, 'Your job is to play the melody and to phrase it in a way that we know what you're going to play so we can play harmony with you. That way, it sounds like a band.'"

Vache was fortunate enough in the 1970s and 1980s to play in the house band at Eddie Condon's on West 54_{th} Street. Condon's was down the street from Jimmy Ryan's, where the legendary trumpeter Roy Eldridge (the musical link between Louis Armstrong and Dizzy Gillespie) was playing. "I learned not to go to Ryan's before 11 o'clock," Vache said. "During the first two sets, Roy was warming up. By 11, he was ready to tear the roof off the joint. So, I'd take my break from Condon's and go to Jimmy Ryan's and order a beer at the bar. Roy would scan the bar, and he would see me—the young blood, the competition. The roof would come off the place. The crowd would be going nuts. Halfway through, I'd go back to Condon's and do my set. And I'd look down at the bar, and there's Roy Eldridge staring up at me. 'Okay, your turn. Show me what you got.' I pulled out every trick I had. Every night, that's what happened. It was always competitive but never demeaning. It was never meant to hurt. It was probably the best teaching experience I ever had. At the same time, I was considered worthy of competition, so it was a shot in the arm as well as being taught a lesson."

DEREK SMITH

Pianist Derek Smith relocated from London to New York City in the mid-1950s and got to know Milt Hinton when both were working in New York studios. "He was very good to me," Smith recalled. "I was sitting at home one Saturday afternoon and he called me and said, 'Get yourself down to Columbia 30_{th} (a legendary New York studio known for its natural acoustics).' Then he said, 'By the way, do you play the organ?' I said, 'Of course. It has keys doesn't it?' But he got me through it. He was playing the bass, so I didn't have to play the feet, and it turned out that it was a big record—it was the New Christy Minstrels, who were pretty hot then. It was just the three of us playing—drums, organ, and Milt. So, I have a lot to thank him for, and he was good to practically every young bass player who came to New York. He took them under his wing."

The only time Smith played regularly with Hinton was at an annual gig they did every summer in the 1970s in Disney World with drummer Bobby Rosengarden. "All year, Disney World would go with a regular trio, and then, for the hottest two weeks of the year, they would import Bobby, Milt, and myself, and we would play for two weeks. It was good for us. We would get away for awhile, and I was a hero to my kids because we got this nice big villa, and they got all the rides for free. We did that for many years."

Smith, Hinton, and Rosengarden made one album together, "The Trio" (Chiaroscuro, 1994), and you can sense Smith's regret that they didn't record together more frequently. "We played all the things we had practiced in Disney World—bossa novas and straight ahead things. And Milt had some nice solos on Duke Ellington ballads. He wasn't what you'd call a real bowing bass player, but he played those things very well. We should have done another album, but we all got busy and went in different directions." In addition to an Ellington Medley of more than 10 minutes, "The Trio" included a Brazilian Medley along with such standards as George Gershwin's "Fascinating Rhythm" and Cole Porter's "Love for Sale".

No musician could talk about Hinton without mentioning Mona, who died at the age of 89 in May 2008. Smith recalls a trip to Iceland. "Rosengarden got this gig in Iceland, and Cab Calloway was going to be there, so that's why Milt was going," he explained. "The people there were all German businessmen working for IBM. They'd never heard of Cab Calloway, but we had a wonderful time. They took us on trips, and we were going up this mountain, a volcano, and Mona couldn't contain herself anymore. She said, 'Milton, get away from that volcano!' She was very protective of him."

Smith remembers the studio era in New York, roughly the mid-1950s through the late 1960s, as a marvelous time. "There's nothing like it anymore," he lamented. "There was a need for musicians; we were all really busy. I was doing 'The Tonight Show,' and then in the morning you'd do some recordings with some singers, and you'd do jingles. But nothing stays the same. The business changed, and all of a sudden there were rock 'n roll bands, and all the entertainers went out to California."

Today, at 77, Smith is still an active, energetic performer and crowd pleaser. At a 2008 solo concert at the Bickford Theater in Morristown,

New Jersey, he played all of the selections from a new CD that hadn't been released yet and then asked for requests from the audience. His personal musical hero is the late pianist Oscar Peterson. "I always loved Oscar Peterson," he said. "I thought he was the best guy I ever heard. Oscar had pulse, drive, technique—anything that came into his head. It's what we're all trying to do."

Smith also experienced playing with Benny Goodman. "I had a great friend, the drummer, Mousey Alexander, who called me one day and said, 'I'm going to get you with Benny.' Before I knew it, there I am rehearsing with this big band, scared stiff, because Benny had this reputation. But I could read, and he put up Fats Waller's 'Stealin' Apples.' The piano chorus was in the key of D, so I passed the test. I didn't hear from Benny for years," he said, "but then, later on, when I'm really busy doing 'The Tonight Show' and doing everybody's record dates, he called me to do weekends. So I went out and played weekends with Benny all over the place. Then, he asked me to go to Australia, and 'The Tonight Show' said they would get a sub for me so I could go. It was a beautiful band—Zoot Sims on tenor saxophonist, Joe Pass on guitar, Peter Appleyard on vibes—and we started out in Sydney, and Zoot got a great big hand, and I got a great big hand; and Benny got pissed about the whole thing. So, we cursed each other out, finished out the tour, and never saw each other again. But everybody's got a similar story about Benny."

CHAPTER 8

The Happy Singer: Helen Humes

"I don't know nothing about singing anymore, and Carnegie Hall is too big to be trying." It is difficult to believe that Helen Humes ever uttered those words in 1973. Five years later in 1978, at the age of 64, Humes exuded unbridled confidence as she frolicked through a typical repertoire—ranging from the bluesy "Don't Worry 'Bout Me" to the winsomely upbeat "Pennies From Heaven."

In the spring of 1973, however, British music writer Stanley Dance met with resistance when he traveled to Louisville to persuade her to participate in a Count Basie reunion at the Newport Jazz Festival in New York. "He called me, said he was going to be in town and would like to talk to me," Humes recalled. "He sat there all night begging me." Reluctantly, Humes accepted the invitation and unwittingly revitalized a career that had been dormant for six years. After that Carnegie concert in June 1973, her star began rising. She toured Europe several times, she appeared regularly at nightclubs in New York and around the country, and she recorded two albums for Columbia Records.

A robust woman with an endearing childlike quality, Humes said she was nervous before the Carnegie concert, but after she went on, things were all right. "Five days later, I was in France touring with Milt Buckner and Jay McShann. (Buckner was a jazz organist who started out on the piano with Lionel Hampton in the 1930s, and McShann was a pianist and bandleader who first achieved popularity in Kansas City in the 1930s). I even made an album over there called 'Helen Comes Back,'" she said.

Humes was asked to do another European tour in 1974, and then she received a call from another old friend, Barney Josephson (no relation to the author), owner of The Cookery, a restaurant and music room in Greenwich Village. Josephson was a veteran of the music business, having run the successful Cafe Society nightclubs in New York in the 1940s. He wanted Humes to sing at his restaurant's New Year's Eve party.

At that time, Humes's aging father was ill. One of the reasons she had stopped singing in 1967 was to care for him. "Before I got ready to come to New York," she recalled, "I said to Papa, 'Mr. Josephson wants me to sing at his club.' My father asked, 'Are you going?' I said, 'If you feel all right.' And he said, 'I want you to go because I know my baby can sing. I got a very nice lady to stay with him; I played the New Year's Eve party, and then on January 3, 1975, my father died." Humes opened an extended engagement at The Cookery later that month and played there regularly during the late 1970s.

Josephson had launched The Cookery in 1955 and operated it strictly as a restaurant for 15 years until jazz pianist Mary Lou Williams persuaded him to add music in 1970. "For 20 years, I had nothing to do with the entertainment business or with talent," he said. "So when I found myself back in the music business, I naturally thought of bringing back the people who had worked for me before. I didn't know anybody but the old-timers. I thought of Helen. I knew she lived in Louisville. I called information and asked if they had a phone number for Helen Humes. A few minutes later, I had her on the phone. I said, 'Come up here. You're going to be singing again.'"

Humes, Josephson felt, was "in better voice" in 1974, than when she worked with Basie. "I called her a happy singer," he said. "She can sing sad songs and make you feel happy. A couple could come in here after having a fight. They could be snarling at each other, and, five minutes after hearing Helen sing, they'll go out holding hands and feeling happy. That's the quality she has."

Josephson first met Humes in the early 1940s after she'd left the Basie band. She was brought to Cafe Society by John Hammond, a record producer and talent scout who is credited with discovering such diverse talents as Benny Goodman and Bob Dylan. In 1975, Hammond produced a Columbia record album for Humes called "Talk of the Town," and later that summer he produced a second album for her. "It's incredible," he said then, "that someone who started performing when she was 15 in 1928 still sounds as youthful and effervescent as she does today." Hammond characterized her as original right from the start. "She was 15 when she made her first record, so she'd have been too young to have any influences," he explained.

The singer agreed with that assessment. "When I was growing up in Louisville, I used to play the piano and sing," Humes said. "I used to just sing the way I felt. I didn't have any records; I just had the piano. People ask me who I've been influenced by. I wasn't influenced by anybody because I didn't hear anybody."

Somebody did hear *her*, though. A Louisville-area blues guitarist whom she simply remembered as "Mr. Weaver" not only liked her singing but did something about it. He wrote to Tom Rockwell, an executive with the now defunct Okeh Records, and in 1928 Rockwell asked Humes's mother to bring her to St. Louis for an audition. John Hammond happened to hear the first record Humes made for Okeh, a song called, "Do What You Did Last Night." Although he had heard the record in 1931, it wasn't until a few years later that he saw Humes in person.

"I used to hang out at a place called the Renaissance Ballroom in Harlem, and the tenor saxophone player was a guy named Al Sears," Hammond recalled. "He played in Vernon Andrade's band. Helen had come in from Cincinnati where she'd been working at the Cincinnati Cotton Club. She started singing with Andrade and Sears. At that time, Count Basie only had a small band in Kansas City, but I brought him to New York in November 1939. He had a male vocalist, Jimmy Rushing, and Jimmy wasn't particularly interested in having any female competition. But we did get Billie Holiday singing with Basie's band in 1937. After she left, the way had at least been paved for having a girl singer. I arranged a session with Basie; Helen sang 'Song of the Wanderer' and some blues, and that proved to Basie—who had once heard her at the Cincinnati Cotton Club—that she was the logical replacement for Billie."

That chance audition earlier in Cincinnati was clearly remembered by Earle Warren. "After I joined Basie, I didn't see Helen for a couple of years. Then she joined us," said Warren, who obviously still nourished a special fondness for Humes. "I used to talk about her and brag about her because she looked good, and she could sing. Everybody had nicknames. She was built kind of strong and had nice hips. So we called her Fanny. 'Course nobody calls her that now but me."

Humes remembered the Basie band members as "a lovely bunch of fellows. They treated me like I was a little girl. But I don't think

I could take those one-nighters and traveling on the bus anymore." The traveling, though, wasn't the only hardship. She also alluded to the racial prejudices of those days, recalling that sometimes she would go out to a store and buy food and make a meal for the band because they couldn't find a restaurant that would serve them.

The racial bias didn't just manifest itself on the road, however. Hammond remembered that in 1936 Helen was in New York when Hammond had her make some recordings with Harry James's first recording band. "They were wonderful records. She was the best vocalist Harry James ever had," Hammond said. "But it wasn't customary in those days for black singers to be with white bands. So that record session never related itself to live performances."

The nuance that differentiates a "jazz" singer from the broader "pop" classification is a subject that has been argued interminably. Hammond believed the mark of a jazz vocalist was "the ability to improvise around a melody, and Helen can do that supremely, and she can do it differently almost every time." Warren believed Humes had "a jumpin,' relaxing" sound. "She can do well with anything—ballads, blues. A lot of people just do one or the other," he said.

And how did she categorize herself? "I just know I'm a singer, and I sing songs the way I feel," said Humes. "I like the ballads—songs that tell a story, that have nice lyrics. My favorite composers are George Gershwin, Fats Waller, and Hoagy Carmichael." Humes had a hit record in 1945, a novelty song called "Ooo Baba Leba" that tended to typecast her as a rhythm and blues singer after she had left the Basie band. She did some touring in the 1950s with vibraharpist Red Norvo. She also recorded several albums in the late 1950s and early 1960s for Contemporary Records, a small jazz label based in Los Angeles, while also making occasional trips to Europe and Australia.

Her career had slowed considerably in the mid-1960s and, finally, in 1967 she called it quits, returning to Louisville to care for her father. She also worked in a munitions factory in the area for about two years. "A friend of mine in Louisville asked me to give her a ride so she could see about a job." she recalled, "I got the job; she didn't. It paid $2.85 an hour, and I stayed one year and 11 months."

Humes has always been considered by insiders to be one of the handful of really remarkable women jazz singers, but real fame eluded her. She never received the widespread recognition accorded to some of her contemporaries. That seemed unimportant to her. It was clear in the late 1970s that she was happy—just as her singing indicated.

Warren, lamenting that "nobody heard of her for a long time," credited her comeback to the general return to popularity of jazz then. "When jazz began to come back, people were wondering what happened to this person and what happened to that person," he said.

Hammond believed the reason for the revival in the 1970s was because "we're finally becoming conscious of our heritage in this country." But Josephson was more direct. "There is respect for older people again," he said. "At one point nobody wanted to listen to anyone past 50. That's changed."

(Adapted from an article that originally appeared in *The (Louisville) Courier-Journal,* July 23, 1978.)

UPDATE

Helen Humes died of cancer in September 1981, in Santa Monica, California. In June 2008, the U.K.-based Acrobat Records re-released a CD called "Today I Sing the Blues," which represented highlights from the first 20 years of Humes's career. Other recently released CDs include "Knockin' Myself Out" (Jazz Legends: 2005) and "1948–1950" (Melodie Jazz Classic: 2004).

Norman Simmons

Norman Simmons accompanied Humes during her appearances at The Cookery. "When I started with Helen, I thought I was subbing for her regular piano player, who had gone to the West Coast," Simmons said. "I didn't realize he had already left. I didn't want to do the gig because Barney would keep people there for months, and I didn't want to get stuck on a regular gig. But, for some reason, I wound up there anyway. I played with Helen up to the time she died. At the time, she was taking chemotherapy. Everybody loved her. She was such a lovable person. When we went out to eat, I had to learn not to order anything because everybody would just be giving Helen stuff. So she'd end up with a bunch of samples of food, and I'd have to finish it."

Simmons, who has accompanied countless singers—from Carmen McRae to Anita O'Day—said he has never heard anyone who has been influenced by Humes. "She's one of a kind," he said.

David Leonhardt

David Leonhardt grew up in Louisville. One of his first gigs, before moving to New York, was as the pianist in the house band at the Fig Tree, a local Louisville jazz club. "The club would bring people in, and one of the people they brought in for a couple of weeks was Helen Humes," he recalled. "She actually had her own pianist, Gerry Wiggins, and he actually did the gig with her. But I sat in and played with her." Leonhardt, who was only 20 years old at the time, remembers Humes as "really nice, a very sweet woman, and she drew more than anybody else at that club, *ever*."

CHAPTER 9

The Religion of Bebop: John Birks "Dizzy" Gillespie

John Birks "Dizzy" Gillespie felt there were several contributors to the development of bebop in the early 1940s. "Monk (pianist Thelonious Monk) and Clyde Hart (also a pianist) were good contributors harmonically," Gillespie said. "Charlie Christian (guitar) and Kenny Clarke (drums) contributed both harmonically and rhythmically. There was Charlie Parker with style. And there was me, with all three."

With the last comment, the rotund Gillespie broke into uncontrollable laughter. It was difficult to keep him serious for too long. The dominant trait in his personality was sheer buffoonery. "I love fun," he admitted unabashedly. "Music is full of fun, but it's hard work, too. There's a lot of hard work behind that fun you're having." Gillespie made these comments while having a frogs legs dinner in the Oak Room of New York's Algonquin Hotel in May 1981, four days prior to a concert being videotaped as part of a Public Broadcasting Service series on the history of jazz. The first four-and-a-half hours of that series, which aired in the fall of 1981, were devoted to bebop.

Bebop, he explained (getting serious again), "was just one of the developments of our culture. Music—especially jazz—can be similar to a religion. It doesn't reveal all of itself at one time." As for the development of bop, "We had no way of knowing that the time was right. There was no assurance about anything. The one thing we did know is that it was time to make a change in the playing of our music. When Charlie Parker came up with the change in the phrasing of our music, that was it, and everything from that point on was with the assumption that it was going to be in that vein."

The real breakthrough, he explained, was, "at a Carnegie Hall concert we did with Ella Fitzgerald in 1947 or 1948. Afterwards, Charlie Parker bought me a rose. It was probably his last dollar." Bebop has settled in as a basic ingredient in jazz, so the natural temptation was to ask Gillespie if he foresaw anything new on the musical horizon. "I'm listening for something new," he confided. "The next thing is going to be the unification of the music of the Western Hemisphere—the blending of the music of Cuba, Brazil, the West Indies, and the United States."

Despite Gillespie's wish for musical unification, one of the acknowledged frustrations of jazz musicians has been the feeling that their music has often been more appreciated in Europe and Japan than in their own country. Gillespie admitted that a wide range of activities is available overseas, but he also believed some misconceptions existed about the opportunities jazz offered in the United States. "I can go to a university in the United States and lecture," he pointed out. (In fact, at the time he had just been awarded an honorary Doctor of Humane Letters degree from Fairleigh Dickinson University in Teaneck, New Jersey.) "In Europe, they don't know what I'm talking about. I appear on TV talk shows here. That would be almost impossible in Europe. I also do voices for animation. One of them, 'The Hole,' won an Academy Award."

Still, some jazz musicians, including Kenny Clarke, migrated to Europe permanently. "I have a friend, Bill Coleman, a trumpet player," Gillespie recalled. "I asked Bill, 'Why do you live in France?' He said, 'Well, Diz, once the French love you, they love you forever.' I couldn't make no answer to that one because I know the situation. In the U.S., you just have to be *up on it!* Otherwise, they'll forget about you in a minute."

(Adapted from an article that appeared in *ELECTRICity*, May 28– June 3, 1981.)

UPDATE

Dizzy Gillespie died of pancreatic cancer at the age of 75 in January 1993. Among the available recordings released after his death were "The Complete RCA Victor Recordings: 1947–1949" (RCA: 1995), "Sunny Side Up" with saxophonists Sonny Rollins and Sonny Stitt (Polygram Records: 1997), and "A Night in Tunisia: The Very Best of Dizzy Gillespie" (RCA: 2006).

Jeanie Bryson

Jeanie Bryson would see Dizzy Gillespie perform "all the time" when she was a little girl. She knew he was her father, and she knew "not to tell anybody." Her first memory of life, she said, was a bus ride from New York to Seattle to see Gillespie perform there. She sat on her mother's lap (her mother being the songwriter Connie Bryson) the whole way to Seattle because her mother only bought one ticket. "I remember looking out the window and seeing purple mountains," Bryson said. "We stayed at Quincy Jones's sister's house."

When Bryson attended college at Rutgers, she thought she wanted to go to law school, but "I was taking all these electives in music, and I kind of shifted my interest to the music classes," she said. She began studying keyboard harmony at Rutgers with pianist Kenny Barron, and by the late 1980s she had developed into an accomplished jazz singer.

In 1988, at the very early stage of her career, Bryson's father and tenor saxophonist Stan Getz came to hear her sing. "It was in New York at a club on 46_{th} Street called Terra Nova," she recalled. "They didn't tell me he was coming. I was downstairs in the bathroom putting on my makeup, and one of the waitresses came downstairs and said, 'Oh my God, Dizzy Gillespie's in the audience.' Stan Getz's son, Steve, was the booking agent for the agency that was trying to get me gigs at the time. He said Dizzy leaned over to Stan and said, 'Oh, she sounds just like me.' And Stan apparently replied, 'No, she doesn't. She sounds like Miles (Davis).' Then everybody laughed, and it was just a really nice moment. It was really nice because that didn't happen very often."

Gillespie's band, Bryson maintains, "*was* his family. His happiness, his joy was making music and being out on the road. I think he was out on the road 320 days out of the year for 50 years. I got to be backstage a lot and see the camaraderie and the friendship and the laughing and joking. Jazz musicians are notorious cutups and jokesters. I'm much more my mother's daughter. My mother actually taught me songs, talked about singing to me, talked about how to interpret a lyric. But I got none of the other stuff from my mom because she was not a performer. Then I would go see my father and see the brilliance onstage and the crowd loving him. It wasn't just music he was bringing to an audience; he was a goodwill ambassador."

In the mid-1970s, Bryson spent a lot of time seeing her father perform in New York. "I was old enough to take the bus into the city myself," she said. "He used to play a lot then at the Top of the Gate in Greenwich Village. He always had everyone around him, and he talked to everyone. He would never turn anyone away."

In 2007, Bryson embarked on a project called "The Dizzy Gillespie Songbook." She gave a series of concerts that highlighted a collection of songs to celebrate what would have been the year of her father's 90$_{th}$ birthday. It was a challenge because much of Gillespie's music did not include lyrics, but she also included some standards that he liked to play but didn't write, such as "Umbrella Man," "Ooh Bob Sh' Bam," "Lover Man," and "I Can't Get Started" as well as Gillespie compositions such as "A Night in Tunisia" and "Birks Works."

Transforming the cafeteria of Metuchen High School in Metuchen, New Jersey, into a cabaret, Bryson had one of the Gillespie Songbook sessions recorded for a DVD, and she hopes it will eventually get wide distribution, both prolonging her father's legacy and perhaps expanding her own reputation as a vocalist. The influence of the late Carmen McRae on Bryson's singing style is apparent, and she pointed out that McRae "also was my father's favorite singer," which is why she included the McRae song, "Beautiful Friendship," in the Gillespie Songbook.

While she would be categorized as a jazz singer today, Bryson didn't start out that way. Although she acknowledged listening to a lot of Dinah Washington when she was young, she also loved pop music. "I listened to Stevie Wonder and Roberta Flack and Phoebe Snow and people like that. I loved the Allman Brothers; I was a real child of the '70s," she said. "My grandfather played a lot of Nancy Wilson; he loved Blossom Dearie and Brazil '66. But as far as jazz singers go, Carmen McRae is the one that really got me. And Billie Holiday, Shirley Horn and Etta Jones."

"For me, a singer's got to really be in the pocket," she continued. "I don't really go much for esoteric, freewheeling ambiguity. I like swing. I love a good blues. As far as ballads go, I want to understand the words. I want to feel what the composer meant. I don't want to do up-tempo things slow and slow things up-tempo. I am not a jazz snob, and I don't think I ever will be. I'm a strong believer in melody, and that's what was so great about so many of the old songs, so many of the standards."

Bryson earned her degree in anthropology at Rutgers, but she credits the jazz department there—particularly Barron—for helping her develop her skills and confidence as a jazz singer. "When Kenny was my teacher, he kept looking at me kind of funny for weeks. Finally, we had a moment alone, and I kind of confessed to him that maybe I could solve his confusion about who I was," she said. "When I told him, he said, 'Oh my God, of course. I remember you running around backstage.' That would have been in 1962 or 1963 when I was about four or five years old."

John Lee

Bassist John Lee literally traveled all over the world with Dizzy Gillespie, but for him one concert in Egypt pretty much defines Dizzy Gillespie, the person. "It was a State Department tour in January 1988 through Africa," Lee recalled. "The first concert in Egypt was in a brand new opera hall. We got there, and the people were dressed so immaculately. At the break, Dizzy told the representatives from the State Department, 'Look, I made this very clear when I signed on to do this. I want the normal people to be able to attend these concerts. You have to make tickets available to them.' And they did. We were in Egypt for a week."

Lee joined Gillespie's quintet in 1984. He received a phone call from another bassist, Bob Cranshaw, who said, "You're going to go to Memphis with Dizzy. Stay by the phone. He's going to call you." Five minutes later, Lee said, "Dizzy called me, and the next thing I know I was at the airport. After the gig, he asked me to come by his hotel room, and he had his schedule laid out for the year. There was a European tour, a Caribbean cruise, a tour of India, etc. He said, 'How would you like to do all those jobs with me?' I had just vowed that I wasn't going to be in that kind of band for awhile, but I said, 'Oh, sure, okay.'" The bassist stayed with Gillespie for eight years until the trumpeter's health began to fail. "In 1987 and 1988, Dizzy revived the big band," Lee recalled. "At the end of 1988, he started the United Nations Orchestra, but the small group was always his staple."

Although Gillespie is most connected with bebop, Lee pointed out that he also "fused Afro-Cuban music with jazz. He was involved in that bossa nova movement that made Stan Getz famous. He made a few attempts at funky styles. By the time I got with Dizzy, a typical show would be, of course a lot of bebop, beautiful ballads, bossa nova, samba, Caribbean music, and funky backbeat music—there was a little bit of everything. It was always fun, though, every night. No matter how hard the travel was, how tired he was, when he hit that stage he was going to have some fun."

Lee estimates the band was on the road about 250 days a year. When asked to describe the hardest stretch, he said, "One time, we did 14 concerts in 15 days in Europe. Then we flew into Newark airport and played at Montclair State University that night. The next morning we caught a flight to Florida to play an afternoon jazz festival and got home about one in the morning. The next night we flew back to Europe, did four concerts. On the fifth day, we flew to Los Angeles, got off that plane, and played at UCLA. We played two more concerts in California, and we ended up in a club in San Francisco for a week. Then we slept for a week. We had 30 performances in 32 straight days. But you know, when you book jazz, you just have to take your chances. You can't wait for the perfectly orchestrated tour."

About a year after Gillespie died, his widow, Lorraine, who died in 2004, called Lee and asked him what they could do to keep Dizzy's music and legacy alive. "I put together this multimedia college clinic program," Lee said. "We would go into schools and try to teach the way Dizzy would have." Lee also went into the studio with pianist Cyrus Chestnut, trumpeter Jon Faddis, and drummer Ignacio Berroa and recorded "Dizzy's 80_{th} Birthday Party" (Shanachie: 1997). "Then, we started getting calls for performances," said Lee. "We also put together a big band, The Dizzy Gillespie Alumni All-Stars, which is led by Slide Hampton (trombonist)." Today, Lee is the program director for "DIZZY: The Man and the Music," the official concert and clinic program celebrating Gillespie's life and work.

As a 19-year-old music student at the Philadelphia Musical Academy, now the University of the Arts, Lee went to an open bass audition with the drummer Max Roach "just for the experience". After the audition, Roach told Lee he had the job. "We had a program in our school that, if the dean approved, you could go on the road," Lee recalled. "On Monday morning he kind of tried to blow me off when I got to his office. I said, 'I want to go on the road for two weeks.' He said, 'With who?' I said, 'Max Roach.' He dropped his pencil and looked up at me and said, 'The drummer?' At that point, he became very encouraging."

The two people who Lee enjoyed working with most throughout his career were Gillespie and the late dancer-actor, Gregory Hines. "Both had the same quality," he said. "They would make people feel good about themselves—from the skycap to the porter in the hotel. The shoeshine guys at the airports around the country all knew Dizzy. He was a very intelligent human being. He had a real sense of people, and he was very encouraging to young musicians, always sharing his knowledge."

Cecil Bridgewater

The first time Cecil Bridgewater heard Dizzy Gillespie play, his initial reaction was that Gillespie was playing "too fast, too high, and too much. I was a teenager, about 15 or 16. I could never imagine that I would ever get a chance to play that music or get a chance to meet Dizzy," he said. Growing up in Champaign, Illinois, Bridgewater was exposed to jazz through his father and grandfather, both of whom played trumpet and played recordings of trumpeters such as Gillespie, Clifford Brown, and Louis Armstrong. After attending the University of Illinois, Bridgewater became a professional musician and moved to New York in 1970. That's when he met Gillespie.

"I was called to teach at Jazzmobile (mobile jazz workshops and performances that brought the music to the inner city). Dizzy would come by the workshops on occasion," said Bridgewater. "You were never a stranger to Dizzy. You met him for the first time, and you felt like you knew him all your life. So, he would sit and talk with me. He would tell me stuff and show me things. He was open, never trying to conceal anything."

Bridgewater believes that Gillespie's contribution to jazz has been understated. "In the history books, people talk about Dizzy as a bebop trumpet player, but he transcended all those periods," Bridgewater explained. "He was there in the '30s with the big bands. He was there in the '40s with the smaller groups, and a lot of the things that he and Charlie Parker did with those small groups was a direct outgrowth of the big bands. They had interludes; they had intros; they had background figures that they played. That all came from the big band tradition. But they changed the focus of it in the kinds of notes and rhythms and tempos that they played. Dizzy evolved from that through the '50s, '60s, '70s, '80s, and into the '90s. To label him a bebop trumpet player is a misnomer. He played the bossa nova and the samba stuff in later years. He could play anything."

In the late 1980s and early 1990s, Bridgewater was a part of Max Roach's group, and Gillespie appeared with them during a tour through Italy. "I was doing my little warm-up exercises, and Dizzy took his horn out and played some stuff. I said, 'Dizzy, what is that?' He said, 'Oh, that's in one of those étude practice books by Schlossberg ("Daily Drills and Technical Studies for Trumpet" Sheet music—1965). You'll find it when you get home; look in the back of the book.' When I got home, I looked it up, and I found the exact exercises he was talking about. So I tried his fingerings, and it was hard," Bridgewater said. "He was in his 70s then, and it made me realize that he was always studying. He was always working on stuff, trying to see a different way of doing things. Even walking down the street in Italy, if there was an open door, he was curious enough to want to go in. He transferred that curiosity to music. Even 'Con Alma,' a tune he played for years and years, he would want to go back and reinvestigate it, maybe change some chords and maybe a couple of notes or something to see what the possibilities were."

Bridgewater, who teaches at William Paterson University in Wayne, New Jersey, and the Manhattan School of Music in New York City, spent more than 20 years with Roach. He was also once a member of the Thad Jones-Mel Lewis big band and has played with an endless list of bands and performers, from Count Basie to Wynton Marsalis. One of his current projects, he said, involves "doing arrangements of some of the master trumpet players. I've put together a group of three trumpet players and a rhythm section. There are a couple of Dizzy's tunes in there. One, in particular—'I Waited For You'—was something Max Roach played with Dizzy singing it. It was fascinating to be around somebody like Dizzy. He was just an amazing musician on all levels—composer, arranger, player. He was a father to all of us. He opened doors and did things that had never been done on the trumpet, just like Louis Armstrong did."

CHAPTER 10

Classical Jazz: George Shearing

"Many jazz musicians feel classical music is just a bunch of scales that are easily understood. And classical musicians and audiences think jazz is nothing but noise. All of these misconceptions are born of ignorance," said George Shearing.

Shearing feels the best way to educate people about the virtues of both types of music is to mix up classical and jazz to draw from both sides and reach a maximum audience. Not everyone has always agreed with him, however. Nearly 30 years ago, the University of Wisconsin Symphony Orchestra's student-staffed directing board decided against performing a jazz-flavored arrangement of Stravinsky's "Rite of Spring," reconstructed by jazz musician and composer-arranger, Don Sebesky. (Sebesky remembers the University of Wisconsin controversy and also recalls that the student symphony orchestra "played my concerto flawlessly, but they had this big meeting with members of the orchestra and decided that it was not 'pure' classical music." Conversely, he added, "the London Philharmonic has no problem playing my music.")

That incident was symptomatic of a larger controversy existing throughout the musical community in the late 1970s and early 1980s—not only whether it was proper to tamper with the music of the masters, but also the entire question of combining elements of classical music and jazz. Shearing, who regularly appeared with symphony orchestras, saw nothing wrong with revising the work of the classical masters as long as it was done in the right spirit.

"I took a theme from 'Scheherazade' (Rimsky-Korsakov)," he pointed out, "and put it in 5/4 time instead of the 6 or 3 it's normally in.

And I even used a kind of Floyd Cramer approach to it." Cramer, a country & western piano player, was credited with developing the "Nashville Sound." Shearing's view of the Wisconsin students' decision was that "while it's dyed-in-the-wool sincere, I find it possibly lacking in humor. I see nothing wrong, for instance, in taking 'Peter and the Wolf' (Prokofiev), making a jazz arrangement of it, and calling it 'Peter Was a Wolf.' Music is music is music."

The classical masters, Shearing felt, would have approved of such dabbling. "There's a jazz feeling in Stravinsky," he pointed out. "In Hindemith, certainly there's jazz. If we go back far enough, we find that Beethoven and Mozart were once considered too far out—they were looking ahead to what would be, but they were being booed."

And Bach, "Bach wrote at least three separate versions of the first complete book of the 48 preludes and fugues," Shearing explained. "While the rules governing the style were maintained, there were three different versions. His mind was not totally settled on a particular order of notation, but because of his creativity and because the composers of those days left great wads of score to the imagination of the performer, there was more room for personal creativity. I think many of these people (Bach, Beethoven, Mozart) would be wonderful jazz musicians if they were alive today. Not the least of whom is Bach. He got thrown out of a few churches for being harmonically too radical. He had two wives and 20 children. How much more of a swinger can you be?"

Shearing, who was blind from birth, always displayed a remarkable versatility in his music. For a great portion of his career he led a quintet, achieving distinction and widespread appeal in the 1950s with such tunes as "September in the Rain," "Roses of Picardy," and his own famous composition, "Lullaby of Birdland."

The latter, he claimed, "was written over a steak in my house in New Jersey in 10 minutes." Having no idea it would become a standard, he wrote the melody because Birdland, the renowned New York jazz club, was sponsoring a radio show and needed a theme. Some music critics and other musicians frequently charged Shearing with being too commercial. He replied to that criticism by describing a typical George Shearing live performance: "Once we get through playing a few choruses of 'Roses of Picardy,' we go to something that really is jazz. But we've gotten the people there on the strength of 'Roses of Picardy.' We reach a wider audience that way. You know," he mused, "we could probably play the most advanced things in the world, but we'd have to keep them between the living room and the office."

(Adapted from an article that appeared in *ELECTRICity*, April 3–9, 1980.)

UPDATE

In March 2004, at the age of 84, George Shearing suffered a serious fall in his Manhattan home, which, according to his wife, Ellie, affected his short-term memory. Nevertheless, he returned home in November 2004, and he was able to travel to London in June 2007 to have knighthood bestowed upon him by Queen Elizabeth II at Buckingham Palace.

"Receiving such an honor as knighthood might show young people what can be achieved in life if one learns his craft and follows his dreams," said Shearing, upon learning of this honor. "A poor, blind kid from Battersea named George Shearing, the youngest of nine, with four years of formal musical training but with tremendous will to make good is to become Sir George Shearing... Now that's a fairy tale come true."

Shearing's last CD, released in September 2005, was "Hopeless Romantics" (Concord Jazz) with vocalist Michael Feinstein. Reviewing the album for Amazon.com, writer and NPR commentator David Greenberger called it "a perfect pairing of vocalist and pianist... These two consummate musicians, a generation apart, are united by the timelessness of the traditions they both draw from."

Dick Hyman

Dick Hyman said Shearing was one of his strongest influences when he was getting started in the 1950s. "He had the new bebop devices down perfectly. His block chord style was always useful, and I was liable to fall into his manner of playing almost by default because he, too, admired and drew from two of my other influences, Teddy Wilson and Art Tatum. Later on, I came to admire his marvelous touch—the most sensitive of any jazz pianist and an ideal that the rest of us ought to aim for." Hyman once suggested to Shearing that perhaps he had developed his "touch" as compensation for not having sight.

"We didn't discuss my theory," Hyman said, "but I am sure it had occurred to him long before I thought of it."

When Hyman was director of the 92_{nd} Street Y "Jazz in July" series in New York, he was able to induce Shearing to appear now and then. "We did some other two piano appearances as well. I would have my piano placed parallel to his so that I could see his keyboard. Once, at the Y, we played with our backs to the audience. I had thought the audience would enjoy seeing both our keyboards. It was very comfortable for us, but there was some criticism," Hyman recalled. "At his New York apartment we would rehearse on the two little pianos he had in his workroom, side by side. He had a grand in his living room, which was sunken and involved a step downward. Sadly, as I understand it, this is how he fell."

Rio Clemente

Rio Clemente, a jazz pianist who studied at the Juilliard School of Music, has always enjoyed mixing classical music and jazz. "The aficionados, the jazz snobs, look upon it a different way. So, I've had to fight that all my life, but that's my style and I'm not going to change it," said Clemente. "If I feel classical music fits into one of my arrangements, I use it—like combining 'My Funny Valentine' and Beethoven's 'Moonlight Sonata.' I did it one time at a concert, and someone said, 'Can you do that again?' I said, 'Do what?' A lot of times things become arrangements even though they're head arrangements; it just happens. And then there are some that are intentional, like the combination of 'Autumn Leaves' with Rachmaninoff."

Echoing Shearing, Clemente pointed out that the classical players, in their day, were the improvisers. "They were the jazz guys. So, the jazz musicians of today are really the classical players of yesteryear. Some people pooh-pooh the combining of classical and jazz, and yet every time I do it, I get standing ovations because people don't expect it."

Clemente, who was approaching his 70_{th} birthday, started playing the piano when he was three years old. "I've always improvised, except I didn't know what the word 'improvisation' was," he said. "I used to listen to Glenn Miller and Artie Shaw because my father had those records. I used to pick up the songs because I had a good ear, but I never thought about how difficult it would be."

His earliest influences were Art Tatum, Erroll Garner, and Oscar Peterson, and later they were Marian McPartland, Mary Lou Williams, and Billy Taylor. "When I studied at Juilliard with John Mehegan,," he said, "he told me to listen to Bobby Timmons, Erroll Garner, and Art Tatum, so I went out and purchased some records." Mehegan, a pianist who died in 1984 at the age of 63, began teaching at Juilliard in 1947.

Today, Clemente's performing venues vary greatly—from soloing in the bar at the Bernards Inn in Bernardsville, New Jersey, to accompanying vocalist Laura Hull at the Metropolitan Room in New York City to appearing at the Gettysburg Jazz Festival. Among his notable CDs, on his own Entemelc label, are "Allegria," which features latin-tinged jazz, "Fascinatin Rhythm," featuring the music of George Gershwin, and "The Bishop Meets the Judge,", showcasing the music of Richard Rodgers and recorded with the late bassist Milt Hinton.

"Some players get older, and they lose the passion," said Clemente. "It doesn't matter today where I'm playing—for 10 people or 1,000. I remember the first time I heard Erroll Garner. I said, 'This guy sounds like he's having a good time.' That's how I play. I have a good time."

BILL MAYS AND MARVIN STAMM

The Inventions Trio consists of a classical cellist, Alisa Horn, and two jazz musicians, trumpeter Marvin Stamm and pianist Bill Mays. Its repertoire ranges from Rachmaninoff to Miles Davis, and in a perfect world its performances would be part of a chamber music series. The problem, said Stamm, is that most presenters fear that if they're not presenting the same piano trios or the same quartets—playing the same music they've played for years—their audience will run away. "That is really sad," Stamm said. "This group has never played anywhere that it hasn't received standing ovations."

The trio started off "as kind of a pipe dream," he continued. "I've known the cellist since she was about four or five years old. Her father, Dr. Howard Horn, and I are very good friends." Stamm, originally from Memphis, would stay at Horn's house in Oakridge, Tennessee, when his high school band was on tour, and they played together in the Tennessee all-state band.

In February 2005, Mays and Stamm were in Memphis as guest artists for the University of Memphis Jazz Week and were invited to the Horn's for brunch. Alisa Horn had graduated from the University of Michigan with a performance degree and was working on her master's degree at Northwestern. "I asked Alisa to play for us," Stamm recalled. "She played one of the unaccompanied Bach cello pieces. Then Bill asked her to play something else."

According to Stamm, Alisa's mother, Jan, suggested the Rachmaninoff Sonata, which she played along with Mays, who sight-read through the first movement. Mays asked her if she knew 'Vocalise,' and she said it was one of her favorite pieces. "He told her to keep playing the melody, but 'don't get thrown off by what I'm doing.' Bill started improvising over the melody, and you saw this big grin on her face. Bill was taken with her playing and said he would love to write a piece for the three of us."

Alisa's father and another doctor, Frank Osborn, came up with the money for a commission so Mays could take four to six weeks in the summer of 2005 to write the piece. According to Stamm, "it ended up being a three-movement, 22-minute piece called 'The Fantasy for Cello, Trumpet and Piano,' which would eventually become the centerpiece of our first CD, 'Fantasy,' on the Palmetto label. Bill also wrote arrangements of 'Vocalise' and Debussy's 'Girl With the Flaxen Hair' for us."

When Alisa was in New York in January 2006, the three musicians went into the studio to, in Stamm's words, "see what it sounded like. It turned out beautifully. A year or so before, Bill and I had recorded the Gershwin Prelude No. 3; we had done 'Baubles Bangles and Beads,' whose melody was taken from the Borodin Second String Quartet; Bill did the Scriabin Etude No. 3, combined with Serge Mahanovich's 'Sometime Ago;' and we did Bach Invention No. 8, combined with 'Ah-Leu-Cha' and 'Scrapple from the Apple.' We had 50 minutes, enough for a CD."

Mays has always been a fan of mixing genres. As a member of the Gerry Mulligan Quartet, he played on the album "Saxophone Dreams" (First Choice Records, 1991), which included "The Sax Chronicles," a seven-part suite written by Canadian composer Harry Freedman for the Gerry Mulligan Quartet and recorded with the Houston Symphony, led by Erich Kunzel. "Harry did a beautiful orchestra suite of several of Gerry's tunes in the style of Stravinsky, Debussy, Bach, and Ravel," recalled Mays. "We performed them first in Italy live and then we recorded them with the Houston Symphony."

In April 2006, Horn was scheduled to do her masters' recital at Northwestern, and she, Mays, and Stamm decided that the trio would perform three pieces. "She played the Rachmaninoff Sonata in the first half of her recital, and we performed 'Fantasy' and the other two pieces ('Vocalise' and 'Girl With the Flaxen Hair') in the back half of her recital," Stamm said. In the meantime, Mays had presented the trio's recording to Palmetto Records, which decided to release it. With the release of the CD, Palmetto "also wanted us to book a tour to promote it, so we booked a two-and-a-half-week tour to California and Washington State. We played in San Diego, Los Angeles, San Francisco, Seattle, and Yakima." The venues included university concerts, house parties, Jazz Alley in Seattle, and a chamber music series.

The repertoire continues to expand. "We've come up with ideas of tunes, and Bill has arranged them for the three of us," said Stamm. "Now we have a repertoire of about 25 pieces, including the 'Delaware River Suite,' which is 32 minutes, seven movements. There are duo pieces for Bill and Alisa, and I do duo pieces from the jazz repertoire. We've added things like 'Bachianas Brasilieras #5, Movement #1;' Bill has written and we've rehearsed the Pavane from the 'Mother Goose Suite;' we've combined Bud Powell's 'Dance of the Infidels' with Miles Davis's 'Sippin' at Bells;' I have an original tune that Bill has arranged; we have several of Bill's original tunes; we have put together a Bill Evans suite of four tunes; and there's a Thelonius Monk suite—in the middle of 'Straight No Chaser,' Alisa performs Miles Davis's solo from *his* recording of 'Straight No Chaser.' We could easily perform two nights in a row on a chamber music circuit and never repeat anything."

Audiences on the first tour were "about half and half, jazz and classical," said Stamm. "In the house parties, they were pretty much jazz audiences; in the universities, more leaning toward the classical side." From some segments of the classical community there is no resistance, he added. At the University of Michigan, Horn's cello teacher was "very anxious to have us come there to play, but the basic faculty members at places like Michigan and Northwestern don't really care one way or another."

When classical audiences first see the trio onstage, "they can't quite get their ears around cello, piano, and trumpet. Most people think of a trumpet player as someone who always plays to the forefront of whatever's going on. Many times, I'm only augmenting the cello sound or the piano sound," Stamm explained. "Bill is classically trained. He will play the Chopin Prelude in E flat and integrate it with 'Body and

Soul,', and it's absolutely gorgeous. It's something that any classical fan—if they didn't know it was 'Body and Soul'—could easily grab hold of as one of their favorite pieces. The music world is very strange. Everyone, from the business end to the musicians, always wants to categorize each other."

The trio's second CD, "Delaware River Suite," was released in September 2008 on Mays's personal label. The title piece is described by Mays as "a seven-movement suite that I wrote dedicated to the Delaware River and lots of places along the way. It's kind of a piece of Americana in that I wrote spoken parts that all three of us do, as if we were sitting around the campfire." Other selections include the previously mentioned Miles Davis/Bud Powell blend of "Sippin' at Bells", and "Dance of the Infidels," an original piece by Stamm called "Charlotte Delights," Django Reinhardt's "Nuages," and Antonio Carlos Jobim's "Zingaro." The trio began a tour on October 3, 2008, with an appearance at West Valley College in Saratoga, California, and ended on December 5 at the Taft School in Watertown, Connecticut. Other venues included both a private concert and a club date at Yoshi's in San Francisco; college concerts at San Jose State and Indiana University; and New York-area performances at the Austrian Cultural Forum in New York City, the Monmouth County Library in Manalapan, New Jersey, and BargeMusic in Brooklyn.

Mays believes Sebesky "opened a lot of doors and opened a lot of minds." He also credits the Modern Jazz Quartet "with their chamber jazz and suites. That was an influence on me. I've always been a classical player, so I'm attracted to people who take classical themes and improvise on them."

CHAPTER 11

Take Five: Dave Brubeck

If Dave Brubeck never again touched a piano, he would be remembered for his quartet's 1960 recording of "Take Five," one of the most popular jazz records of all time. On December 6, 1980, however, he wasn't even able to rest on his 60$_{th}$ birthday. That day, the San Francisco Symphony presented a special concert to mark the occasion, and the following day, December 7, he played his Christmas work, "La Festa de la Posada," for the fifth consecutive year at the Fifth Avenue Presbyterian Church in New York.

Brubeck first became a major figure on the popular music scene in the 1950s when he developed into something of a cult figure on college campuses. Many of those college students remained his fans through the years, but he continued to be buoyed by his ability to still excite young audiences. In the summer of 1979, his quartet played aboard the Queen Mary, which was docked in Long Beach, California. "We came on around 10 PM," Brubeck recalled. "Around 1 in the morning, Al Jarreau came on, and Stevie Wonder came out of the audience to perform with him. There was a total mixture of people, and that audience was digging everything."

No matter what else he accomplished, though, Brubeck's earmark will always remain "Take Five," a record that made musical history on two different fronts. That single and the album on which it was featured, "Time Out," were the first jazz releases to sell more than 1 million copies, and the manner in which "Take Five" was played represented a break from the traditional 4/4 rhythm that was identified with jazz. The wide acceptance of the uneven 5/4 rhythm of

"Take Five" and other tracks on the LP paved the way for more unconventional jazz.

Although the alto saxophonist Paul Desmond is listed as the composer of "Take Five," Brubeck maintained that "it was a group thing. Paul contributed the most, but Joe Morello was very important. None of us ever thought the album would have that kind of commercial success. All we were trying to do was make an album with different time signatures."

Despite the pioneering effort "Take Five" represented, Brubeck was sometimes disparaged by jazz critics, who felt his music didn't "swing." Though accustomed to such criticism, the mention of it still caused him to bristle. He pointed out that there have been other targets of the same insinuation. "According to certain critics, guys who couldn't swing included Duke Ellington, Stan Kenton, and Art Tatum—so I'm in good company."

The person who best understood his music, according to Brubeck, was Desmond, who died of lung cancer in May 1977. "He said I touched on so many things that other people made their style out of," he said. "And most of the avant-garde pianists—if you get them away from where the critics can hear them—will say I had something to do with the way they play."

The relationship between Brubeck and Desmond was special. "If we were riding in a car and something came on the radio that the other guys would want to turn off, Paul and I'd simultaneously say, 'Leave it on.' We'd even make the same mistakes unintentionally," Brubeck explained. "One of the last interviews Paul gave was with the BBC. I heard it after he was dead. He said he used to try and trick me all the time—playing the least likely note to see what I would do. He said I'd always resolve it and set up for the next note. It's a good thing I didn't know what he was doing—I was sweating for 30 years trying to keep up with him."

(Adapted from an article that originally appeared in the New York *Daily News*, November 30, 1980, used with permission.)

UPDATE

Nearly three decades later, the memory of Desmond remains strong. "Paul is like a family member you always keep talking about," said Brubeck. "He was very close to all the members of my family. Our sons called him Uncle Paul, and, actually, they thought he was my brother when they were little."

Brubeck recalled Desmond's last concert with him in February 1977, at Lincoln Center's Avery Fisher Hall. "Paul wanted to play so badly that he got out of the hospital, and blood transfusions gave him the strength to play that night. It was really emotionally so tough for all of us and for all his friends who came backstage because they knew what he was going through. At the end of the concert, I said, 'Paul, we've got to do an encore.' And the last thing he said was, 'No, Dave. Leave 'em wanting more.'"

In July 2008, the 87-year-old Brubeck had just finished a tour of Canada with his current quartet—alto saxophonist Bobby Militello, drummer Randy Jones, and bassist Michael Moore. Militello and Jones have been with him for more than 30 years, and "newcomer" Moore joined in 2001, replacing longtime Brubeck bassist Jack Six, who wanted to spend more time with his family. Brubeck is delighted that his quartet continues to be so busy, but he does acknowledge that "traveling is harder now because of all the hassles at the airport. It takes hours out of your day—getting the instruments through. Sometimes, people want to search all the drums. You can see why they have to do it, but it sure makes life harder for the guys in the band."

Audiences today are, a cross-section, he said. "Say we're playing the Newport Jazz Festival. There's a complete mixture of young people, teenagers and college students; their parents; and sometimes grandparents. Like any other group that's been able to survive, you have to mix it up and play the things the audience knows; and it's also important to do something new. If you don't play the old things, they'll be really disappointed; they want to hear 'Blue Rondo a la Turk' and 'Take Five.'" Brubeck's live performances in 2008 included annual appearances at Harvard's Sanders Theatre and at the Berklee College of Music Performance Center, Chicago's Ravinia Festival with pianist Ramsey Lewis, and Jazz at Lincoln Center and the Blue Note jazz club in New York.

In 2007, he released a solo album on the Telarc label called "Indian Summer," which was named album of the year by Bloomberg News. Reviewer Douglas Lytle wrote that Brubeck "invests all of the songs with the kind of soul that only 86 years of living can bring to chestnuts like 'Georgia on My Mind' and 'Spring is Here.'"

In the midst of his busy 2008 touring schedule, Brubeck was asked to participate in two television documentaries. One is an eight-part music series for the Public Broadcasting System, the other is a Polish TV documentary about the Brubeck quartet's visit to Poland in

1958. Brubeck still marvels at the memory of "how many people who came to the concerts in 1958 said it changed their lives. In this documentary, they talk about how it was one thing that brought courage to them to be the artists they wanted to be."

He had traveled to Poland and other countries as part of a program President Dwight Eisenhower called "People to People." "What he had set up with John Foster Dulles is that we would play in many of the countries along the periphery with Russia," recalled Brubeck. "So, Poland was the first country. We played 12 concerts in Poland. We then skipped over to Turkey, then to Afghanistan, Iraq, Iran, India, east and west Pakistan. The idea was to put on a friendly face in places like that."

One of Brubeck's greatest memories is "going to Russia three times during the Reagan-Gorbachev summit, playing my mass in Moscow with the Russian National Orchestra and the Orlov Choir. The people were out in droves to hear us. They wanted us to play in stadiums, like we were a rock group. Jazz is very strong in all parts of the world now."

Brubeck is very enthusiastic about a young pianist named Taylor Eigsti, calling him "fantastic." The 23-year-old Eigsti gained notice with a 2006 CD called "Lucky to Be Me," recorded on the Concord label, and has followed it up with another Concord CD called "Let It Come to You," which features tenor saxophonist Joshua Redman as a guest artist. He has been featured on the covers of *Jazzis* and *Keyboard* magazines, and has made an appearance in the *Downbeat* magazine critics' poll the past two years.

When Brubeck was even younger than Eigsti, his first influence, he said, was Billy Kyle, the pianist in the John Kirby Sextet from 1938 to 1942 when Brubeck was in his late teens and early twenties. In the 1950s and 1960s, Kyle spent nearly 13 years with the Louis Armstrong All-Stars. Other influences on Brubeck included Teddy Wilson, Art Tatum, and, before that, Fats Waller.

"And, Cleo Brown," Brubeck added. "Do you know who she was? Look her up because she was very important to me. I worked with her when I was 19." Brown played in the Chicago area in the 1920s and, according to www.allaboutjazz.com, she replaced Fats Waller on his New York radio program on WABC in 1934. Brubeck sometimes played during the intermissions of her shows.

Upbeat about the future, Brubeck believes "there are such great things going on worldwide in all the arts, and especially in jazz." He's confident today's young musicians will keep the tradition and spirit going, adding, "There are so many wonderful musicians who come to places like the Berklee College of Music, the Brubeck Institute, North Texas State, and to all of the places that are teaching jazz studies."

CHAPTER 12

Duke's Man: Norris Turney

It was Wilmington, Ohio, in the 1930s, and the system was segregation. "Back in those days, recalled Norris Turney, "the only black people who were into extracurricular activities had to be athletes—basketball players and football players. Nobody black in my hometown ever played music in the school."

Turney vividly remembered the day his father changed all that. "I'd just gotten into seventh grade. I was coming to school one day, and I met my father. I couldn't imagine why he was going there. He'd had a couple of tastes—I could tell he was feeling good. He said, 'I'm going to see the superintendent of schools.' He was going to ask him if it was all right for me to take music lessons."

About two or three weeks after his father's visit to school, Turney came home one afternoon to find Luther Jones, the Wilmington High School music director, waiting for him with an old C melody saxophone. "I was in the junior high school band in four weeks—the only black that had ever been in the band," said Turney. "The next year my parents bought me a new alto."

Turney's early musical training and his ability eventually landed him a job in the Duke Ellington band in the late 1960s and early 1970s, a period he considered the "highlight" of his career. As he looked back on his formative years in Ohio, the soft-spoken Turney said he always knew he wanted to be a musician. "My brother, sister, and I would always have an orchestra. We'd make paper horns, blow through kazoos," he recalled. "My brother would play on pots and pans, and we'd give concerts in the yard. So I guess my parents figured, 'Maybe we'll take a chance and get him a horn.' In those days, for them, that was a very hard thing to do. I think my father paid $25 for my first instrument, and that was a whole lot of money." Both of Turney's parents liked music. "My father used to sing. My mother studied piano when she was a young girl. She had an old player piano, and my favorite piano roll was a thing called, "Cow Cow Boogie."

During the summer months, Turney's musical skills on saxophone were nurtured during vacations in Cincinnati. "That was my mother's home, and I heard bands down there," he said. By the time Turney was in high school, he was visiting Cincinnati regularly, getting jobs at "a lot of little joints around the West End. I worked at this place on Sixth Street called the Green Tavern. Another place was called Wade Central, on the corner of Central Avenue and Wade Street." But there were also gigs on the outskirts of the city. "I worked with a guy named Virgil Tucker in Hamilton, Ohio. I think we made a dollar and a half a night." His first real "professional" job was with another Cincinnati club, The Cat and the Fiddle, on Central Avenue, where he was hired full-time after graduating from high school.

A couple of years later, in 1941, Turney hooked up with A. B. Townsend, who led the house band at Cincinnati's Cotton Club. "They had a chorus line, shake dancers, comedians, everything," he remembered. "We went to work on Friday night, played a show, came back Saturday morning and played what they called a dawn dance. That started around 2 in the morning. We'd come back Saturday night and play a matinee on Sunday afternoon. We were there from Friday night through Monday, because on Monday afternoons we played what was called a 'blue Monday.'"

All the while, Turney was developing his own individual style on alto saxophone. His first real influence was Chu Berry, a tenor saxophonist who had been featured in the 1930s with Fletcher Henderson's band. Berry, who died at 31 in a car accident, was known for his tender, mellow tone. After high school, Turney started listening to Coleman Hawkins, the dominant tenor saxophonist of the 1930s. Toward the end of World War II, he left the Townsend band and went to St. Louis to join another bandleader by the name of Jeter Pillars. "We were playing at a club called the Riviera," he said. "It was a fantastic club —a great big place with balconies and floor shows. Big acts came in there, and we were the house band."

By the time he was playing with Pillars in St. Louis, Turney was paying attention to several alto saxophonists—Benny Carter, leader of a renowned big band in the 1930s, Johnny Hodges, one of the stars of the Ellington band, and Willie Smith, who played with

Jimmie Lunceford. Turney felt he was especially influenced by Smith, a musician somewhat underrated by the general public but whose floating, happy tone helped distinguish the Lunceford sound throughout the 1930s.

After Pillars, Turney moved to New York in 1945 and joined a band led by Tiny Bradshaw. Shortly after that, he joined Billy Eckstine and, for the next 24 years, made his living playing around New York. Although he often played jazz—with New York City-based rehearsal bands, as a freelancer with small groups in club settings, and as leader of his own quintet—he also found it necessary to play other kinds of music. He played tenor sax with pop groups, spent a year with Machito, a Latin bandleader, another year with Ray Charles, and did some appearances at resorts in New York State's Catskill Mountains.

Like many African-American musicians of his generation, Turney suffered indignities while traveling on the road in the 1940s and 1950s. "Now you can stay in any hotel you want, but back in those days you had to go across the tracks to the black neighborhood. You had to find somebody's house. The people who booked you always had a list of the people you could stay with. That was just the normal thing for black people in those days," he explained. "I remember the first white hotel I stayed in down south was the Peachtree in Atlanta in 1967. I was with Ray Charles. Before that, you had to find somebody's house to stay in or a black hotel. That was just a way of life... I never had any problems with it."

In 1969, the 48-year-old Turney received a phone call from Mercer Ellington, Duke's son, who was the band's business manager. "He called me to see if I could come with the band for a couple of weeks because Johnny Hodges was sick." That, said Turney, "was the turning point in his whole career, although at the time I didn't realize it. To this day, I don't know how he got my name, but I suspect it was either Stanley Dance or Billy Eckstine." The five years he spent with Ellington opened a lot of doors for him. "Since that time, I've done Broadway shows, jazz gigs, recordings, a few television things." In his sixties, he was finally doing what he wanted to do all his life.

Turney's first date with Ellington was a sacred concert in Washington, Pennsylvania. "I had never heard his sacred concerts before," he said. "Duke gave me a solo that Johnny had played and said, 'If it doesn't work out, I'll play it on the piano.' I was in the band six or eight months before he'd call on me and say, 'Try this.'" After awhile, Ellington began writing parts for Turney to play on the flute. "I enjoyed playing the flute, but I really wanted to play alto. He put me on the flute, especially after

Johnny had passed away. When anyone left the band, Ellington would never pass those solos onto the same instrument."

One night shortly after Hodges's death, Turney casually remarked to his wife, Marilee, that he was going to write a song for Johnny. "I got out my tape recorder and started playing, just like him. I did it in a half hour," he recalled. "It seemed like the notes just came out. I don't know where they came from. To tell you the truth, I never really tried to sound like Johnny. Nobody in the world sounds like Johnny. Nobody ever will." The resultant tune, called "Checkered Hat," a Hodges trademark, is a haunting ballad that all but cries out in anguished memory. It was recorded once with Ellington's band on an album called "Toga Brava Suite" (United Artists), which is out of print and difficult to find. It also appears on another recording called "Boys from Dayton (Master Jazz), equally hard to track down.

In the mid-1980s, Turney toured Europe with a group led by drummer Oliver Jackson and recorded on the Concord Jazz label as part of the Newport Jazz All-Stars, a sextet that also included pianist George Wein, founder of the Newport Jazz Festival, bassist Leroy "Slam" Stewart, drummer Jackson, cornetist Warren Vache, and tenor saxophonist Scott Hamilton. His top priority, though, was the development of a group called The Duke's Men, a small band of Ellington alumni dedicated to keeping the composer/conductor/pianist's creations alive through performances and recordings. The group premiered in the summer of 1984 at the Lush Life jazz club in New York's Greenwich Village, and the positive reaction convinced Turney and his fellow musicians to convert what had been a one-shot project into a permanent arrangement.

Reviewing that engagement in its August 23, 1984, edition, *The New York Times* critic Jon Pareles wrote that "the solos were something to hear. In solid swing tradition, Duke's Men focused on relaxed, conversational melody... But the standout soloist was clearly Norris Turney on alto saxophone. He gave every phrase the romantic swagger of vintage Ellington."

(Adapted from an article that appeared in the Cincinnati *Enquirer Magazine*, June 9, 1985.)

UPDATE

Norris Turney died in January 2001 in Beavercreek, Ohio, at the age of 79. His last recording as a leader was "Big, Sweet 'n Blues," released in 1995 on the Mapleshade label. It featured "Checkered Hat" as well as another Turney original composition, "Blues for Edward." He also appeared on "Echoes of Spring," a recording released in 1997 by pianist Red Richards on the Sackville label. Duke's Men continues to operate today under the direction of trombonist Art Baron.

Art Baron

Duke's Men was founded in 1984 when trombonist Art Baron was 33 years old. "I was learning to be a bandleader with a lot of guys who were a lot older than me," he recalled. "There were guys in their sixties." In addition to Turney, band members included bassist Arvell Shaw, vocalist Milt Grayson, trumpeter Barrie Lee Hall, and baritone saxophonist Joe Temperley.

"I knew Norris had led his own band, but he acquiesced to the idea of me leading this band," said Baron. "So, one night, I'm calling up 'A Train,' and it was a little fast. After we finished playing, Norris said, 'You know, that was fast.' I said, 'Yeah, you're right.' I was learning how to count off tempos. Then, at the end of the night, Norris said, 'You know, *A Train* was too fast.' He did this probably five or six times. It got to be hysterical."

"I had gotten a commission from Lincoln Center to write a piece for Duke's Men," he continued. "It was all original, and part of it was a ballad. We rehearsed several times; we did a sound check; everything was fine. There were several pieces of music, and I glued all the pages to cardboard, so they wouldn't blow away. I had Norris featured on part of the ballad, and he starts going off the page. It didn't sound weird, but it wasn't the standard ballad. But he just caught it and came back to the page. I didn't know where he was going because he was flying. He was just feeling it."

Turney, Baron said, "was a real gentleman, but there were times when he would step out of character and let loose." One time in particular involved a night the band was led by Gunther Schuller, a composer/conductor who moved easily between the classical and jazz worlds but who did not allow musicians much flexibility when he was leading them. "Norris was playing second alto, without a solo," Baron recalled. "I love Gunther, but he was a very restrictive conductor. We were kind of playing in strait jackets. At the end of the concert, the audience wanted an encore. Norris stood up and said, 'Hey, everybody—C Jam Blues. Ah 1, ah 2 . . . .' Norris took a bunch of choruses, and it got totally out of control. Norris was one of these guys—if something needed to be done, he did it. It made a good concert great."

One characteristic of Turney's that could be frustrating was his propensity to walk very slowly. "I would try to walk as slowly as Norris, and I couldn't do it," said Baron. "One night, I had done this arrangement for the Duke's Men based on Ellington's arrangement of 'Mood Indigo.' It started out with clarinet, bass clarinet, and trombone. The sax didn't come out until after the trombone solo. It was relatively new for the band, and I said, 'Norris, remember, I need you in there right after my solo.' So, out of the corner of my eye, I saw him coming up to the mike. He was walking really, really slow, but I thought he looked like he'd just about make it. Then, he had this look on this face, 'Why did I come up here?' and he left. So I ended up playing the lead alto part on trombone."

"One time," Baron continued, "the Duke Ellington Society asked Norris to lead a band at Sweet Basil's in Greenwich Village, and when you're leading a band so much is going on in your mind—right brain/left brain stuff. He's introducing the band, and he can't remember my name. He looks at me and says, 'What's your name, man?'"

Baron joined the Ellington band in 1973 at the age of 23. "Jimmy Maxwell, the trumpet player, was a dear friend of mine, and he told me Mercer needed someone to play trombone. "At the time," he remembered, "they had a small band during the week at the Rainbow Grill, but on Sundays they'd go out of town and do a gig in other cities, such as Washington, D.C., and Boston, with the full band. For whatever reason, Murray McEachern, the regular second trombone player, couldn't make those gigs. When I got on that band bus people had told me to be careful where I sat. Some of those guys had their seats for 50 years. So, I waited for people to get on the bus, and I hear a booming voice say, 'You sit here, boy;' it was the third seat on the right. I wouldn't move out of that seat for years. But those guys were so nice to me. I was a hippie with long hair. We all had these dinner jackets we'd wear for the gig, but on the bus I was in jeans and a t-shirt. But they never had an attitude about me."

JOE TEMPERLEY

The first time Joe Temperley saw the Duke Ellington band was in England in 1959. The 78-year-old Temperley, a baritone saxophonist and bass clarinetist, was born in Lochgelly, Scotland. In the late 1950s he was playing with a band led by British trumpeter Humphrey Lyttelton, and he recalls that "we used to follow the Ellington band around. They did about 25 or 26 concerts in England in 1959, and I must have seen about 20 or 22 of them. Every night, they would come into a pub after the concert, and they would see us there."

Temperley's opportunity to actually play with the Ellington band came 15 years later. "I was very friendly with John Gensel, the pastor of Saint Peter's Church. When Harry Carney died, John Gensel asked me to play at Harry's funeral." Ellington, Temperley said, referred to Gensel as "the shepherd of the night flock." Harry Carney, a baritone saxophonist, was a fixture in the Ellington band from 1917 until his death in 1974, a few months after Ellington died.

"I played 'Sophisticated Lady' at Harry's funeral, and Mercer Ellington was there, and that's how it came about," Temperley said. "Next thing I knew, I was in the bus, traveling with the band." Playing with the Ellington band meant a lot to Temperley because Harry Carney had been his idol for years.

Turney was in the saxophone section of the Ellington band when Temperley joined it, and the two would continue to play together in the pit orchestra of "Sophisticated Ladies," the Broadway show based on Ellington's music, and the Lincoln Center Jazz Orchestra, of which Temperley is still a member. "When I first went with the Ellington band, Norris was the lead alto player," said Temperley. "We did 'Sophisticated Ladies' for almost two years. And then after that, Duke's Men started. It was Norris and me and Art Baron on trombone, Arvell Shaw on bass, and either Aaron Bell or Richard Wyands on piano and Ronnie Cole on drums. That particular band didn't stay together all that long because we worked very sporadically, more like a pickup thing."

"The more Norris drank, the quieter he got," Temperley remembered. "We'd be on a bus at 5 o'clock in the morning, going to the airport, and all of a sudden Norris would say, 'Do you want a taste?' It's 5 o'clock in the morning. The last thing I want to do is start drinking vodka. I'd say to Norris, 'It's a bit early.' And he'd say, 'It isn't early; it's just a little bit late.' He was a great friend of mine. I loved him dearly."

Temperley has been a member of the Lincoln Center Jazz Orchestra for 20 years. He believes the band and its home, Jazz at Lincoln Center, on Manhattan's Upper West Side, are helping to keep jazz alive. The ultimate aim of trumpeter Wynton Marsalis, founder and leader of Jazz at Lincoln Center, Temperley said, "is to build a new jazz audience. He doesn't get nearly enough credit. He works very hard at it, and it pays off. We're starting to get a lot of young people coming to our concerts, and we do an Ellington high school festival every May. That helps a lot; 650 kids come to New York to take part in it. That does a lot for young people appreciating jazz. This place is thriving, and it all has to do with Wynton."

Virginia Mayhew

When tenor saxophonist Virginia Mayhew first moved to New York from San Francisco in 1987, Duke Ellington's grandson, Edward Kennedy Ellington III, was tending bar at Sweet Basil's, a jazz club in Greenwich Village. "He was also a black belt at the karate club I joined," she recalled, "so we ended up becoming good friends.

Shortly after his father, Mercer Ellington, died in 1996, Edward Ellington and his sisters created the Duke Ellington Foundation, and they decided to put together a band that became the Duke Ellington Legacy band. "When he asked me to be the bandleader and musical director, I was thrilled," said Mayhew. "Norman Simmons agreed to be the pianist, and we have been evolving ever since."

The band released a CD, "Thank You Uncle Edward," in 2007 (Remma Recordings) that included, in addition to Mayhew and Simmons, Edward Kennedy Ellington III on guitar, vocalist Nancy Reed, Temperley on bass clarinet and baritone saxophone, and Wycliffe Gordon on trombone. The tracks range from well-known Ellington compositions like "In a Sentimental Mood" to lesser-known pieces such as "Mainstem" to an original Mayhew composition, "Toe Tickler."

"We're the only Ellington band in existence with a singer, so that makes us really different, and Edward is there telling stories about his life on the road with his grandfather. The 'Uncle' in the CD title reflects Duke Ellington's reluctance to admit being a grandfather. It was inconsistent with his image as a ladies' man, so he made Edward call him Uncle Edward," Mayhew said. "When we first started out, we played more of the Ellington hits, but Norman has written arrangements for some of the more obscure Ellington and Billy Strayhorn compositions, and we also add a few things that are not Ellington."

One example of the latter is a Simmons arrangement of "Don't You Worry 'Bout a Thing," the Stevie Wonder hit. In addition to

"Toe Tickler," the band's repertoire includes another Mayhew original, "Tempo Minor Blues." "There's some stuff you know and some stuff—unless you're a really big Ellington fan—you probably never heard," Mayhew said, emphasizing that the Ellington Legacy Band is not a museum band. "The goal is to have new arrangements. We're not trying to recreate the Duke Ellington big band. We want to take his music and make it 'today.' We're just trying to make it our take on Ellington. His music is perfectly suited to that because it's such great music to work with. There is so much music in his library."

Mayhew, who grew up in the San Francisco area, remembers being asked in the fifth grade what instrument she wanted to play. "I said, 'saxophone,' and they said, 'Girls don't play saxophone.' They gave me a clarinet, and I grew to love the clarinet, but when I was a junior in high school they needed an alto for what they called the stage band—the jazz band. So I went to my clarinet teacher and asked, 'Can you give me some lessons on the saxophone?' He got really excited, but he also said, 'You have to go up to the Keystone Korner and hear some of the great saxophonists.'"

She followed his advice and began frequenting the venerable jazz club. "The first saxophonist I fell in love with was Dexter Gordon," she said. "When I first heard him, I didn't know anything, so what got me was that it was just so swinging and emotional and powerful and beautiful."

Mayhew hasn't made a conscious effort to listen to the Ellington saxophone players, but one who really influenced her was Ben Webster, who was "one of the first tenor players that I really listened to a lot. He had such a distinctive style, and I think that how he affected me was his passion and how beautiful he played ballads, with that breathy tone. You just have to take your impression of him, though. If you try to copy him, you're just going to sound corny."

Other saxophonists who impressed her at the Keystone Korner were George Coleman and Archie Shepp, but her mentor in San Francisco was a trumpet player named Johnny Coppola. "He introduced me to a lot of people," she said, "and lent me a bunch of records, from really early stuff to very contemporary stuff. He introduced me to Lester Young and Zoot Sims and Coleman Hawkins."

Aside from the Ellington Legacy band, Mayhew plays in a quartet with Simmons, who was her teacher at the New School for Social Research, and she leads a septet, which released a CD titled "A Simple Thank You" (also on Remma) in March 2008. She also co-leads an all-female salsa band called Cocomama, and on most Sunday nights she can be found playing with bassist Carl Thompson at a Brooklyn club called Downtown Atlantic. "A Simple Thank You" contains mostly Mayhew originals (one notable exception is Thelonius Monk's "Rhythm-a-ning"), and everything on the CD is arranged by her. There are four horns, guitar, bass, and drums with "some odd meter stuff," she added. "It's one of the directions that jazz can take and still maintain its integrity." The album is both modern and swinging, perhaps reflecting the influence of Dexter Gordon, and the final track is the stirring "Sandan Shuffle," the title tune from a previous release.

Mayhew began working on "A Simple Thank You" in 2005, but the project was delayed when she was diagnosed with breast cancer. The CD's liner notes express "an extra special thank you to those who were really there when I needed you," and, fortunately, she was able to get back to work in 2006. She manages to squeeze in a little teaching in between gigs and writing/arranging commitments, teaching one day a week at Greenwich House in Greenwich Village, where she founded a jazz workshop. She also has some private students, "all ages, from six to 60," she said. "As soon as they get around on their instrument at all I have them start improvising."

Norman Simmons

Pianist Norman Simmons grew up in Chicago when the main thing on the radio was the big bands. "I was particularly influenced by Duke Ellington, and I still am. When I first heard Duke, I wasn't even an active musician at the time. I was very much influenced by Jimmy Blanton, the walkin' bass," Simmons said. "Of course, Duke had wonderful soloists like Lawrence Brown and Johnny Hodges, and his music was songs. So those two elements—melody and Jimmy Blanton—got to me because I'm a rhythm section man. Duke didn't play a lot of piano, and when Sonny Greer was in the band, he was not a banging drummer, so the balance of the band was between Jimmy Blanton and the soloists."

"There are things about it that have carried on in my playing and arranging from that point on," Simmons continued. "My style of accompaniment came from the idea of being orchestrated behind some kind of a lead. Someone else is going to lead, and then I can orchestrate behind them. So when I'm writing arrangements, that's one of the formats that I will use—the lead voice and the bass line."

A lot of singers, Simmons said, "really like the bass player because the bass player has the freedom of lines that don't cross over the voice. The piano player is right on top of their voice." Simmons never actually met Ellington, but "I had circumstances where I was around him." He *did* know Turney and remembers him as being "quiet and reticent. I remember that quiet smile he had on his face all of the time. He didn't seem to talk a lot, but when he came to play, he'd take no prisoners."

In the 1950s when *Ebony* Magazine had a launch party in Chicago, Simmons's band played at the event, "and Duke was there, and he complimented me, and he sat down and played. Ben Webster was in my band, and one time he took me down to where the Ellington band was rehearsing." Simmons and Webster played together in the 1950s as part of the house band at a Chicago club called the Beehive.

"I also played with my trio at the Blue Note in downtown Chicago opposite the big stars—Dave Brubeck, George Shearing, Earl Hines, Sarah Vaughan. One time, Duke was going to be coming in the next week, and Billy Strayhorn was in town, so they gave Strayhorn the gig to play the week before Duke came in. I was on opposite him with my trio," Simmons recalled. "Strayhorn had been playing 'A Flower Is a Lonesome Thing,' and I asked him for a copy of it. I was playing a song that I had recorded with tenor saxophonist Paul Bascomb called 'Jan' that had sort of become a hit, and he said, 'Yeah, I'll give you a copy. Would you give me a copy of Jan?' I said, 'Yeah, I can really hear Johnny Hodges playing that.' He gave me a copy of 'Flower' in his handwriting. I've got it at home. He also sent me a copy of 'Moon Mist.'"

Simmons moved to New York in the late 1960s and started traveling with vocalist Dakota Staton in 1967, and that led to a career accompanying a long list of vocalists that included Ernestine Anderson, Joe Williams, Maxine Sullivan, Helen Humes, Carol Sloane, and Anita O'Day. However, he is best known for his work with Carmen McRae. In 1997, he was honored by the National Jazz Museum in Harlem, which described him as "a consummate musician, best known for his ability to connect with jazz singers... Much more than just an accompanist, Simmons is an extremely accomplished soloist, arranger, composer and educator... Simmons insists he enjoys helping others excel. 'I always get a lot of satisfaction knowing that I pushed someone up to the skies.'"

Over breakfast at a diner near his home in Lakewood, New Jersey, Simmons complained that too many of today's vocalists are "performers instead of singers. All they want to do is improvise; there's no singing. It gets away from the interpretation of a song for the sake of the notes. A lot of young musicians are going through that, too. They focus on notes before they ever get a style."

When pressed, though, he singled out a couple of his favorite contemporary vocalists. "One of the best out there is Cynthia Scott. She is very solid," said Simmons. Scott had worked as a Raylette with Ray Charles, and that experience, Simmons feels, was important. "In the old days, singers were with big bands. Those were great experiences. Today, singers are jumping around too much. I knew Cynthia in Dallas. She came up to New York and was at The Supper Club for years, but nobody knew she was there. I took her to Japan with me, and we recorded an album there. She is one of the unrecognized singers with experience behind her. When she started to record, she would include all this popular stuff. I told her, 'You got to make a jazz record. You can't bring the stage on the record; you can't bring a performance on the record because you ain't got no visibility. It's got to be about singing.'"

The Japan album was called "Boom Boom" and received critical acclaim among fellow musicians. Guitarist Russell Malone described Scott as a "great vocal instrument, with great choice of material and great soul and swing." Vocalist Mark Murphy wrote, "Cynthia swings her socks off and then continues to serenade us with her jazzy so-in-tune contralto that goes in and out of so many wonderful old chestnut songs." Simmons, writing in the liner notes, said, "There are very few jazz singers left made of the real thing, and she is definitely one of them."

One singer with whom Simmons has not worked but whom he admires is Ann Hampton Callaway. "There's something good and right in her voice," he said. Another singer that "has it" is Vanessa Rubin. Callaway, whose most recent CD is "At Last" (Telarc: 2009), is that rare singer who can combine two styles—cabaret and jazz.

Rubin, who recorded a tribute album to Carmen McRae in 1994 ("I'm Glad There Is You"/Novus), was praised by *The Washington Post* for having an "affinity for hushed balladry and brash extemporaneous singing." Her 2001 CD, "Girl Talk" (Telarc), was praised by Amazon.com for showing "respect for her predecessors while bringing something fresh to the music."

Reiterating that "orchestrating" rather than piano playing was his first major influence, Simmons said that all changed when he met Oscar Peterson. "That was in 1951. He came to the Blue Note. Flip

Phillips and Bill Harris, tenor saxophonists, had just left the Woody Herman Band, and they had the gig there. Their regular piano player had to take off, and I got a chance to take the piano player's place on that gig. Oscar and bassist Ray Brown were opposite us. So, I'm coming off the stage, and Oscar's getting ready to come on stage; and he just grabbed my arm and sat me down at a table beside the stage and said, 'I see you're having some problems with your technique.' He sat me right down at the table and gave me instructions. Plus, I was sitting there all week long watching him. He made me see the difference between what I was doing and what he was doing. He was playing the piano and sweating; and I'm posing. Because, you know, with the Ellington Band, it was a chord every now and then. So my solos were never really well constructed. Just watching Oscar and what he showed me began to turn my whole world around."

CHAPTER 13

Singing the Chords: Jon Hendricks

As a 14-year-old in 1935, Jon Hendricks was at the vortex of Toledo, Ohio's entertainment scene, working as a singer at the Waiters and Bellmen's Club. Art Tatum was his accompanist there, and, said Hendricks, "I learned everything from him." Toledo was a hip, entertainment-conscious town in the 1930s, recalled Hendricks. "It was a centrally located area, and the gangsters who ran the roadhouses—and who earlier on used to run illegal whisky—would all come to Toledo to relax. The town was wide open."

In those days, Hendricks, like most other vocalists, would sing the popular songs of the day—"Love Letters in the Sand," "Mighty Like a Rose," and "I Cover the Waterfront," to name a few. But, he pointed out, "singing all those songs at an early age, you soon learn to distinguish a good lyric from a bad lyric. And singing a bad lyric is very frustrating if you have any literary taste. It wasn't long before I felt that certain lyrics I was singing could use a little help. So I would start to 'amend' lyrics that I was singing. And then it wasn't long before I was writing my own. I still can't sing a song that doesn't communicate to me a sensible message."

Of particular importance was his ability to hear chords. "I would hear and sing chords, as opposed to learning to sing the melody. Every singer learns to sing the melody, but only musicians learn to sing chords on their instruments. I learned to sing the chords with my voice and was accepted by the musicians." In the 1950s, Hendricks's lyric-writing ability and ear for the chords skyrocketed him to international fame as a member of the ground-breaking jazz vocal group, Lambert, Hendricks & Ross.

His next step in Toledo was to get on the radio. He was hired as the male lead singer for a vocal group, the Swing Buddies, who had a twice-weekly program on a local station, WSPD. "I was a 16-year-old high school kid. The Swing Buddies were grown men, but they had lost their lead singer, and they couldn't find anybody, so they auditioned me. They were on the radio every Monday and Wednesday, and they were sponsored. I was making $125 a week as a 16-year-old in the middle of the Depression. I was rich."

In 1986, looking more like a diplomat than a musician in a double-breasted, pinstripe suit that smacked of Savile Row, Hendricks said he continued to sing in and around Toledo and Detroit until 1942, when he entered the army. Sipping a Perrier in the bar of New York's Roosevelt Hotel, he grimaced at the memory of what was obviously a bitter experience. "It was miserable," he recalled. "You were supposed to be fighting to teach Germany democracy, and this you were supposed to do under segregated conditions, which was actually a denial of your whole purpose. It was reprehensible to me. I still am angry at the whole miserable experience."

After the war was over, he returned home, got married, and enrolled at the University of Toledo, where he intended to study law. "I had finished high school, and I took my pre-law at the University of Toledo and entered the law college. Under the GI bill, which expedited things, you could cut it from eight years to five."

But a one-night concert by Charlie "Bird" Parker at Toledo's Civic Auditorium in 1950 changed everything. "I had been scatting around Toledo for years," Hendricks recalled (Scat is singing in wordless syllables, improvised to imitate the sounds of musical instruments.) "Though I was too shy, my wife asked Bird if I could scat with him, and he said, 'Yeah,' so I went up." After he sang, Hendricks started down from the bandstand, but Bird grabbed him by his coattail and told him to sit down. "We had this conversation on the bandstand," Hendricks continued. "He said, 'Man, what are you doin'?' I said, 'I'm gonna be a lawyer.' He said, 'You're no lawyer. You're a jazz singer.' I said, 'What do I do about that?' He said, 'Come to New York.' I said, 'Well, I don't know anybody in New York. That's a big city.' He said, 'Well, you know me.' I said, 'Well, where will I find you?' He said, 'Just ask anybody.'"

Two years and four months later, Hendricks went to New York with his wife, Connie, his son, and a set of drums. He learned that Parker was appearing at the Apollo Bar in Harlem. "So I went there, and as I walked in, he was playing 'The Song is You.' Right in the

Singing the Chords: Jon Hendricks

middle, he says, 'Hey, Jon, how you doin', man? You want to sing some?' And he went right back to the song. I almost fainted."

Parker spread Hendricks's name around the city, and as a result he was readily accepted in jazz circles. But he still wasn't able to earn a full-time living in music. While working for a newsprint company, he was having lunch in Washington Square Park when he heard 'Moody's Mood for Love' on the radio (saxophonist James Moody's adaptation of 'I'm in the Mood for Love," using lyrics by King Pleasure). "I thought, Wow! I had been a songwriter for some years, but this opened up possibilities for stretching out, that you didn't have to stop at 32 bars. I really was excited by this. So I sat down and wrote a lyric to Jimmy Giuffre's 'Four Brothers' (made famous by Woody Herman's band). That got a record date on a little record label, and they asked me who I wanted with me. I said Dave Lambert because I had heard Dave Lambert with Buddy Stewart." Lambert and Stewart had both written and sung lyrics to instrumentals while members of Gene Krupa's band in 1944 and 1945.

Nothing much happened from the recording of "Four Brothers," but it started the association between Lambert and Hendricks. Eventually, "Dave had the idea for me to lyricize a bunch of Count Basie things that we should record," said Hendricks. "Since we were starving and not doing anything, I said okay. I wrote four songs, and we got a gig from a young guy named Creed Taylor, who was making his record-producing debut with ABC-Paramount Records. So, I wrote the other six songs. Dave hired 13 singers, but they couldn't swing, and we were in the hole for $1,250."

A solution presented itself, however. "There was one girl in the group—Annie Ross—who had come to New York from her native England in a revue called 'Cranks.' We figured we could use Annie because she was hip enough," Hendricks said. Ross had previously done her own jazz vocalese in a 1952 recording called "Twisted," in which she fit lyrics to a tenor saxophone solo by Wardell Gray.

The trio's album, "Sing a Song of Basie," was recorded in 1957 using a multi-taping technique devised by Lambert that enabled the singers to imitate the horns of an entire big band. "After the recording we went our separate ways, except by that time since I had gotten divorced, Dave and I were living together," Hendricks recalled. "Then, one day I picked up *Downbeat* magazine and found that 'Sing a Song of Basie' was Number 13. So I called up an agent and lined up an audition for Willard Alexander (who handled most of the big bands, including Count Basie, Woody Herman, and Harry James).

He began to book us, and we went from obscurity to Number 1 in about two months. It was really meteoric."

The group made its first public appearance in August 1958 at the Randalls Island Jazz Festival in New York, and "within a few months, it had become the most sought-after new singing group in jazz," according to "The Encyclopedia of Jazz" (Bonanza Books: New York). *Time* magazine called Hendricks "the James Joyce of Jazz." Not only did Lambert, Hendricks, and Ross break new musical ground, they pioneered in another respect as well. Hendricks was black; Lambert and Ross were white. Although bands and even small music groups had become racially mixed by that time, the idea of a mixed vocal group was still of doubtful acceptance.

"That's what deterred Dave and Annie at first," Hendricks said. "I never looked at things like that. I was a bit myopic in not realizing the rest of the world did. I couldn't understand why they looked at each other and kind of smirked when I broached the idea that we go and sing." Because of their instant success and wide appeal, the group's racial daring was generally overlooked. There were, however, exceptions. By 1959, Hendricks had remarried. His wife, Judith, was white. "When Lambert, Hendricks & Ross got booked into the Flamingo Hotel in Las Vegas in 1959, Willard said, 'Don't take your wife.' I didn't say anything, but I took my wife," Hendricks said. "I took her to dinner in the restaurant of the hotel, and I saw people looking at me from behind pillars. And the waiters would stand still and hardly approach my table until I waved at them. I still didn't understand what the hell was going on. After about a week or so, I finally got the message; the rest of my group told me. I haven't been back to Vegas since."

At one point during the height of their success, the trio did a tour called Jazz for Moderns with six integrated groups. "We asked for and received nonsegregated clauses in all the contracts," said Hendricks. "This was the '60s, but well before civil rights. But we were the Number 1 jazz vocal group in the world. If they wanted us, that's what they had to do to get us."

Lambert, Hendricks & Ross's reign at the top of the jazz world lasted five years, from 1958 to 1962. A half hour before a concert in Frankfurt, West Germany, in 1962, Ross collapsed from exhaustion and, shortly after, left the group. She was replaced by a Ceylonese singer, Yolande Bavan, but in 1964 the group broke up for good. The Frankfurt experience, though, stood out in Hendricks's mind as both an upsetting and ultimately satisfying memory. "The joint was packed," he remembered. "I went out and announced, in German, that Annie was sick and that Dave and I would do the concert. We didn't have time to rehearse who knew which parts of Annie's. We'd look at each other, and Dave would say, 'I'll take it' and vice versa. We got a standing ovation."

More than 20 years after the golden years of Lambert, Hendricks & Ross, Hendricks savored the memories and appreciated the success more than he did while it was happening. "It was an amazing group. I've never seen anything like it—before or since. I still live off the reputation of that group. It seems like we lasted 20 years, but it was only five." After the group dissolved, Hendricks worked as a solo, settling in Mill Valley, California, outside of San Francisco. Lambert was killed in an automobile crash in 1966. Ross, after keeping a low profile for many years, became active again on the New York cabaret scene.

In 1968, Hendricks and his family moved to London. The move, he said, was motivated by two experiences. "I had gone on tour in 1967 and passed through race riots. That didn't spur me to move out of the country, but it did shake me up a lot. Then I came back to our home in Mill Valley to find that the rock movement, having hit San Francisco, meant a proliferation of dope that was very widespread. My 10-year-old son was able to buy a bag on the high school grounds from a 16-year-old. So I went to the Mill Valley chief of police and I told him, and he said to me, 'We know, but we're not the San Francisco police department, we're Mill Valley. We can't bust these children because their parents are the ones who pay us.'"

Hendricks called Ronnie Scott's, a well-known London jazz club, and secured a 30-day gig; he took his children and enrolled them in school there. "My 30 days was extended another 30 days," he said. "Two weeks into that, *Melody Maker* magazine (a British music publication) came out with its international jazz critics poll, and I was the Number 1 jazz singer. So I stayed five years."

In 1973, Hendricks returned to Mill Valley and opened a musical revue in San Francisco called "Evolution of the Blues." Originally written by him as a concert for the Monterey Jazz Festival, it traces the blues from their origin to the present day, singling out and showcasing the various major influences along the way. Hendricks developed it into a theatrical format while he was in London. "I expected to be able to work at home five or six weeks. It ran five years, plus a year in Los Angeles and eight months in Chicago," he said.

Hendricks moved back to New York in the 1980s and created a new musical group called Jon Hendricks and Company, which included his wife, Judith. He kept up a busy performing schedule in the 1980s and made an album, "Love," on the Muse label. He wrote material for a number of pop performers, among them Barry Manilow, the Pointer Sisters, and the Manhattan Transfer. One Manhattan Transfer album, "Vocalese," consisted entirely of Hendricks's compositions.

All of his accomplishments notwithstanding, however, Hendricks knew that without the phenomenal success of Lambert, Hendricks & Ross, nothing unusual might have happened. "It's very difficult for an artist to leave the scene and come back, but I never had a struggle. This is testimony to the strength of Lambert, Hendricks & Ross," he said. "I'm only now beginning to realize the weight of what we did. People I meet in the business now—they tell me how I put them through college, how they tried to sing along with the albums in their dorms. I get that all the time, and it's really heartwarming. I'm really honored."

(Adapted from an article that appeared in the Sunday magazine of the *Toledo Blade*, February 16–22, 1986.)

UPDATE

In 2008, at the age of 86, Jon Hendricks was still improvising. He created a new vocal group called L, H & R Redux, consisting of himself, his daughter Aria, and her childhood friend, Kevin Burke. "Anyone who ever liked Lambert, Hendricks & Ross is going to feel it's back," he said. "It's two boys and a girl singing vocalese with three voices."

The group premiered in July at the New York jazz club, the Jazz Standard, and, according to Hendricks, "We had standing ovations every show. Then, we went up to Boston and did the Regatta Bar in the Charles Hotel. It was unbelievable. We did two full houses each night to standing ovations. Then we did the Providence Jazz Festival. The mayor gave us the key to the city." Stephen Holden, writing in *The New York Times* about the Jazz Standard opening of July 5, 2008, described Hendricks as "one of the most joyous performers I've ever seen ... an intrepid musical missionary for a difficult style that has its own set of complicated but flexible rules ... "

Hendricks conceded that "the audiences were overwhelmingly older people indulging in something nostalgic to them, but they were happy to see and hear it." Some of the fans of the original Lambert, Hendricks & Ross brought their adult children with them.

"They wanted their children to experience the thrill that they experienced. It was people so glad to hear the music they fell in love with."

For that reason, he insists the group perform the tunes the original group made famous, such as "Centerpiece" and "Jumpin' at the Woodside." "But I did add some new things that were mostly duets between my daughter and me," he said. "Like 'Four.' She loves that. She did Miles and I did Horace Silver's piano solo." "Four," a Miles Davis composition, was recorded on a Prestige 1954 album called "Blue Haze." In addition to Davis and Silver, the track included Percy Heath on bass and Art Blakey on drums.

Hendricks, looking years younger than 86, lives in New York's Battery Park City with his wife, Judith, and also spends eight months a year in Toledo, where he is a professor of music at the University of Toledo. "It's the best of both worlds," he said. "They gave me a distinguished professorship; they gave me tenure and a doctorate in the performing arts, and they give me gigging privileges, which means when I get a gig, I put my teaching assistant in the class."

Teaching jazz is a double-barreled challenge for Hendricks, as he is constantly educating the classical community as well as his students. He put lyrics to Rimsky-Korsakov's "Scherazade" and took it to the Toledo Symphony. "We performed it at the Cathedral of St. John the Divine in Toledo, and it was the hit of the season," he said. Hendricks also wrote a jazz version of Rachmaninoff's Piano Concerto #2.

He tells his jazz students to be proud of their music. "We spend millions of dollars on buildings called opera houses to prove that we're cultured. We subsidize Shakespeare acting companies," but when Europeans come to the United States, he added, they want to hear jazz. "The United States," he charged, "is the only nation that does not acknowledge its cultural output. The number one culture in the world today is jazz music."

Hendricks also reminds his students not to forget the past. To illustrate, he told the story of the legendary tenor saxophonist, Lester "Prez" Young. "Lester Young played everything—alto, baritone, tenor saxophone. He finally settled on tenor, but he didn't like the sound that everyone was playing—the Coleman Hawkins big heavyweight sound. He wanted something lighter, more airy. So, he was on the road one time with another tenor saxophonist, Buddy Tate. His room was next door to Buddy's. So, Buddy puts on this record that had just come out—Bix Beiderbecke and Frankie Trumbauer (trumpet and tenor saxophone), and Prez heard Frankie Trumbauer through the wall. He jumped out of bed, put on his pants, banged on

Buddy's door, and said, 'Who is that?' Prez went out and bought that record and got his sound. He got his sound from Frankie Trumbauer and ignored Coleman Hawkins. Now, dig that!"

DAVID LEONHARDT

In 1982, David Leonhardt was a 22-year-old jazz pianist from Louisville trying to make it in New York. Jon Hendricks needed a pianist for his group and held an open audition. "It was a gig that people wanted to have because it was a full-time jazz gig," Leonhardt recalled. "Jon had a group with his daughter, Michelle, his wife, Judith, and another guy, and they were working quite a bit. He had the audition one afternoon in a jazz club, and about 40 pianists came."

Leonhardt got the gig. He explained why. "The reason Jon hired me—he actually told me about this later—is that I was the only person who came to the audition in a three-piece suit. Jon is a real smart dresser. He's really into image. He once told me, 'When you walk out of your hotel room, you're onstage. So, you always have to present an image. When you're in the lobby, you're representing me, and you're representing the band. You always have to look good.' I knew that about him, so I thought, 'I'm really going to dress sharp.' Everybody else was in blue jeans and t-shirts. I think Jon knew I wanted the gig. He liked the way I played as well, but I firmly believe if I didn't have that suit on, he never would have hired me."

The four years he stayed with Hendricks had an enormous impact on young Leonhardt's career. "For four years I was working full-time as a jazz pianist, traveling to Europe and South America and all across the United States and Canada. We were doing all the jazz clubs and festivals. It was a really good band. The drummer was Marvin 'Smitty' Smith, who is now the drummer on 'The Tonight Show.'" Leonhardt said the experience helped him in several ways. "It helped me in terms of my skill level; it helped me learn how to present myself in a concert, how to speak, how to act, how to structure a set; and it helped me with my reputation. By the time I finished that four-year period, everybody in New York knew who I was. I wasn't famous, but it helped me get my foot in the door."

Hendricks, Leonhardt believes, has had an impact on "any jazz singer who scats. When I got into the band, Bobby McFerrin had just gotten out of the band. That was when he was an unknown. Then, we did some gigs with him. I remember we did a tour on the West Coast that included Bobby when he was just starting to get well-known, Janis Siegel of Manhattan Transfer, and Dianne Reeves when she was just getting started. So, you can imagine—it was a heck of a concert. They were all influenced by him, and then there were the fledgling singers, the ones you've never heard of. In the '80s and '90s they were all over Jon when he was in New York. That was good for me, too. I would get a lot of gigs because they would see me with him, and they would hire me."

Today, Leonhardt, who lives in Easton, Pennsylvania, has his own trio, which performs between 20 and 30 concerts a year at various venues, such as college campuses and music festivals. His wife, Shelly Oliver, is a well-known choreographer and tap dancer, and sometimes "we'll do a 10-piece thing with five musicians and five tap dancers. It's a lot of fun. The musicians are onstage with the dancers, and there's a lot of high energy and improvisation."

Leonhardt released a trio CD called "Explorations" (Big Bang Records) in August 2008. Other CDs include "In the Moment" and "David Leonhardt Plays Gershwin," both released in 2005 on Big Bang. He also played piano and wrote arrangements for the 2007 album, "Life," recorded by tenor saxophonist David "Fathead" Newman (Highnote), who died in January 2009 at the age of 75. Leonhardt had been playing with Newman for about 20 years, and they did about five CDs together. "Explorations" is an eclectic album with selections ranging from Leonhardt originals to Horace Silver's "Peace" to James Taylor's "Fire and Rain" and Jerome Kern's "Yesterdays."

JANIS SIEGEL

Janis Siegel first worked with Jon Hendricks in 1979 when the vocal group, The Manhattan Transfer (which she was part of) contacted him to write lyrics for "Birdland," a jazz tune made popular by the instrumental group, Weather Report. That was for an album called "Extensions" (Atlantic/wea), and "Birdland" won a Grammy Award for The Manhattan Transfer. In 1985, for another album, "Vocalese" (Atlantic/wea), the group decided to do the whole album with Hendricks. "He's our mentor; mine in particular. We commissioned him to do a lot of new stuff for that, and he came out on the road with us. It would be like a master class after the show."

Hendricks, she believes, is one of the greatest scat singers ever. "Jon and the whole legacy of Lambert, Hendricks & Ross have really had a big influence on The Manhattan Transfer," Siegel said. "As a vocal arranger, I've always been in awe of Lambert as well. To me, it was the thrill of a lifetime to take Jon's lyrics and actually be Dave Lambert on the 'Vocalese' album. That's probably my favorite thing to do—to adapt instrumentals to vocals, creating vocal orchestras. That was Dave Lambert's job. It was such a great team."

CHAPTER 14

Traveling with King Louis: Arvell Shaw

Arvell Shaw could never forget the first time he saw Louis Armstrong perform. It was at the Comet Theater in St. Louis. "I was still in grade school," he recalled, "and I had to raise hell for three days before my mother would let me go. My parents were very old-fashioned. My father was a Baptist minister, and they thought jazz was the devil's music."

Shaw, who would eventually become Armstrong's bassist, always cherished the memory of that concert. "He did four shows, and I must have sat through all four of them. I made up my mind. I said, 'One day, I'm going to play for Louis Armstrong,' although I never did think it would happen." Shaw had no way of knowing that his childhood fantasy would turn into reality, but he did know that he had a special attraction to band music.

"One of the biggest days of the year for me when I was growing up was one Sunday a year that they'd have a big benefit for the orphans in St. Louis—it was called Orphans' Home Day. They used to have a big parade, and it was my first chance to hear all of the bands that were around town—the Shriners, the Knights of Pythias, American Legion. My uncles were all Masons," he continued, "and they would be in the parade that day. I was about six years old when I saw the first one, and I guess, in my subconscious, I said 'That's what I want to do. I want to be a member of a band.'"

Shaw's first musical training took place when he attended John Marshall School. He also played in a children's band at the First Baptist Church. "My first music lesson was actually on trombone," he said, "but I didn't take too well to the trombone, so the band leader said, 'We'll try the trumpet.' I got nowhere with the trumpet, so he said, 'We'll try you on the tuba, and that one stuck.'"

Later, the band director at Sumner High School turned out to be "one of the biggest influences in my life. Mr. Henderson—for the life of me, I can't remember his first name—was a great teacher, one of the best. The older I get, the more I realize how good he was. I realize how patient he was because we were pretty rugged to get along with." Another musical outlet was the American Legion post. "My uncle, George Pruitt, was a veteran of the first World War, so he got me into the drum and bugle corps at Tom Powell Post No. 77. We got to be pretty good; we became state champions of Missouri."

In his last year in high school, Shaw began playing bass fiddle in addition to tuba, and his proficiency on that instrument landed him some weekend jobs with Fate Marable, a piano player who led bands aboard the Mississippi riverboats. His next stop was with the Navy. "The armed forces had just been desegregated, and they came through all the schools to recruit because they needed some black musicians," he said, adding that it was during his three-plus years in the Navy that he permanently switched from the tuba to the bass. "I was inducted as a tuba player in the Navy band, but they used to have small groups play for the officers club, and they needed a bass fiddle. I told the bandmaster I played the fiddle, so he said, 'You got the job.'" On weekends he would travel from the naval air station at Quonset Point, Rhode Island, to Boston or New York, and if Armstrong was playing at the Apollo Theater in Harlem or one of the theaters on Broadway, Shaw would always go see him.

About six months after Shaw's discharge from the Navy, Armstrong came to St. Louis to play with his big band at the Club Plantation. That's when fate intervened on Arvell Shaw's behalf. "The bass player who was with him, Al Moore, had to go home to Philadelphia because his wife was pregnant. He was going to take a leave of absence for a few months, so they called the union in St. Louis and asked them to send the best bass player they had. I guess it must have been me at the time," said Shaw. "Louis asked me if I could finish out the engagement."

Shaw stayed with Armstrong's big band for about a year until the trumpeter decided to break it up in favor of a smaller group. "He decided to try it out in a place called Billy Berg's in Hollywood. He was going to use Jack Teagarden on trombone, Barney Bigard on clarinet, Big Sid Catlett on drums, and Dick Cary on piano. I guess his agent asked Louis about a bass player, and he had liked me with the big band, so he said, 'What about that young kid who was with my big band in New York?' So I got a call from Joe Glaser, his agent, who said, 'Louis Armstrong is starting a small band in California and wants you to go out there. Do you want to join?' I tried to control myself. I said, 'Yes' and tried to be cool."

"When I got there and went to take my instrument to the club," Shaw continued, "I looked at the marquee and almost fainted. They had up there, 'Louis Armstrong All-Stars: Jack Teagarden, Barney Bigard, Big Sid Catlett'—all these guys I'd been admiring for years. And there was my name at the bottom. I was about 20 years old, and the first night at work I was scared to death. I'll never forget the first tune of opening night. It was 'Muskrat Ramble.' The band played one chorus, then the pianist took a chorus, and Louis looked at me and said, 'You got it.' I guess he thought, 'Throw him out in that deep water, sink or swim.' That was the beginning." Shaw was to remain with Armstrong off and on until the trumpeter's death in 1971.

The Louis Armstrong All-Stars were a smash at Billy Berg's, and from that beginning their popularity soared. Some of the personnel changed through the years, but the essence of the group remained its swinging New Orleans-style jazz. The All-Stars went on from Hollywood to the Roxy Theater in New York, the Nice Jazz Festival in France, and the Blue Note in Chicago. But the scope of the band's appeal manifested itself on the first European tour in 1949.

"The promoters had no idea how famous Louis was," Shaw recalled. "The first stop was Stockholm. We had landed in Shannon, Ireland, on the way, and they radioed from Stockholm that there was a crowd gathering at the airport. By the time we got to Copenhagen, which was the next stop, they said the crowd had grown to such proportions that they had to keep the plane in Copenhagen for two hours so they could clear the Stockholm airport. By the time we got there, something like between 40,000 and 60,000 people were in the airport. Originally, we had only about 10 or 15 dates booked, but we were such a smash in Sweden, the dates just kept piling up—Belgium, Switzerland, Holland, Germany. A tour that was supposed to last two weeks stretched into three months. In 1950, they booked us back for another tour that lasted six months. That's the way it was, year in, year out. Then we started going the other way, too—Japan, Hong Kong, Australia." Traveling with Armstrong, Shaw said, "was like traveling with the President of the United States. He was like a king, but there was nothing pretentious about him."

Armstrong's disarming candor caused some nervous moments when, on one trip to Rome, the All-Stars had an audience with the Pope.

"Thousands of people greeted us at the airports and train stations," Shaw recalled. "Louis created such a sensation that Pope Pius wanted to meet him. So we were in the Sistine Chapel—Louis, his wife, Lucille, and the band. The Pope was asking Louis about his life and asked, 'Mr. Armstrong, do you have any children?' And Louis, said, 'No, we don't have any children, but we're having a lot of fun trying.' There was shocked silence for a minute because all the diplomatic corps was there. I looked at Pope Pius, and I could see he was trying to suppress a laugh, but he couldn't, and he let out a guffaw. Then everybody started laughing. But it was touch and go there for a minute. Nobody else could get away with that but Louis. But that's what he thought, and he said it."

During its travels, the band encountered relatively few racially related problems, probably because of Armstrong's prestige. Nevertheless, before the civil rights legislation of the 1960s, the black musicians often weren't able to stay in the same place as the white musicians. "We'd get to a town, especially in the South, and they'd go to the white section, and we'd go to the black section," said Shaw. "That's the way it was in those days, and that's what we were accustomed to." One scar that does remain is the memory of when the All-Stars were prohibited from playing a concert in New Orleans because the band was racially mixed. That, according to Shaw, is "one of the reasons Louis didn't want to be buried in New Orleans. They wouldn't let him play because Jack Teagarden was in the band. That really hurt him. They named a park after him. They've got big statutes of him. He really loved New Orleans, but he figured, 'How could they do that to me?'"

After Armstrong's death, Shaw led his own group, the Arvell Shaw All-Stars, and performed with bands led by Benny Goodman and Teddy Wilson, played in the orchestra for such Broadway hits as "Ain't Misbehavin'" and "Bubbling Brown Sugar," and appeared at numerous European jazz festivals. A towering figure with a silvery beard, Shaw resembled a gentle giant as he reminisced while relaxing in his suburban Long Island home with his Swiss wife, Madeleine, and their daughter, Victoria. Madeleine had been a journalist and met Shaw when she was interviewing Armstrong for a magazine.

Filled with a seemingly endless stream of stories about life with Louis Armstrong, Shaw recalled the time "we were playing at the Chez Paree in Chicago, and we got a call from New York that they wanted Louis to fly the band back on our day off to record. We got to New York, and they gave us the music, and Louis played it and said,

'What is this? You mean to tell me you brought me all the way from Chicago to record this?' But we made the record, and about two months later, we were doing some one-nighters out in Iowa and Nebraska, and we kept hearing the audience calling, 'Hello Dolly! Hello Dolly!' The first time, Louis just kind of fluffed it off, but it was persistent. The next night the crowd again called, 'Hello Dolly! Hello Dolly!' And Louis said, 'What is this 'Hello Dolly?' Billy Kyle, the pianist, said, 'Louis, remember that record date we did a few months ago? Well, one of the tunes is *Hello Dolly*. It's from a Broadway show.' So we had to fly the music out and learn it. And the first time we did it in a concert, pandemonium set in."
(Reprinted with permission of the *St. Louis Post-Dispatch*, copyright July 10, 1983.)

UPDATE

Arvell Shaw died of a heart attack at the age of 79 in December 2002. In his later years he had suffered from glaucoma, but he continued to perform almost up to the time of his death. According to www.jazzhouse.org, the Web site of the Jazz Journalists Association, Shaw's "rock solid rhythmic foundation, highly accomplished soloing and engaging personality suited Armstrong's requirements perfectly."

An obituary published in *The Guardian* on December 18, 2002, recalled Shaw's appearance with the Louis Armstrong band in the movie, "High Society:" "In Bing Crosby's genial routine for 'Now You Has Jazz' in the 1956 film, 'High Society,' each of Louis Armstrong's bandsmen was introduced in turn, with bassist Arvell Shaw ... especially prominent. His eager, animated persona, bearlike frame and propulsive bass style had obvious visual appeal, as well as musical merit, making him a natural for a concert and movie attraction like the Armstrong All Stars."

DAVID OSTWALD

David Ostwald's favorite Louis Armstrong story takes place in Toronto. "There was a fan who Louis had met the last time he had been there, and the fan invited him to dinner. Then the Mayor of Toronto came backstage and said to Louis, 'I want to take you out to dinner,' and Louis said, 'Sorry, I've already got plans.'

That translates into the way he thought about everything. There weren't any boundaries for him. He knew how to touch the basic human instincts that everyone feels. No one has ever done that."

Ostwald is an attorney who also plays the tuba. He leads the Gully Low Jazz Band (aka Louis Armstrong Centennial Band), which appears every Wednesday evening at the Birdland jazz club in New York City. To say he admires Louis Armstrong would be an extreme understatement. "Some people have a St. Christopher medal," he said. "I have a St. *Louis* medal, or pendant, whatever you want to call it. My son's middle name is Armstrong."

When Ostwald was six or seven years old, growing up in Philadelphia, his mother gave him a series of records on the Riverside label— "The Child's Introduction to ... fill in the blank. One of them was to orchestral instruments; another was the introduction to jazz, narrated by Cannonball Adderly. One of the things on there was 'Chinese Blues,' which Louis played with the King Oliver Band. It was a great record. Then it wasn't until I was 15 when I got my first Armstrong record. I went to the Sam Goody music store to pick up a Bach double violin sonata, and I saw this two-sided record, half was Ella Fitzgerald and half was Louis. I figured I'd get it because I had some vague memory from when I had that child's record. So, I listened to it, and one of the tunes on it was 'Swing That Music,' and it was like an epiphany. I thought I had died and gone to heaven. After that, I just bought every record I could."

His own playing on tuba, though, was only classical. In college, at the University of Chicago, Ostwald continued to play in classical orchestras. As a tuba player, "I'd have to wait for one note, and if I was off by one measure, I'd miss my one note. It got a little tiresome. Then, some fellow orchestra members asked me if I wanted to play in a jazz band. I said I was scared to because I'd always read music; I'd never improvised. And they said, 'Neither have we.' So, we got this book that had eight tunes in it and had each part written out. We thought that was a good place to start, and that's what we did. We got some gigs playing in 'pass the hat' bars in Chicago, and we just kept working on it. The band wasn't great, but it was a start."

That was in 1976. After graduating from college, Ostwald came to New York in 1977, and the first night he was there he went to Jimmy Ryan's jazz club on West 54_{th} St. It was a Sunday night, and the trumpeter Max Kaminsky was playing. "I haven't really played classical music since," said Ostwald, who began visiting different clubs and eventually started getting gigs. "I began to notice that there were tunes that were called at a certain tempo that I might have done differently. You can't say to the leader to do it differently; you'd be out of work real fast. So, the answer was to get my own band."

"The idea was jelling, and I went into this club I used to hang out at on 88_{th} Street and Third Avenue called the Red Blazer Too," he continued. "Sometimes I used to play with some of the bands, and I finally said to the owner, 'If you ever have any openings, I have a band I'd love you to consider.' He surprised me by saying, 'Can you start next Friday night? What is the name of your band?' I had to not miss a beat and come up with a name, and I'd been singing 'Gully Low Blues' in my head before I came in. I had a week to get the band together, and I began calling the guys who I had fantasized having." He recalls that the band the first night consisted of Randy Reinhart on cornet, Joe Licari on clarinet, Joel Helleny on trombone, Jim Lawyer playing banjo, and Fred Stoll on drums.

The Red Blazer Too gig lasted until 1984, when the club closed. Ostwald, who had enrolled in New York Law School in 1979, said the club reopened in 1986 on West 46_{th} Street, "so we were there for a few years, and every week we had different musicians. It's like that now. We have a rotating group of musicians. Except for a few years in the '90s, we've had steady gigs one place or another. Birdland is the most thrilling, though, for a bunch of reasons. Normally, in the jazz clubs we've played in the past, there was not a 'quiet' policy. That's one reason why it's really nice to play there; it's like a concert setting in a jazz club. Also, what's cool about it is that, in 1949, when the original Birdland opened, they called it 'the birthplace of bebop.' At the time, the critics were stoking the embers of animosity between the beboppers and the 'moldy figs,' which is what they called the guys who played our kind of music. At the time it was beyond comprehension that there would ever be a banjo-tuba band at Birdland. So, when we got the gig here, it was really cool—a banjo-tuba band at Birdland!"

Ostwald is quick to point out that those acrimonious days are over. "All the guys in my band except for banjo player Vince Giordano and me certainly play bebop." Ostwald's band plays from 5:30 to 7 PM at Birdland, and the crowd is a mix of regulars who come after work and tourists. Sometimes there are surprises. "My rabbi, who kicked me out of Hebrew school a month before my bar mitzvah, I met here 25 years later at a gig. He's here tonight. We always try to do different things," said Ostwald. "We're supposed to do things that are associated with Armstrong. It's not like we'd get arrested if we didn't, but we're expected to. I wouldn't say it's limiting because there's so much stuff."

Ostwald emphasized that, as great as the music was, there was more to Louis Armstrong than his music. "The more I read about him, the more I realized how his mindset was really the opposite of most people," he said. "If people were different, it didn't matter to him. People had to earn his *dis*respect, rather than the other way around. He liked hanging out for three hours after a performance signing autographs, and—from what I understand from people who had this experience—these were not friends of his, just people who went backstage to see him. They felt like they were the only people in the world he was talking to."

Ed Polcer

"There's Louis, and there's everybody else as far as I'm concerned," said cornetist Ed Polcer, who still gets "goose bumps" when he thinks about the one time he heard Louis Armstrong in person. "It was at Basin Street East, around 1956 or 1957. I was in college at the time. Just hearing him come into the room playing 'Sleepy Time Down South'—he was bigger than the room. It was like being in the presence of God in a way."

Polcer's beginnings in jazz were formulated when he was at Hawthorne High School in Hawthorne, New Jersey, in the early 1950s. "This fellow got me to play in a 'dixieland' jazz band," he recalled, "and we had more or less the Eddie Condon concept of jazz—collective improvisation. You just get together without a bunch of charts in front of you, and you play tunes and you think choruses. At that time, kids were dancing to what we were doing."

Collective improvisation, Polcer said, "stood with me my entire life. I really prefer that kind of thing rather than soloing." Louis Armstrong, however, "had everything going. He had collective improvisation. He had soloing. He had a very simple attack. When I say 'simple,' it was very understandable by the public. That's why I stayed my entire life with classic jazz, as opposed to going into bebop or more progressive things."

Polcer played one summer with Arvell Shaw at the Promenade Café in Rockefeller Center. Another bassist, Red Balaban, had arranged the gig, and, "Red ended up playing banjo or guitar some of the time," Polcer said. "Arvell wasn't as talkative as you might expect about Louis. He was just another musician who loved playing. The Armstrong that I enjoyed most was what I heard in the '50s with his All Stars. I just liked Louis's simple, collective improvisation. My favorite Armstrong album is 'Louis Armstrong Plays W. C. Handy' (originally recorded on July 12, 1954; available on Sony). It's very simple, direct music. It shows in very simple fashion what a clarinet is supposed to do, what a trombone is supposed to do. You have a leader who's dynamic and a bass player who's pumping out those notes—boom, boom, boom. Armstrong's All-Stars were really the epitome of that whole genre of music. It has stayed with me forever."

In the mid-1950s, with the emerging popularity of rock 'n roll, Polcer said a lot of the jazz players were hurting for work. "I was living in New Jersey, and I was hosting a lot of things for the New Jersey Jazz Society," he recalled. "I'd have to make two trips into New York with my van—one to go pick up the guys to bring them to the gig in New Jersey and another one afterwards to bring them back home again, but I got to know a whole bunch of players. Arvell Shaw was one of the bass players. Others included pianist John Bunch, drummer Joe Corsello, and trombonist Lou McGarrity. We had something going on every week with great players. I always liked the solid style of jazz we were playing because I thought that it was music people could move to—whether they got on the dance floor or not. I just think that getting people involved, making music they can somewhat understand as well as move to has always spurred me. Louis Armstrong and Benny Goodman were always asked what kind of music they played. And they always said, 'It's dance music,' meaning, to me, that it's music that makes you want to swing."

Polcer graduated from Princeton with an engineering degree and continued his "day job" while playing three to five jazz gigs a week. Then, in 1973, he got a call from Benny Goodman. "That was the catalyst," he said. "I packed in my day job and went into music full-time." He stayed with Goodman for a year, and from 1975 to 1985 he and Red Balaban ran Eddie Condon's jazz club in New York. "We were open seven nights a week, plus Wednesday and Friday lunches," he recalled. "The regular band was there Monday through Saturday, from 9 PM to 3 AM at first. Gradually, we changed the closing to 2 AM and then to 1:30 AM. Sunday nights, we had it open to other bands. It was a glorious 10 years."

Today, Polcer estimates he does about 200 gigs a year. "I travel probably three or four months out of the year." In 2008, he released an album called "Ed Polcer & his Swingtet presents Lionel, Red & Bunny" (Blewsz Manor Productions). "I realized that Lionel Hampton, Red Norvo, and Bunny Berigan were all born in 1908, so 2008 would have been their 100_{th} birthdays," he said. "Benny Goodman's

100$_{th}$ birthday would have been in 2009, and Red Norvo hired Benny Goodman, and Benny realized the wonderful concept of the xylophone and the clarinet being a wonderful trade off. So, Benny, in his famous 1938 concert, hired Lionel Hampton. All of a sudden, the clarinet and vibes became something. Red Norvo tied to Benny Goodman tied to Lionel Hampton. And you also have this young guy, Bunny Berigan, playing this trumpet solo, 'King Porter Stomp.' So, they're all passing their ideas onto one another." Featuring John Cocuzzi on vibes, the album has an all-star band, including two of the clarinetists carrying on the Benny Goodman tradition—Dan Levinson and Ken Peplowski. The opening track is "King Porter Stomp" and, among the other standards is Berigan's signature, "I Can't Get Started."

Polcer believes rock 'n roll became so popular in the 1950s and 1960s because jazz musicians—and specifically those playing bebop—"tended to forget that jazz was a music that resonated with a lot of people. If you get too much into yourself, too much inner contemplation, you're forgetting about the public. From that point on, jazz became something that was peripheral."

The ability to capture an audience is perhaps best exemplified by a performance Polcer remembers doing with another trumpeter, Charlie Shavers. "Charlie Shavers and I were hired to play this gig up in Connecticut in the early '70s," he said. "The feature of this concert was the young and veteran trumpeters playing together. It was at a country club, and the mini-concert was supposed to be played over dessert, so the country club folk could pay a little attention to what we were doing instead of talking. I got out there and said, 'I want to pay tribute to another great trumpet player, Bunny Berigan.' I'm playing, 'I Can't Get Started,' and I'm halfway through it and the people are still talking. I hit the high note at the end, and I get a smattering of applause."

"Charlie puts a mute in his horn, and he starts strolling. He starts playing a ballad, and he goes over to one table and starts playing in this lady's ear. He walks to the next table and starts playing to the table. In half a minute, the entire room shut up. They were afraid they were going to miss something that was going on in the other corner of the room. By the time he strolled back to the bandstand and made a beautiful flourish, he got a standing ovation. Charlie Shavers was a hell of a technician. He could finger notes all over the place. But if you're playing notes that people like, it's show business."

Bria Skonberg

"Louis Armstrong is my American idol," said twenty-four-year-old Canadian trumpeter/vocalist Bria Skonberg. She made that comment during a concert in April 2008 at the Bickford Theatre in Morristown, New Jersey, where she was co-leading the Borderline Jazz Band with veteran trombonist Jim Fryer.

Skonberg, of course, never met Armstrong. He died in 1971; she was born in the mid-1980s. "I really wish I could've met him, but I feel that he communicated so much through his music and impressions he made on people," Skonberg said. "Just by listening to him and hearing stories about him, I feel a connection. Louis played for *people*, and I've tried to model a lot of my approach to music and life in the same humanitarian way. He, out of anyone, had a right to sing the blues from the cards he was dealt early on in life—being born into an unsteady home life, but he didn't let that hinder his positive outlook or work ethic. I was dealt a royal flush in terms of family, location, and timing; and learning from people like Louis has taught me not to take any of it for granted."

Originally from Chilliwack, British Columbia, Skonberg's first exposure to music was through dance and piano lessons, but she began to take up the trumpet at age 11. The decision, she said, came naturally and easily—"Have you seen me dance?" she asked. "Seriously, I was following in my older siblings' footsteps of joining the school bands, and since my dad had played a bit of trumpet in high school, I went in that direction."

Skonberg became a serious follower of Armstrong about four years later. "I started playing traditional jazz at Chilliwack Senior Secondary about that time," she said. "Chilliwack has hosted a Dixieland jazz festival every May for the last 20 years, and I really must give credit to my teachers, Rob Hopkins and Gary Raddysh, for getting me and so many other young people into the festival playing this kind of music. The high school group is now called the Big Bang Jazz Band, aka The 51_{st} Eight. They played some direct transcriptions of Louis's work, such as 'Potato Head Blues,' Cornet Chop Suey,' and 'Mahogany Hall Stomp.' I fell in love with Louis's sound, phrasing, authoritative lead playing, and joyous personality. So I bought many compilation CDs, and I'd sit in my room trying to copy what he did."

About the time Skonberg started listening to Armstrong, she met Australian multi-instrumentalist Simon Stribling, who had just relocated to Vancouver. Stribling fed her recordings of all the great trumpeters and opened her ears to the world of hot jazz, and the Vancouver Dixieland Jazz Society sponsored Skonberg at a youth jazz camp, which, she said, changed her life. "That's where I really fell in love with the music and where I am now an alumni counselor/teacher," she explained. "When you're young, you play what's put in front of you. I think a lot of young people would be interested in playing classic jazz if they were given the opportunity to play and listen to it by their school teachers. It's not so much teaching kids that's the challenge right now as teaching the teachers where to start a student's music education. Classic jazz is the most logical starting point since it's focused on melody, rhythm, blues, emotion, lyrics, and ensemble playing."

Skonberg confesses that, as a teenager, "teenage angst" drew her to Armstrong's recording of "Little Girl Blue," but "my other favorite is 'I Gotta Right to Sing the Blues' from the '30s. His out chorus still gives me the shivers. You can learn so much from any era of his playing. I love the All Stars from the late '40s and '50s. By that point, it was all about 'minimum input and maximum output' as Simon would say. Every note Louis played had such impact that just a few in the right spots would send the song over the top."

It is clear that Skonberg has adapted the "minimum input and maximum output" technique. Her playing seems effortless and swinging at the same time, and her onstage authority, for someone so young, is unquestioned. She has never met anyone who played with Armstrong regularly, but a "wonderful" local Vancouver pianist, Rice Honeywell, got to sit in with Armstrong's band once in 1950 when he was only 18 years old. Skonberg relates the story. "Rice went to see Louis play in Quebec, and when the band came back from a break, Earl 'Fatha' Hines was nowhere to be seen, so Rice snuck up on stage and played the piano behind Louis. Barney Bigard, Jack Teagarden, Arvell Shaw, and Cozy Cole gave him looks like, 'Yeah, man, go for it!' After a couple of choruses, Rice felt some hands lifting him up from his armpits, and 'Fatha' Hines said with a smile, 'All right, boy, it's my turn now.' " The biggest compliment was that Louis didn't even turn around!"

GREGORY RIVKIN

Eleven-year-old Gregory Rivkin, growing up in Russia, was taking classical trumpet lessons when a relative introduced him to the music of Louis Armstrong. "A husband of a cousin of my stepfather was a jazz collector," he recalled. "He introduced me to Louis Armstrong, and I liked it from the first moment—first of all because of the sound on the trumpet and second of all because he improvised. Both of my parents are musicians, and I said to my mother that I would like to become a jazz musician from that moment on. She didn't like it and said, 'If you would like to become a trumpet player, you'd better stick with classical music.' Jazz musicians—especially brass players—had a bad reputation in Russia because of the drinking habit."

Rivkin, now 31, is an emerging jazz talent on trumpet, supplementing the early influence of Armstrong with the modern styles of Miles Davis, Freddie Hubbard, and Woody Shaw. When he first heard the music of Armstrong, he considered it "a hybrid version of ragtime, although the critics called it New Orleans jazz. Since I was also taking classical piano lessons, I had been introduced to several pieces by Scott Joplin. I was familiar with what ragtime was; I just didn't know the correct definition and where the work came from. So, to me, Louis Armstrong played in that style. And he also played popular songs, which you would call jazz standards. But he played them in a hybrid manner, mixed with blues—and plus he added improvisations. That was the music I understood and that I wanted to play."

Shortly before Rivkin's family emigrated to Israel in 1990, the same relative introduced him to Miles Davis, giving him the record, "Bags Groove." "That was how I got introduced to modern jazz," Rivkin said. Subsequent influences were Hubbard and Shaw as well as Lee Morgan, Clifford Brown, Chet Baker, and Tom Harrell. However, his instructors in Israel continually underscored the importance of concentrating on traditional jazz. One college instructor urged him to "keep digging New Orleans musicians. Learn to improvise melodically. You have to go backward before you can go forward. You have to develop your own links to the information that you want to get from certain musicians."

Today, Rivkin would describe himself as "a product of hard bop in the '60s." The CD he released in 2006, "Soft Colors" (Eroica Classical Recordings) reflects this style, and in the liner notes he wrote, "The target of this project is to deliver a top-notch 'Hard-Bop' to the listener, mine and each of the musicians' independent voices within this style." However, the early influence of Louis Armstrong has never left Rivkin. "If you put me in a Dixieland band today and tell me to improvise, I could do that," he said.

CHAPTER 15

Beyond the Big Bands: Gerry Mulligan

In 1978, baritone saxophonist Gerry Mulligan surprised a Newport Jazz Festival audience by appearing with a rejuvenated version of his 1950s concert jazz band instead of with his quartet. That was a one-night project, but for Mulligan the lure of the big band was evidently too much. Shortly after the Newport concert, he brought it back to stay. The fruits of that effort could be heard on a 1981 album, "Walk on the Water" (DRG Records), a release that presented the band in swinging versions of Mulligan originals, Duke Ellington's "Across the Track Blues," and the George Bassman-Ned Washington standard, "I'm Getting Sentimental Over You."

But the big band was only one facet of Mulligan's activities in the early 1980s. He frequently led a quartet or quintet, and he spent a considerable amount of time composing and arranging. "When I was first attracted to music, it was the bands that did it," he explained. "I loved the bands, but it's never really been a goal of mine to keep a band together 52 weeks a year since an important part of my activity is arranging and composing. I like to work both ways: with a small band and with a big band. They're two totally different ways of playing. I like to play within the restrictions of the big band, and I also like the freedom of the small band."

Mulligan first gained widespread recognition with arrangements he wrote for Miles Davis's band in the late 1940s. Then he made jazz history in the early 1950s when he unveiled his now famous pianoless quartet at a small Los Angeles club called The Haig. Although Mulligan had been rehearsing a band without a piano, the opportunity to showcase it in public developed almost by accident. "I had worked as the off night, opposite Erroll Garner," he recalled. "They had a beautiful piano in the place for Erroll. When Erroll was finished with his engagement, they were bringing in Red Norvo's trio, which consisted of Red on vibes, Red Mitchell on bass, and Tal Farlow on guitar. No piano."

"They weren't going to have a piano in the club," he continued. "They said that, for the off night, they would get a little spinet or something that didn't take up much room and wasn't very expensive. I said, 'Forget it. I'll put a group together without a piano, and we won't have to bother with it at all.'" The quartet (Chet Baker on trumpet, Chico Hamilton on drums, and Bob Whitlock on bass) was an almost instant success, playing what Mulligan described as "improvised counterpoint—having the two horns operate over the bass line."

By the early 1980s, Mulligan ranked as one of the giant figures in jazz, playing and writing music that was both modern and swinging. Although he was a perfectionist in everything he undertook, he never lost sight of the need for music, above all else, to be fun. Some jazz, he complained, "has become so bloody serious and self-conscious—so terribly aware of its social importance—that it's just become pompous beyond enjoying it. It's lost any sense of the joy of music. It isn't a joy to hear some cat struggling for 20 or 30 minutes on a solo."

Relaxing in his Darien, Connecticut, home 45 minutes from New York City, the bearded musician could have been mistaken for a college professor as he continued to discourse on the state of popular music at the time. "The whole aspect of the music scene has changed so much," he pointed out. "Jazz is less connected with pop music that it was 20 years ago." This, he felt, was particularly true with regard to music played on the radio. "Everything is so pigeonholed that it's very difficult to get out of the damn pigeonhole once they put you in it," he said, his voice reflecting just the slightest trace of bitterness.

"There are tracks on that record ("Walk on the Water") that could and should be played in the programming of a pop program, but now stations are known for being hard rock, for being middle of the road, for being country. It's so rigidly categorized that it makes audiences that much more narrow in their awareness of what's going on," he continued. "It's an odd thing. All of the readily accessible media for communication have made people more narrow instead of making them more broad." (Mulligan would have probably welcomed such relatively recent developments as the iPod, satellite radio, and digital cable.)

If radio was a culprit in Mulligan's mind, then television was a monster. Television people, said Mulligan, "don't care about sound. It's incredible the complex machinery that goes into making the television picture, and they put those tiny little speakers in there. Television is very hard on music. It eats music up. It's like a great gaping maw. You just keep shoving the music in, and it chews it up and spits it out and wants more."

Despite its drawback, Mulligan did feel that television, handled correctly, had possibilities. "For years I've been wanting to do a variety show based around a band," he said. "I would have guests—singers and comics—and present things in a grown-up way. Probably the most successful musical show on television was 'The Lawrence Welk Show.' I don't see why a show like that can't be done based around another kind of music."

If Mulligan's vision of a television variety show had ever developed, his biggest problem probably would have been finding time for it. His big band was doing two six-to-eight-week tours a year. He toured Europe regularly with a quintet. He was planning more albums. He did a triumphant Kool Jazz Festival concert in the summer of 1981 with Mel Torme and George Shearing that they hoped to take on the road. And, finally, there was his budding career as a singer.

In 1979 at a concert in Carnegie Hall dedicated to the American popular song, Mulligan sang in public for the first time "since I was a child singing in a choir. I felt it was kind of a stunt, but the thing is, I've gotten to enjoy it. I saw George Shearing the other day, and we were joking about it. I'm the only singer I know who *only* sings at Carnegie Hall. I don't even sing in the shower."

Torme and Mulligan were working on lyrics to some of Mulligan's compositions, with plans for Mulligan to do a vocal album, which apparently never materialized. One other goal of Mulligan's was to have his big band perform in Nashville because he felt his style of jazz had a lot in common with country music. "I sometimes think," he reflected, "a swinging band like mine could be very popular in Nashville. When you hear a lot of the best of country groups, they swing in a way music is supposed to swing. It's fun."

(Adapted from an article that appeared in *ELECTRICity*, December 10–16, 1981.)

UPDATE

Gerry Mulligan died at the age of 68 in January 1996 of complications following knee surgery. The last three recordings made before his death were "Dragonfly" (Telarc: 1995), which featured several guest performers, including cornetist Warren Vache and soprano/tenor saxophonist Grover Washington; "Dream a Little Dream" (Telarc: 1994), a album containing mostly standards, including the title tune, "Here's That Rainy Day," "Georgia," and one of Mulligan's signature hits, "My Funny Valentine;" and "Paraiso" (Telarc: 1993), Brazilian-flavored jazz featuring Brazilian vocalist Jane Duboc. An almost endless catalog of Mulligan recordings remains available today. Some of the more notable include "Walk on the Water" (DRG: 1980 and 1992) featuring his reconstructed big band, "The Original Quartet with Chet Baker" (Blue Note: 1998), and "Quartet" (Polygram: 1993) with alto saxophonist Paul Desmond.

Bill Charlap

"It's been said about Gerry Mulligan that he shot for 42_{nd} Street and overshot—ending up on 52_{nd} Street," said pianist Bill Charlap. That, he added, is why he and Mulligan connected so well. Charlap, recognized as one of the preeminent jazz interpreters of American popular standards, was part of Mulligan's quartet for two years. "There was a deep part of Mulligan that understood popular songwriters," Charlap pointed out. "As a composer, he was very tuneful. Although he was certainly writing jazz music, his music was very singable. And it was influenced as equally by Charlie Parker as it was by Richard Rodgers or George Gershwin. So we *got* each other in that way. We understood each other."

According to Charlap, Dave Brubeck once described Mulligan's music as having the past, present, and future—all at the same time. "Mulligan loved the history of the music. He loved Charlie Parker, and he loved Jimmie Lunceford. And he could hear it all very well," Charlap explained. "He was able to think like an arranger, and he was one of the most important arrangers in the history of the music. He had an ear that could hear Stravinsky as well as James P. Johnson. He appreciated all of it. And, beyond that, he was able to hear things that were theater music. He got it all. So, in some sense, we didn't have to discuss things. I understood, and he understood that

I understood very well. I played with him for two years in the late 1980s, and it's all one big good memory."

BILL MAYS

Pianist Bill Mays moved from Hollywood to New York in 1984. He was hired by Mulligan on the recommendation of drummer Rich DeRosa, and just before moving to New York was also among several jazz musicians, including Mulligan, who recorded "Paradise Café," a jazz album made by pop vocalist Barry Manilow, based on many of composer Johnny Mercer's unused lyrics.

Musically, what Mays remembers most about Mulligan was his "great melodicism, the sense of putting on a musical show in the best sense of the word. He was really great at programming. Most of the music we played was his. I think we only played a few standards—things like 'Georgia on My Mind,' 'My Funny Valentine,' and 'Satin Doll.' Everything was very arranged. On one song, I knew I'd only get one chorus, and on another song, I'd only get eight bars. At first, I felt kind of limited until I really got into his mind and the way he thought about music and presenting music. It taught me a really valuable lesson about making smaller, more concise statements musically."

"Gerry was the most erudite, well-read, articulate musician I've ever met," Mays continued. "He was really brilliant, and he always really took care of the musicians. He always made sure I didn't have to deal with poor pianos. I remember we did a gig somewhere in Europe, and they didn't have a good piano. He said, 'We're not going to do a concert unless you have a proper piano.' "

Mays first became aware of Mulligan when he heard his pianoless quartet, which, he said, "paved the way for the bands we see nowadays that have odd combinations, such as guitar, drums, and horn." He didn't play much with Mulligan's big band, although there was one occasion when he did that was somewhat memorable—although not necessarily in a positive way. "We went on a jazz cruise to the Caribbean with the big band on the USS Norway. We could bring our wives; it was going to be a paid vacation. But everyone was really angry because Gerry decided to call big band rehearsals every morning at 10 o'clock when we all wanted to be out on the sun deck. So, there was a bit of a rebellion."

Trombonist Keith O'Quinn, a regular member of the big band, recalled that Mulligan was "very meticulous about what he wanted.

He would rewrite things constantly. Sometimes, we would have rehearsals where we would do nothing but rehearse backgrounds to use behind the soloists."

"Another thing about Gerry that some people don't know was that he could sit down at the piano and play with a certain degree of facility," Mays added. "He often would close the program by playing a solo version of 'Darn That Dream.' I think he also wrote a Broadway show with Judy Holiday." Holiday and Mulligan, who had a seven-year romantic relationship, *did* work together on a musical version of "Happy Birthday," based on a play written by Anita Loos, best known for writing "Gentlemen Prefer Blondes." The play was never produced, but four of the songs— lyrics by Holiday, music by Mulligan —were released on an album, "Holiday With Mulligan" (DRG: 1980).

Mays played with Mulligan for five years, left awhile, and then came back for a few months. "It was great to come to New York with a steady gig," he said. "We got to play in some places I've never been back to, like Uruguay, Paraguay, Panama, Brazil. We were once in a club in Norway, and he insisted that there be no serving of food while we were on and absolutely no smoking. We played a place in Wales that was an old dairy barn and still had some of the stalls where the cows were."

Currently very active playing and composing for the Inventions Trio, the classical-jazz hybrid that includes trumpeter Marvin Stamm and cellist Alisa Horn, Mays also recorded a new live album in September 2008 at the Kitano in New York with tenor saxophonist Jed Levy and drummer Billy Drummond. One of his compositions, a song called "Judy," was featured in the 2008 Coen Brothers movie, "Burn After Reading."

The first pianist Mays heard live was Earl 'Fatha' Hines. "I loved the way he used the whole keyboard. Right after I heard him, I went to the Blackhawk in San Francisco and saw Wynton Kelly with Miles Davis. That was it," he said. "I was 16 at the time, and I was hooked."

Rich DeRosa

As associate professor for jazz arranging at William Paterson University in Wayne, New Jersey, drummer Rich DeRosa insists that his students write baroque counterpoint. "Baroque counterpoint is the hardest to do. After you master that then you can start to relax the rules a bit," DeRosa said. "Since most of the students are coming from the jazz side of things, I try to use something that's more familiar to them to get them into the baroque thing. And that's Gerry Mulligan and his pianoless quartet. It's very much the same kind of sound; it's all about counterpoint. Chet Baker was playing the melody on trumpet. There was the bass line and drums stirring brushes. And Gerry had the creative part; he was creating the counter lines. So, the bass notes are in counterpoint to the melody, and Gerry's pianoless quartet exemplifies that perfectly."

The influence of the pianoless quartet was enormous, said DeRosa, but the other part of Mulligan's legacy, he believes, was how he transformed the baritone saxophone. "Gerry was about melody," he explained, "and he took the baritone saxophone and gave it delicacy, grace, and beauty. So, if I'm dealing with a student who plays baritone sax, I'll ask them, 'Do you know Gerry Mulligan?'" Mulligan's playing, DeRosa said, combined "the exploration of the high register while also making the low register graceful. It's hard to do on that instrument. There were times when I heard Gerry play, and he would play so delicately you would almost think it was a bassoon. He was amazing as a creator of melodies and counterpoint."

DeRosa first met Mulligan in the late 1970s when the drummer was still in college at Jersey City State (now New Jersey City University). "He heard some of the music I had written, and in the rejuvenation of his concert jazz band, he needed an assistant," DeRosa said. "I would go up to his house in Connecticut and help him, copying parts, assembling the books, proofreading. It was a fortunate experience for me. When he put together a rehearsal, I played drums."

DeRosa toured with the band in 1979 and remembers that "we would play some of the pieces from his early band, but here was this opportunity for Gerry to write all this music, things like 'Walk on the Water,' '42_{nd} and Broadway,' and 'Song for Strayhorn.' Then, in 1980, he asked me to join his quartet. I wouldn't say he was rough on rhythm players, but he was specific; he wanted certain things. He wanted the band to play for the sense of an arrangement. It's something I still subscribe to today. Sometimes, you get in those freer settings and you say, 'I just want to do what I want to do, stretch out.' But he used to say things like, 'You can't let the solos get too long because you lose the arc of the piece.' That's something in my teaching that I continue to stress with my students."

When DeRosa was playing with Mulligan, he always put Mulligan's intentions first. "He would ask me to do certain things, and I would do them even if I thought it wasn't something I would do. I think he really appreciated that. With Gerry, you weren't just a rhythm player, you had to bring a sense of arranging into it. And what made it more difficult, it wasn't your own arranging. Pianists had to be aware of a register. 'Don't get in the upper register when I'm playing behind you,' he would say. 'I'm a low instrument.' He wanted more of a darker, fuller sound, and, of course, he was hearing texture and register and all these other things. That's why he had great pianists: Mitch Forman when I joined him, then Harold Danko, Bill Mays, Bill Charlap, and, finally, Ted Rosenthal. They had the ability to hear beyond the piano."

DeRosa, who recorded one small group album with Mulligan, "Lonesome Boulevard" (A&M: 1989), was busy in 2008 both writing and performing, in addition to his teaching. He had just finished writing an arrangement for harmonica player Toots Thieleman that was to be performed with Wynton Marsalis's Jazz at Lincoln Center band in October, and he had succeeded the late Joe Cocuzzo as the regular drummer with Warren Vache's trio.

Mulligan, he recalled, "didn't really like playing clubs. He liked the concert hall. I understood why. You have undivided attention. You may not have the intimacy of a club, but Gerry made his own intimacy. One time we played, 'Song for Strayhorn' in a concert, and there was a hush in the hall."

"Gerry loved all those Broadway shows and tunes," he added. "That accounts for his melodicism and for his passion. He was theatrical in the best sense of the word. And there were misconceptions about his playing that he would get upset about. 'I'm not a *cool* player,' he would say. 'I love to swing.'"

CHAPTER 16

Musical Chameleon: Dick Hyman

For Woody Allen's 1983 motion picture, "Zelig," pianist Dick Hyman composed a number of novelty songs, including "Doin' the Chameleon" and "Chameleon Days." Although the titles referred to the film's main character, portrayed by Allen, they could just as well have referred to Hyman, a musical chameleon who is as comfortable with ragtime as he is with modern jazz and whose activities have ranged from scoring films to playing solo jazz piano concerts to writing original classical compositions.

Hyman, who studied with jazz pianist Teddy Wilson in the 1940s, first became associated with Woody Allen when he was asked by guitarist-composer Mundell Lowe to play piano in the score of the 1972 film, "Everything You Wanted to Know About Sex and Were Afraid to Ask." "I didn't see Woody for some years after that," Hyman recalled. "Then I played piano in 'Manhattan' in various cafe or nightclub scenes. Then, after that, I got a call to play some silent-movie kind of stuff for 'Stardust Memories.' That little scene was improvised, and therefore I became, for the first time, a composer for Woody—in that 18 seconds of music. It was just something I threw together. In that film, I also played considerable solo pianos. One thing led to another, and I got involved in arranging music and composing a lot of the underscoring and a number of songs." All of his assignments from Allen, Hyman said, were given "without quite revealing what the plot was all about. Woody has some very secretive ways of operating."

In "Zelig," Hyman composed the music for other original songs such as "You May Be Six People But I Love You," "Reptile Eyes," and "Leonard the Lizard." In "Broadway Danny Rose," he was the arranger for singer Nick Apollo Forte. Hyman also wrote some incidental scene music. In "Purple Rose of Cairo," he wrote the full score, and in "Hannah and Her Sisters," he played piano. Hyman's credit in "Radio Days" was as musical supervisor.

"Radio Days," released in 1987, took place in the early 1940s, and the music is crucial to the story because the omnipresent radio is central to everything that's going on. Part of the score, explained Hyman, "is just the old records themselves, which Woody selected. And they're very effective—things by Benny Goodman and Tommy Dorsey and Harry James and Duke Ellington. And they work very well. The rest of the score is newly recorded and arranged and, at times, it's hard to tell it apart from the other music, which is what we were trying to accomplish. We did, for example, all of the music for the nightclub scene, all of the dance music there; Mia Farrow's Relax commercial ('Get regular with Relax'); Diane Keaton's song; the kid singing in the manner of Frank Sinatra; some of the old-time radio theme songs; the little girl singing, 'Let's all sing like the birdies sing,' the soap opera stuff; and the mystery shows and the quiz game shows. So, in addition to the recorded classics, there was a lot of music to be done."

Hyman's efforts did not go unnoticed. Janet Maslin, writing in the February 1, 1987, edition of *The New York Times*, commented, "Dick Hyman, the musical supervisor, who is responsible for several dozen extremely well-chosen songs, plus a very hummable laxative jingle, is—with no pun intended—one of the film's unsung heroes."

The aspect of "Radio Days" that Hyman considered particularly significant was "the reminder that there was so much more live music in those times. There was so much more employment of individual musicians. Every one of those programs used an orchestra. Although 'Radio Days' is set about 10 years before I got active, that time was still going on in the 1950s. I was reminded that a show that now would be using prerecorded tapes over and over, very likely done on synthesizer, in those days would have had a 12-piece orchestra. I think it's too bad that we've lost that. You can't fight technology and economics, but I do find that regrettable."

Composing and arranging music for films was just one facet of Dick Hyman's varied agenda in the 1980s. He often played solo and duet jazz piano in concert, at clubs, and on recordings; and he accompanied dozens of singers in those settings; he performed his original compositions with classical orchestras, including the Baltimore, Indianapolis, and Austin symphonies; he produced concerts, such as the 92$_{nd}$ Street Y Jazz Festival and Piano Spectacular, a full-day at Waterloo Village in Stanhope, New Jersey, which was part of the JVC Jazz Festival in New York; he led larger musical groups, such as his own Perfect Jazz Repertory Quintet; and he also arranged and composed music for Broadway shows, television programs, and specials.

"I have always tried to keep a balance between the playing and writing," he said. "I want to continue that way—one seems to help the other." On the day of his interview he was scheduled to do a duet-piano concert of stride music with another jazz pianist, Dick Wellstood, at the Church of the Heavenly Rest in uptown Manhattan. "I do a lot of this kind of thing," he said, "with Dick or Roger Kellaway or Derek Smith or cornetist Ruby Braff, but what I do most is solo piano." He also toured with a Paul Whiteman package—a recreation of Whiteman's Aeolian Hall concert of 1924 at which George Gershwin's "Rhapsody in Blue" was introduced.

His most well-known involvement with the Broadway theater was his role as arranger for "Sugar Babies," the long-running vaudeville-inspired revue that starred Ann Miller and Mickey Rooney. "I have fooled around with original shows," he said, "but they never came to very much. Film is more interesting to me and more productive. I also have written other things for performance. I wrote a violin sonata, which we premiered in March 1987, in Mamaroneck, New York, at the Emilin Theatre. Yuval Waldman was the soloist. So composing is not limited to films, although films are certainly the most demanding and the most widely seen vehicles."

When you are a jazz player, he explained, everything you improvise is a composition. "Sometimes improvisation can be captured on tape, and it works very well, but most of the time when you play jazz, you're improvising on other people's material. The skill you develop doing that is the stuff of composition for me. And I refer to it constantly in everything I'm trying to write."

Hyman, in a sense, let his music speak for itself. His demeanor was understated, and he might even have passed for an accountant or academic as he chatted over a large midday meal at a coffee shop on West 42$_{nd}$ Street. "I've always resisted attempts to limit me to one particular groove," he said. "It seems there are so many interesting ways of approaching music. I don't see why I have to stay in one particular mode. But my personal jazz piano style centers somewhere around the era of Art Tatum and goes forward and backward from there. However, I like many things, and I try to incorporate them into my music to some degree—Chick Corea, Bill Evans, of course, and Oscar Peterson."

A native New Yorker, Hyman became aware of music early in life via his uncle, Anton Rovinsky, a classical pianist and teacher. After studying with Teddy Wilson in 1944, the result of winning a scholarship in a radio contest, and spending a hitch in the navy shortly after World War II, Hyman made his professional debut in 1948 at a Harlem club called Wells. He subsequently worked for bands and/or combos led by Victor Lombardo, Tony Scott, and Red Norvo; spent two months working with various groups at Birdland; and gathered some experience playing in the staff orchestras of New York radio station WMCA and the NBC network.

In 1957, he became a full-time freelancer, eventually leading him into studio work as a conductor, pianist, organist, and arranger. "It seems like I always knew that I would be a musician," Hyman said. "But it wasn't exactly clear that it would go precisely along the lines that it has. I was very happy when I broke into New York studio work. I liked the variety and challenge. I found myself playing soap operas and game shows as well as jazz piano programs and complicated concert stuff on big variety shows. I found that pretty stimulating, and more and more, I came to do my own programs as the conductor or leader and arranger. And all of that led to the composition, too. So, it's all been one great jolly collection of impulses."

While Hyman was saddened by the paucity of live music in broadcasting, he did find some bright spots, such as the live band on "The David Letterman Show" and the soundtrack of the 1980s TV hit, "Miami Vice." "I think that's remarkable music-making," he said, "in that one guy, Jan Hammer, created the entire score in his studio. With the most sophisticated electronic equipment, he was able to create the entire thing on his own. And it worked wonderfully. It really was good writing."

(Adapted from an article that appeared in the Sunday magazine of the *Toledo Blade*, May 17–23, 1987.)

UPDATE

At the age of 81, Dick Hyman had not given up playing the piano, but what he was doing was "reducing the amount of organizing and directing I do in order to focus on composing." In the last few years, his compositions have included a cantata setting for choir and orchestra of Mark Twain's "Autobiography," a ballet for another Mark Twain project, "The Adventures of Tom Sawyer," a sextet for piano, clarinet, flute, viola, bass, and drums, and a trio for piano, violin, and cello, which he premiered in late 2007.

Hyman moved permanently to Venice, Florida, in 1993, and "although I frequently fly elsewhere, we are content here. I continue to balance playing and composing, believing that, for me, the latter comes from the former. What I no longer do—and the field is vastly diminished in New York—is the run-of-the-mill miscellaneous studio work that kept me so busy along with my jazz career." He hasn't been in touch with Woody Allen since Allen began doing films in England after "Melinda and Melinda" (2004). In the latter film, Hyman played solo piano in a living room scene. Hyman believes he's influenced a number of European stride pianists with whom he has played and recorded. He has recorded duo-albums with three of them—Louis Mazetier, Bernd Lhotzky, and Chris Hopkins.

His earliest influences, Hyman said, were Fats Waller, Art Tatum, and Teddy Wilson; later influences were George Shearing, Erroll Garner, and Bill Evans. "These days," he added, "I like Bill Charlap." Charlap has succeeded Hyman as director of the Jazz in July series at the 92_{nd} Street Y in New York City. "His natural style is not like mine, although he can do astonishing note-for-note versions of some of my arrangements."

CDs released in 2008 include a reissue of an old vinyl album Hyman did with cornetist Ruby Braff and the entire 'History of Jazz' (formerly 'One-Hundred Years of Jazz Piano'), which he recorded as a CD-ROM in the middle 1990s. Now, without the graphics but with printed text, it comprises five CDs and a single DVD in a box. It was scheduled for release by Arbors Records in the spring of 2008.

RANDY SANDKE

The summer 2008 JVC Jazz Festival in New York included a tribute to Hyman, and one of the musicians participating in that event was trumpeter Randy Sandke. "The thing that always impresses me about Dick," said Sandke, "is that he is always himself." Sandke recalled a recording session with Art Garfunkel of music Hyman had arranged. "Garfunkel decided he want to change something. I remember how cool Dick was. He gave everybody notes, and we made the changes. He was totally unflappable. I've never seen him lose his cool."

Hyman, added Sandke, was also indefatiguable. "He's totally ageless. I used to work with him in Oregon." Hyman, until stepping down in 2007, was jazz advisor for the Oregon Festival of American Music. "We had 14-hour days, from 9 AM to 11 PM, with a reception afterwards. I would be dead. He was in much better shape than me—he had unbelievable stamina."

Bill Charlap

Dick Hyman's comment, "These days I like Bill Charlap," while discussing Bill Evans, Erroll Garner, and George Shearing was, to Charlap "an honor. He is an overwhelmingly complete musician, and he's certainly one of the most important pianists in my lexicon of great artists I look up to."

Hyman is a distant cousin of Charlap's on his father's side of the family. "I've known him since I was in my early teens. My mother called him and said, 'I want you to meet my son.' I was looking for a teacher at the time. Though he wasn't able to take me on as a private student—he just didn't have the time—he sent me to Jack Reilly, which was actually a lucky break because Jack was a fantastic teacher." Reilly, a jazz pianist and educator heavily influenced by Bill Evans, is known for compositions incorporating elements of both jazz and classical music.

Hyman, though, would give Charlap some practical experience. "Dick would take me around to various record dates, film scores, and solo piano recitals. I was a fly on the wall, and it was a great learning experience. I'm still learning from him all the time. I think that one of the amazing things is that—in his eighties—he is still at the very top of his game. That's an inspiration, and it's kind of incredible."

Dan Levinson

In the spring of 1987, Dan Levinson was about to graduate from New York University. Levinson, who played the clarinet, recalled that he really didn't know what he was going to do with his life. "I was interested in these older jazz styles, and I was planning a tribute to the Original Dixieland Jazz Band, and that was really all I had planned for after graduation," he said.

Originally from Los Angeles, Levinson wanted to stay in New York but didn't know if it was feasible. "I had gotten to know Max Morath (a ragtime pianist-entertainer) and I called him up on a whim because I had happened to enjoy one record he had done," Levinson said. "He was very kind; he invited me over, and he said, 'You know, Dick Hyman lives upstairs, and I think he's looking for an assistant.' Sometimes I look at that phone call I made to Max Morath and realize it was most important phone call I made in my life because it led to a job with Dick Hyman and led to me being able to sustain myself as a musician. I met virtually everyone I know in the music business through Dick."

For the next six years, Levinson worked out of Hyman's office on West 42_{nd} Street. The job, he said, "was as much as I wanted to make of it or as little as I wanted to make of it. That worked out very well for me because I was a budding clarinetist; that was clearly what I wanted to do ultimately—and he knew that from the beginning. He was very understanding of the times I needed to take off. In fact, during the six years I worked for him—until he permanently relocated to Florida in September 1993—I took off an entire year and lived in Paris; and he offered me the job when I returned."

Levinson spent a year as a street musician in Paris with a quintet organized by West Coast cornetist Dick Miller. "I wouldn't trade that experience for anything," he said. "We traveled all over Europe. I really got to know my instruments. I came back and was able to work with professionals." By that time, Levinson was also playing alto saxophone.

In addition, while in Paris his group included a young female singer named Madeleine Peyroux, whose career eventually took off in 1996 with a debut album called "Dreamland" (Atlantic/wea). *Time* Magazine called it "the most exciting, involving vocal performance by a new singer this year." She has been compared to everyone from Billie Holiday to Patsy Cline.

Levinson remembers her as "an enthusiastic but crazy young singer. I mean crazy in a good way. She was determined to sing, and sometimes, against her mother's wishes. The band was called the Riverboat Shufflers. We would take occasional trips to other places. Once, we went to Zurich, and her mother forbade her to go. We were there for a day, playing on the street, and here comes Madeleine Peyroux. She snuck out of the house. I don't know how she did it, but she had to sing. She was just developing her style then. Who knew she would go on to become a million-selling artist? She and I have stayed in touch sporadically over the years. I'm very proud that I had a chance to perform with her way back when she started."

The decision to play saxophone as well as clarinet was actually based on Hyman's advice. "One of the first suggestions Dick made to me was shortly after I began working for him," Levinson recalled. "I was doing this tribute to the Original Dixieland Jazz Band and trying to play like their clarinetist, Larry Shields. Dick said to me, 'You know, Dan, you can't make a living playing like Larry Shields. You really have to play saxophone as well.' I asked, 'Why? Benny Goodman didn't play saxophone.' Dick said, 'Well, he did when he first started out in the 1920s, and, besides, Benny Goodman is Benny Goodman.' I said, 'Well, Kenny Davern doesn't play saxophone.' Dick said, 'And he suffers because of that. He doesn't work as much as he could. But even Kenny will play baritone sax if I twist his arm.' So, I got my hands on an alto. I took some lessons and got relatively proficient on it."

That was the first little bit of advice Hyman gave him. "He also showed me little tricks about improvising," Levinson continued. "He had an exercise that he wrote about in one of his keyboard articles called, 'Practicing a Continuous Melodic Line.' It's much easier to do on a piano than on a wind instrument because on a wind instrument you have to breathe. But it helped me with improvising. One day he sat down and wrote out a bunch of complex jazz rhythms for me to practice. So, he did have a great deal of musical influence on me over six years."

In addition to his foray to Paris, Levinson took time off to play in New Orleans at the Royal Sonesta Hotel on Bourbon Street and other New Orleans jazz venues. Hyman, he said, discouraged him from doing that. "He said, 'When you leave town so often, people stop calling you for jobs because they can't depend on you to be there. You really need to stay in town and build your career here and then, later on in life, there will be plenty of time for traveling.'"

Levinson decided to go anyway. "All I wanted to do at that point in my life was to play, so I took this job playing five nights a week against his recommendation. I wrote him a long letter saying I didn't want to lose his respect, and he wrote back saying, not only would I not lose his respect but, 'as long as you want it, this job will always be yours.' He's the greatest gentleman I've ever had the pleasure of knowing."

The first concert Levinson ever played with Hyman was at a 92_{nd} Street Y tribute to Frank Teschemacher, a legendary clarinetist in the 1920s who died very young. "It was in July 1992, and I was still rough around the edges, but Dick thought I would be a good fit," Levinson said. Aside from the opportunity it presented him musically, it enabled him to meet other musicians and producers "on a different level."

By 1990, Levinson had been working fairly often as a musician, although he admits that "the jobs were not all that prestigious. Starting a year after I began working for Dick, I was doing little jobs around town with Dixieland groups. When I came back from Paris, that work gradually increased. By the time Dick moved to Florida, I had a lot of work and was traveling a bit. Fortunately, I've never needed a secondary job since then."

When Levinson first started playing, his influence on clarinet, he said, was Kenny Davern. "I also enjoyed listening to Benny Goodman, but my real focus on Benny Goodman came a little bit later. Then I realized that I was sounding too much like Davern, not in a good way, but in a way that sounded like I was trying to copy him. So, I had to get away from that and find my own voice. I had to do that with Goodman, too. I had to put the records away. It's an ongoing struggle, finding your own voice; and it doesn't help that I'm constantly called upon for Benny Goodman tributes."

"But what I've tried to do," he continued, "is assimilate him and Davern and others who have influenced me and create something, so that when I play solo it sounds like it's in the style of Benny Goodman but not a replica of one of his solos. Virtually every jazz musician I know doesn't want to be told they sound like somebody else. And every member of the public thinks when they tell a jazz musician he sounds like another jazz musician, they're complimenting him."

Today, Levinson's schedule is varied and busy. He often plays with Vince Giordano's Nighthawks, a band led by bass saxophonist/banjoist Vince Giordano that is dedicated to playing the music of the 1920s and 1930s. "There's a bandleader up in Albany named Don Dworkin who I do a lot of work with; I'm up in Saratoga every year working at the track with the band there; there's a group in Germany called the Swing Dance Orchestra that I perform with; and I also work for Stan Rubin, a bandleader in New York who doesn't play the clarinet anymore. So, he has me come in and play the clarinet while he leads the band."

In early June 2008, Levinson led a tribute to Davern at the Bickford Theatre in Morristown, New Jersey, and the same week he performed with Hyman and Bob Wilber in a concert for the Sidney Bechet Society at Symphony Space in New York. Hyman's playing, he said, is amazing. "He's 81, and he hasn't lost anything. He played incredibly, very fast tempos, and he did things I've never heard a pianist do. But that's why he's Dick Hyman."

CHAPTER 17
Flying High: Maynard Ferguson

In the early 1950s, a 23-year-old trumpet player was the scream (literally and figuratively) of the Stan Kenton band, attracting a sizable popular following because of his wild, screeching high notes. The critics, though, complained that Maynard Ferguson was too undisciplined.

In the late 1970s, Maynard Ferguson was still hearing complaints from the critics—but not from his fans. By adapting the big band sound to the music of contemporary young America, Ferguson suddenly turned into a pop music star. He was nominated for a Grammy Award in the pop/instrumental category for his hit recording of "Gonna Fly Now," the theme from the movie, "Rocky," and he was named the number 1 pop instrumentalist of 1977 in *Billboard*, the music trade newspaper.

The recording of "Gonna Fly Now" happened almost by accident. Peter Philbin, a young executive with Columbia Records in Los Angeles, had attended a press screening of "Rocky." After he heard the soundtrack, he contacted Jay Chattaway, Ferguson's coproducer and arranger. "Jay phoned me," Ferguson recalled, "and said, 'You'd better get over here and listen to something.' That's how it all came about."

Did Ferguson envision the "Rocky" theme becoming a hit single? "For the first time in my life I did smell that as a possibility," he said. "We were already getting attention from departments at Columbia that we normally wouldn't get attention from. To show you how unthinking I was about Top 40, my daughter, Kim, called me one day all excited and said, 'You're 89 with a bullet.' I said, 'What's a bullet?' In the old big band days, 'the bullet' meant you were getting fired. They'd say, 'I hate to tell you this, man, but I think you're gonna get the bullet.'" In the music trade papers, a bullet meant a recording was climbing in the charts.

Ferguson found himself in the unusual position of appealing to the children of people who were his fans 25 to 30 years earlier. "The parents just love it. They have so little identity with the music of their children," he said. "You know, I have kids who come up to me and say, 'Mr. Ferguson, I have every album you've ever recorded—all seven of them! I don't tell them I've actually recorded something like 50 albums."

Like other artists who have combined jazz and rock, Ferguson was constantly confronted by critics who felt he had diluted the purity of the music in order to make a buck. "One critic," he said, "wrote that 'this obvious use of rock rhythms was a disappointing departure from his greatness of before.' I'd never had a good review from that guy—so what 'greatness' was he talking about?"

Ferguson pointed out that there have always been members of the music establishment who resisted change. "When Louis Armstrong left the King Oliver band in order to be more creative, there were people who said, 'How dare he?' Then, we went to the swing era with Benny Goodman and Count Basie. People said, 'How can jazz not have a Dixieland beat?' Then, they attacked Dizzy Gillespie and Charlie Parker as being 'impure.' I don't impose my musical philosophy on other people. It's very important, I think, to leave the people that do not wish to change alone and still admire them as the great artists they are."

His first "rock fusion" album contained such hits of the day as Laura Nyro's "Eli's Comin'" and Jim Webb's "MacArthur Park." The album was originally recorded with an all-British band that Ferguson had assembled after he had taken a hiatus from music in India. "I did a record and returned to India," he recalled, "but a couple of guys from Blood, Sweat & Tears came over to England, heard the album, and brought it back to Columbia Records. That caused things to happen. Suddenly, the album was released in this country. Then I got a call from Willard Alexander, a booking agent for most of the remaining big bands. He said, 'Maynard, I don't know if you know it, but you have an album that's starting to make a little noise. How would you like to do about four weeks touring in this country?' We did a second tour of eight weeks and, by the third and fourth tour, I started losing some of my British musicians. They were married with families and couldn't spend that much time in the United States."

Ferguson insisted he would continue to change his music, despite the fact that it might disappoint "purists," and he felt he had given impetus to a possible revival of big bands in the United States. "There are 30,000 to 40,000 stage bands in high schools and colleges around the country," he said. "What we've done is give a lot of encouragement to these young kids. We're the first big band to be in the Top 40 in 20 years."

(Reprinted from an article that appeared in *The Trib*, January 26, 1978.)

UPDATE

Maynard Ferguson died at the age of 78 in August 2006, in Ventura, California, of kidney and liver failure caused by an abdominal infection. The obituary in the *Washington Post* on August 25, 2006, described him as "a trumpeter of phenomenal range and endurance" who "possessed a dazzling virtuosity that spanned classical music, jazz, rock, disco and Indian ragas. With an ebullient personality to match his dizzying flights on trumpet, he remained a popular and influential force in music to the end."

Ferguson's last recording, "The One and Only," was recorded three weeks before he died and released in May 2007 by Contemporary Productions. At least four other Ferguson CDs were released in 2007. Three were on the Wounded Bird Records label: "M. F. Horn 2," "M. F. Horn 3," and "M. F. Horn 4 & 5—Live at Jimmy's." The fourth, "The Essential Maynard Ferguson," was a two-disc set from Sony.

DON SEBESKY

"Every trumpet player I know reveres Maynard Ferguson," said Don Sebesky. A trombonist in Ferguson's band in the late 1950s, Sebesky also made major contributions to the band as a composer and arranger and eventually gave up playing to do that full-time. Ferguson's band "was the smallest it could be and still be considered a 'big' band, Sebesky said. "It had three trumpets, two trombones, four saxophones, and piano, bass, and drums. Then, Maynard would be the sixth brass player—he could play trumpet, trombone, or French horn. He was great as a high note player, and he had really reached his peak with the Stan Kenton band. Kenton allowed him to do what he did best."

Everyone, Sebesky said, "wanted to write for Maynard because he provided a lot of opportunities to write. He allowed guys like me to come up with our own ideas. He gave the writers a nice forum—it was almost like a lab band." Sebesky recalled Ferguson as being "so low-keyed and likable. He was a nice guy toward all the musicians. The only time I saw him get angry was one time we were playing at a prom in the Midwest, and Maynard was playing a ballad with his eyes closed. Some kid who was drunk bumped into him and bashed his horn into his lip. I never saw him get so angry."

The Ferguson band's appearances at the legendary jazz club Birdland were particularly memorable to Sebesky. "There was continuous music," he recalled. "The main attraction might be Miles Davis or the Hi-Los; then when they finished, we would go on. There was never a break. There was even a part of the club for people who didn't drink." His favorite Ferguson album was a record comprising tunes made famous by other people, such as Basie's "One O'Clock Jump" and Tommy Dorsey's "I'm Getting Sentimental Over You."

Sebesky left the Ferguson band in 1959 to join Kenton's band, but he kept writing for Ferguson for about 10 years. He continued to concentrate on writing and arranging and established a reputation as one of the most gifted and well-regarded arranger-composers in the music business.

Ferguson's "Rocky" period, Sebesky believes, meant the band "was no longer a pure jazz band." He remembers seeing Ferguson in concert in the spring of 2006 at West Morris Mendham High School in Mendham, New Jersey, where Sebesky lives. "The band had six horns and a synthesizer. It was kind of formulaic."

Randy Sandke

Fifty-eight-year-old jazz trumpeter Randy Sandke recalls listening to Maynard Ferguson when he was in high school. "I loved his band. I took a friend to one of his concerts, and my friend got a nosebleed (from the stratospheric high notes). I don't believe Ferguson has gotten his due. He always had great bands and great writing. And he made a lot of memorable records," said Sandke. "When he got into rock, I stopped listening. I don't fault him for that; he was trying to survive. After all, in the '70s, Duke Ellington and Count Basie were making arrangements of Beatles' tunes.'"

To Sandke, Ferguson's classic period was the early 1960s. "He tends to get written out of the history books, but he had very hot jazz bands. The focal point of his style was his range. He had phenomenal control. He had a really huge sound up and down. He was always very musical, but not the kind of player I'd like to listen to in a small group setting. He was a bit limited as an improviser, but he was a guy you could recognize in one note. His bands had an identity of their own, and he always led a happy band."

DENIS DIBLASIO

Baritone saxophonist Denis DiBlasio joined Ferguson's band in the 1980s after receiving his master's degree from the University of Miami. He eventually became the band's musical director. "I grew up loving his music," DiBlasio said. "He was a hero. As a kid, I saw him in the men's room at Brandy's Wharf in Philadelphia and said to him, 'I'm going to be in your band someday.'"

Ferguson, DiBlasio pointed out, loved to show off the members of the band. "If you wrote a chart, he would introduce you. If we were playing in someone's hometown, he would give that person more solos. He got that from Kenton. That's why so many of us showed up for his 80_{th} birthday memorial concert in St. Louis."

That concert was held on May 1, 2008, at the Touhill Performing Arts Center in St. Louis. It was organized by Ed Sargent, Ferguson's former tour manager, and St. Louis music promoter and Contemporary Productions president, Steve Schankman, who was Ferguson's last manager. In addition to DiBlasio, other musicians who performed included trumpeter Eric Miyashiro, who came all the way from Tokyo, trumpeter Walter White, trombonist Steve Wiest, and a rhythm section comprised of Chip Stephens on piano, Brian Stahuski on bass, and Dave Throckmorton on drums.

It's difficult to characterize Ferguson's playing, DiBlasio believes, because "he truly loved to play the trumpet, and he would play any style. He would have fun playing any kind of music. He just wanted a vehicle to play his horn, and he really loved physicality. Guys would come in with convoluted stuff, but if it worked he would do it. What the band played reflected what the band wrote."

DiBlasio is currently director of the jazz department at Rowan University in Glassboro, New Jersey. In 2000, Rowan presented Ferguson with an honorary doctorate degree. DiBlasio wrote on the Rowan

Web site: "It was a dream come true for me to be one of the people that helped make the event happen. To give something back to a man that gave so much to myself and others was not only a natural thing to do but a necessary one. Maynard had over 70 recordings in his career; books have been written about him; he's been on countless television shows, played for royalty and was all over the world many times... What could I give him that he didn't already have? The answer was an honorary doctorate from a university."

At the time Ferguson was given his doctorate, a decision was made to create The Maynard Ferguson Institute of Jazz Studies at Rowan, which is headed by DiBlasio. The goal of the Institute is to further the training of young jazz musicians and support the Rowan jazz program. DiBlasio emphasized that, in addition to being an outstanding musician and performer, Ferguson was "one of the best jazz educators on the planet. Maynard liked young guys because they were hungry. He liked the energy of young guys. The problem with kids today is that they only know Charlie Parker, and they think everyone else sucks. "

In February 2008, while performing at the Jazz in the Wood series at the Collingswood Community Center in Collingswood, New Jersey, DiBlasio participated in a question-and-answer series with the audience. According to the *Philadelphia Inquirer* (February 17, 2008):

> "Someone asked DiBlasio how he focused on the baritone sax, a larger, deeper-sounding instrument than its alto cousin. 'I had an offer to perform with Maynard Ferguson, who needed a bari player,' said DiBlasio. He said he wasn't sure whether he should take the gig, until he asked his father for advice. 'You play with him even if you have to play bagpipes!', his father advised.

On the www.maynardferguson.com Web site, there is a feature, created by his former musicians, called "Road Stories." DiBlasio appears in those stories quite frequently, and one of his recollections encapsulates the exuberant and unpredictable nature of Ferguson's personality: "We were in his pool, which was just off the back of his house. I had some manuscript papers by the shallow end, and 'Boss' was in the pool with his horn. When he would play, he would put the bell underwater so it sounded like a double C gargle. He said he practiced like that sometimes so we wouldn't disturb the neighbors. I remember Boss playing 'Shuffle Monk' while I was underwater to check out the effect. It was a riot!"

Steve Schankman

Steve Schankman met Ferguson in 1973 and recalled that "in the '70s and up to around 1988, we were friendly but not close friends." In 1988, though, Schankman's wife booked Ferguson to play at her husband's 40th birthday party. "I had stopped playing the trumpet for about 10 or 15 years because I was building my company, Contemporary Productions," said Schankman. "I had six weeks notice because it was decided that I would be playing with Maynard (at the birthday party). So, you think of a trumpet section with the likes of Wayne Bergeron and Roger Ingram and *Steve Schankman*. Something wasn't right about this picture. I spent that next six weeks getting every recording of Maynard's I could put my hands on, and I started practicing. And that night, I played with them. It was quite the night. We talked a lot, told stories. We got even closer over the later years."

"I never met the jazz greats like Miles Davis or Dizzy Gillespie," Schankman conceded, "and Maynard wasn't Miles Davis or Dizzy Gillespie. But he put notes on trumpets that no one did before him. There were other trumpet players who could play high notes, but it wasn't about the notes he played, it was about the shape of the note and the sound that he could make happen. He became this great high note trumpet player, but he also had this sound which nobody has reproduced." Schankman had taken over management of the Ferguson band in 2003, and the band was planning an Asian tour in 2006, when Ferguson became ill. Schankman was able to speak to him shortly before he died, and he remembers the moment vividly. "I told him, 'You'll go down as the greatest stratosphere trumpet player of all time, the guy that made 'Rocky' famous. In my mind, you'll go down as one of the most wonderful people I ever knew.'"

CHAPTER 18
Growing Up With Jazz: Stanley Cowell

Art Tatum changed the course of jazz piano in the 1930s. His inventive technique and harmonic diversity set the standard for a whole generation of jazz pianists to follow him. Stanley Cowell, who grew up in Tatum's birthplace of Toledo, Ohio, only met Tatum once, but that meeting made an indelible impression on his life.

Cowell's father (also named Stanley) and a local trumpeter, Francis Williams, had been boyhood pals of Tatum. "Art came to town once on a visit, to see his sister, and my father saw him and invited him by the house," Cowell said. "My father insisted that he play, and I don't think he really wanted to play. He had a way of choosing titles that reflected the way he felt, so he played, 'You Took Advantage of Me,' and he played the hell out of it. He played it so strongly and so powerfully that my mother left the room and went into the kitchen, kind of shaken and seemingly upset. I asked her what was wrong, and she said, 'Oh, that man plays too much piano.'"

Though only six years old at the time, Cowell had already been taking piano lessons for two years. He didn't attach that much importance to Tatum's visit then, but more than 30 years later he savored the memory. "I never met him again after that," he said. "He was dead by the time I really recalled the experience. I kind of tucked it away and forgot all about it. Later, I may have heard the piece and remembered, or maybe I read his obituary and remembered it."

Although Tatum undoubtedly influenced Cowell, his modernistic playing seems to also have been touched by a variety of other piano styles, ranging from the pure bebop of Barry Harris and Bud Powell to the avant-gardism of Cecil Taylor. In the early 1980s, Cowell was described by *Downbeat* magazine as "a fine composer and a keyboard performer of considerable range and depth...a musician capable of almost anything."

In 1982, his musical activities were centered in two spheres. He was the pianist in the Heath Brothers quintet, touring and recording with tenor saxophonist Jimmy Heath, bassist Percy Heath, guitarist Tony Purrone, and drummer Akira Tana; and he was an associate professor of jazz studies at Lehman College in the Bronx, New York.

He was also involved in another project, the fruits of which were seen in the movies. Cowell served as piano coach for Howard Rollins, the actor who portrayed Coalhouse Walker in the movie version of E. L. Doctorow's "Ragtime." Rollins played the piano a little, but the trick, said Cowell, was to make him look like a professional player of the ragtime era. "With great difficulty he could play the notes, but it would have taken him two years to work up a performance of one of those pieces that was really a performance," Cowell explained. "I just had to get him to understand that he didn't have to play every note exactly. That was the hardest thing because he had the music, and he was trying to read it; and I was trying to get him to get the overall proportions, the overall look of the piece—the oompah oompah bass figure in ragtime. I was trying to get him away from reading the notes to just dealing with the shape of the phrase." The result: "He did great. He worked hard. We worked twice a week for about two months. Then a new batch of music came down about six months later, and we worked again."

Cowell's formal music instruction was classical, but by the time he reached high school he had discovered jazz from records he had heard around his house and from concerts he attended with his brother-in-law, Archie Finch. "I saw the Billy Taylor Trio; I saw Stan Kenton; and I saw Don Shirley, who is really not a jazz pianist, but he had a presentation that is like jazz."

At 14, he was a featured soloist with the Toledo Youth Symphony, but he was also trying to play jazz as much as possible and had begun to play combo gigs around town with some of the local musicians. He also used to sneak up to Detroit as much as possible. "In addition to the Tatum experience, the real experience of the Detroit pianists and the Detroit musical scene was probably one of the most important influences," said Cowell. "There were so many musicians there at the time. So much was happening." One of the hot places was the Club 12. "I went there, and that's where I first saw Yusef Lateef (tenor saxophone, flute). That's when I first met Barry Harris, Joe Henderson (tenor saxophone), Roy Brooks (drums), Frank Gant (drums), and Terry Pollard (piano, vibes). I even sat in one night there."

Cowell went on to college at Oberlin, majoring in music, but he was somewhat frustrated by the attitude of the school toward jazz. "When I first got there," he remembered, "the dean of the music school, at his opening address, said, 'This is a Bach, Beethoven, Brahms school. All that other stuff—keep it out of here.' That surprised me because Dave Brubeck had gotten a lot of popularity because of a record, 'Jazz at Oberlin'."

Nevertheless, Cowell was able to continue playing jazz, albeit outside of the classroom. "You couldn't play jazz in the practice rooms. It was done outside," he said. "There was a guy named George West who had been with a group called the Airmen of Note. He had a big band, and he had arrangements; and there was a jazz club there. I met people that I began to associate with, who wanted to play. We'd play small group stuff. A guy named Howard Storch and I went to the Notre Dame Collegiate Jazz Festival one year, and it opened up a lot of interests for me as to what was happening at the universities around the country."

After finishing at Oberlin in 1962, Cowell accepted a piano-tuning fellowship for graduate work at Wichita State. "I hated piano tuning. I did it to help put me through school, but I hated Wichita State," he said. "They had the same kind of ethnocentric view toward music. Any interest I was going to generate toward undergraduates about jazz was suspect, subversive almost." Cowell quit Wichita State and shortly afterward received a composition scholarship to the University of Southern California. But, he said, "I got too busy performing out there with jazz players. We played all day and all night, and I just really dropped out of classes." He stayed at Southern Cal for about a year and then returned to Toledo in 1964 when his father suffered a heart attack.

In January 1965, Cowell picked up his graduate studies at the University of Michigan, from which he eventually earned a Master of Music degree. "During that time I played in Ann Arbor with a trio, and I was associated with some musicians in Detroit," he said. "We called ourselves the Detroit Contemporary Four or Five or Six—whatever number it took. We were kind of experimental. It was part of that explosion sociologically and musically that was related to Martin Luther King's death and the frustrations and racial tensions of the time."

In 1966 Cowell moved to New York City, where he "did a lot of things like accompanying unknown singers, writing arrangements, and doing occasional studio work for films and commercials." His first real jazz connection was with avant-garde alto saxophonist Marion Brown. In 1967, he was hired by drummer Max Roach and, "from that point on, everything just opened up." There were jobs with Miles Davis, flutist Herbie Mann, vibist Bobby Hutcherson, tenor saxophonist Stan Getz, trumpeter Donald Byrd, and tenor saxophonists Clifford Jordan and Sonny Rollins.

Cowell hooked up with the Heath Brothers in 1974. Jimmy Heath is a tenor saxophonist who developed out of the bebop tradition. His brother, Percy, a bassist, was one of the founders of the Modern Jazz Quartet in the early 1950s, remaining a member of that heralded group until it broke up in 1974. After the Modern Jazz Quartet's "farewell concert" at New York's Lincoln Center, Cowell recalled that, "Jimmy had the idea to try and put the brothers together. A third brother, drummer Albert Heath, played with the group initially but later went his own way. Percy was maybe a little reluctant. He wanted to retire at that point—he wanted to fish. But he agreed to it." The group was critically acclaimed and enjoyed better-than-average commercial success.

Although having great respect for the bebop tradition, Cowell pointed out that "bebop is also the most difficult for a listener." The record industry in the 1980s, he explained, was "more interested in having something that would cross over into radio airplay—something that is more akin to fusion, that has the broken beat, the kind of rock-funk beat to it. So Jimmy wrote a lot of those types of songs—at least one or two on each album—in the interest of that large group of record buyers who were not necessarily into the music of jazz."

Cowell also made some albums on his own, most notably "Talkin' 'Bout Love," a 1979 record on the Galaxy label that featured original material cowritten by him and Bowling Green State University faculty member John Scott for a musical called "Karma," which was presented in 1977 at the Afro-American Total Theater in New York.

Despite the fact that jazz is considered an improvisatory art, Cowell confessed that what a jazz musician plays in public is "never off the top of your head. You develop over the years a certain pattern and vocabulary of musical ideas which you reuse. I tell my students, 'You get up; you're going to play for people. You already know what you're going to say. Then you present your ideas in a coherent fashion. And when you're extra creative, sometimes something comes that is seemingly from above; but usually, unless you're a genius, that doesn't happen all the time.'"

(Adapted from an article that appeared in the Sunday magazine of the *Toledo Blade*, July 14, 1982).

UPDATE

In January 2000, Cowell accepted a piano professorship position at Rutgers University's Mason Gross School of the Arts in New Brunswick, New Jersey. He eventually became director of the jazz studies program there. His permanent residence is in Upper Marlboro, Maryland, however, so he travels between both locations and has been very active, with his wife Sylvia, producing concerts in Prince Georges County, Maryland.

In the spring of 2006, Cowell took a sabbatical from Rutgers in order to work on an orchestration commissioned by the Philadelphia Museum of Art. "The commission in 2005 was for a septet based on the museum's Asian art collection," he explained. "I did a 12-part suite for different works of art from India, China, and Japan, and we premiered it at the museum in December 2005. So, to justify my sabbatical, I began orchestrating that work, cutting it down to six movements, still based on musical elements from the three major Asian cultures, but inspired by the works of the permanent collection there, which is pretty vast."

"I've sent it to the conductor of the Toledo Symphony, and I've done a synthetic version of it just to illustrate tempo," he continued. "It features three sections of an orchestra—no percussion—and a jazz septet, ostensibly the Rutgers jazz faculty, musicians such as guitarist Vic Juris and trombonist Conrad Herwig. They're looking at fall 2010 to possibly perform it at Rutgers. The conductor of the Prince Georges Symphony Orchestra, Charles Ellis, also has the score. I have a feeling he's going to do it first. We may use some of the guys from the University of Maryland or other local jazz musicians rather than my Rutgers colleagues. It depends on the budget and/or the ability to get these guys there."

There is a precedent in classical music for a relationship between music and art, Cowell said, pointing to Mussorgsky's "Pictures at an Exhibition." "That would be my takeoff point," he said, "but Duke Ellington and Chico Hamilton also produced works inspired by artwork. Dave Liebman (tenor saxophonist) also did one, but his was based on a 20_{th} century modern collection."

When a representative of the Philadelphia Museum of Art suggested the project, Cowell chose the Asian collection partly because of his interest in Asian history. "I'm a practicing Buddhist," he said, "and there are two Buddhist temples, one Chinese and one Japanese, represented in the artwork. The Indian artwork is generally religion-based, too."

The combination of classical music and jazz began to develop in the mid-1950s, Cowell said, with the third stream movement spearheaded by conductor Gunther Schuller, bassist Charles Mingus, and trombonist J.J. Johnson because "jazz musicians wanted to be respected on an artistic level. The first manifestation of that would have been somebody recording with strings. That has continued as jazz musicians developed the same resources that classical musicians and composers have. It's just that classical players had to grasp jazz techniques. There was a period where jazz players did not accept classical players to be able to do anything except read the notes. You either became very specific about what you wanted rhythmically or you had to find someone in the first chair who could simulate the long short, long short, swing eight—that kind of thing."

Cowell remembers when he first premiered a piece with the Toledo Symphony in the early 1990s "the first violinist asked me, 'Do you want me to swing these notes?' I'd gone to great detail to write everything out exactly as I wanted it played." Even today, he added, "I don't know if you can trust for an orchestra to really swing without everything being written out."

Teaching today is a real challenge, Cowell said, because "these guys can play. The first week of my jazz improvisation course I usually have them play standards. They're already professional-level musicians. Ultimately, I want them to write vehicles that will take them out of the nightclub and push them to bigger venues incorporating orchestras, male choruses, church choirs, dance groups."

When Cowell arrived at Rutgers, a rift had developed between the jazz and classical areas. "There was no effort to connect the classical and jazz programs," he said. "Part of my tact in writing pieces for brass choir and classical ensembles was to repair that rift." He wrote a piano concerto that he believes "created some respect for the jazz musicians. Then I began to write other works. It showed that jazz musicians have a side that is not limited to the idiom. Ideally, our students should come out of here with the ability to do a variety of things."

CHAPTER 19
Horn of Emotion: David Sanborn

David Sanborn indirectly owes his career to the St. Louis (Atlanta) Hawks professional basketball team. It was during a concert following a Hawks basketball game in 1956 that the 11-year-old from the St. Louis suburb of Kirkwood was inspired to learn how to play the alto saxophone. "They used to have concerts after the game, and this one was by the Ray Charles band," Sanborn recalled. "The band did about an hour before Ray came on, and I heard the alto saxophonist Hank Crawford play. He just knocked me out."

Sanborn, at the time, was recovering from polio, and doctors had advised him to learn a wind instrument to build up his lungs and help regulate his breathing. Until that night he was undecided about which instrument to choose, but Crawford's sound "just really cut through," he said. "It had an emotional quality to it that really appealed to me. I think that was probably the reason I wanted to play the alto saxophone—because of that emotional, from-the-heart kind of sound to it."

Sanborn has appeared on record and in concert with an endless string of pop vocalists, including James Taylor, Linda Ronstadt, and Paul Simon, and he was once a member of the house band on NBC-TV's "Saturday Night Live." In the 1980s he also ranked as high as second on alto saxophone in *Downbeat* magazine's readers' jazz poll. The emotional quality he recognized in Hank Crawford's playing in the 1950s became the embodiment of his style. Composer-arranger Gil Evans characterized Sanborn's playing as having "that great cry." *Downbeat*, reviewing his 1979 Warner Brothers album, "Hideaway," described his sound as "penetrating, yet satiny sensuous and romantically evocative."

Sanborn's personality is laced with humility. Of his high *Downbeat* ranking, he said, "I grew up reading that magazine. It's a little embarrassing to finish ahead of people that I consider to be better players than myself, but I still feel flattered. I'm not egotistical enough to admit to not liking it."

He acknowledged that his playing was pretty emotional. "It was an emotional experience when I heard Hank Crawford," he said. "He didn't have to play too many notes. He just manipulated the space in a real masterful way." The saxophone, Sanborn explained, "is a combination of a brass and woodwind instrument. The alto saxophone has a kind of aggressiveness to it, and the reediness sort of balances it off. It's close to the human voice. With the alto, you can get a lot of expressiveness because of the reed quality—and you can get the projection of a brass instrument."

The haunting, passionate side of Sanborn was evident on his solos on such hit records as Linda Ronstadt's "Ooh Baby Baby." The upbeat side of Sanborn came through in his feverish licks on songs such as "Trouble in Paradise" from John David Souther's 1979 Sony album, "You're Only Lonely." But Sanborn has always been a musician who could glide easily in and out of several musical worlds—from jazz to rock to soulful rhythm and blues. It was in the latter category that he sharpened his musical acuity after getting off to a somewhat inauspicious start as a music student in the Kirkwood school system. After the Ray Charles concert, he had enrolled in a beginner's course at the Osage Elementary School so he could play in the school's band. "I really didn't learn how to read music very well," he said. "I just kind of faked it. For awhile I wrote the fingerings above the notes and just kind of tried to follow the flow of what everybody else was playing. We played little marches and "The Dance of the Fairy Queen"—things like that. I more or less stumbled through it, playing mostly by ear."

Sanborn was also in the band at Kirkwood High School—but just barely. "I kind of learned my parts from the guys sitting next to me," he explained. "I was always last chair; I couldn't read, and I didn't have a legitimate approach to the instrument. I was just kind of messing around, playing along with records and stuff." By the time he was about 14, Sanborn had gained enough confidence from playing along with records to start hanging out at teen centers. "The Sunset Teen Town is one I remember. They had various bands—people like Jules Blattner and the Teen Tones, Albert King, and Little Milton."

A little later, he started spending time in an area of St. Louis called Gaslight Square, gravitating to a little club called The Other Side. "There was a piano player there named Rick Bolden, who I became friendly with. It turned out he was playing with Albert King," Sanborn recalled. King, a guitarist, was considered a major blues figure in the Midwest in the 1950s and 1960s. His best-known record was "Born Under a Bad Sign," released on the Stax label in 1967. The *Contemporary Music Almanac 1980/81* (Schirmer Books: New York), in fact, described him as "a key figure in the postwar St. Louis blues scene."

Sanborn, through Bolden, worked his way into King's band. "I kind of snuck in the background" he recalled. "Albert had four or five horn players who were just playing lines like 'doo dah.' Once in awhile one of them would take a solo." After playing with King, Sanborn began working gigs in small towns—roadhouses on the highway between Davenport, Iowa, and St. Louis. "All the time," he said, "I was gradually learning about the instrument. It was a great experience."

His introduction to jazz evolved through his acquaintance with Phillip Wilson, a St. Louis drummer. Sanborn started playing jazz with Wilson and his contemporaries. "I really didn't know what the distinction was at that point (between jazz and blues); I pretty much played what I'd always played." Wilson helped Sanborn get a job at the Blue Note, a club outside of East St. Louis, Illinois. Sanborn shuddered slightly at the memory. "We played from midnight to 6 in the morning, seven nights a week. That was quite an experience. It was the summer before I was a senior in high school."

Sanborn attended Northwestern University, where he studied saxophone more formally, and then moved on to the University of Iowa, playing in the jazz band there as well as studying and playing contemporary classical music. He never actually earned a college degree, though. "I always felt like an outsider at school," he said. "I just didn't have the discipline to learn the instrument the way they wanted to teach it."

So, in the summer of 1967, Sanborn took off for San Francisco. "I was walking down the street in Haight-Ashbury, and I ran into Phillip Wilson. He had just joined the Paul Butterfield Blues Band. I went down to see them at the Fillmore, and I said, 'Gee, this is great. I'd love to play in this band.'" Once again, Sanborn managed to sit in, not only in live performances but in a recording session as well. He eventually joined the Butterfield Blues Band and stayed on for almost five years. Then he moved to the East Coast, played with such pop superstars as Stevie Wonder and David Bowie, and landed a recording contract on his own with Warner Brothers Records.

"I think it's absolutely necessary for me to play in a lot of different contexts," he said. "It keeps my playing fresh. My records are kind of the distilled versions of all these inspirations and styles and types of music that I listen to." Although he came to be closely identified with jazz, Sanborn conceded that he didn't have roots in jazz. But, "now that I'm beginning to understand more of the vocabulary of jazz and bebop, I'm learning how to navigate through the harmonic aspects of it. I have a feeling, an affinity for the music."

On the other side of the coin, "You hear a lot of the old jazz players who will play rock 'n roll. But there's a certain kind of stylistic thing to playing rock 'n roll that a lot of people—especially saxophone players—don't understand. It's a nuance. It isn't playing flat out hard and loud. It's playing intense. Dynamics. I think that's what a lot of musicians lack, period—a sense of dynamics."

(Reprinted with permission of the *St. Louis Post-Dispatch*, July 25, 1980.)

UPDATE

If David Sanborn is remembered for one accomplishment, he would like it to be his efforts in breaking down the barriers between different types of music. "Common ground, that's what interests me—on a musical level, on a sociological level, on a human level," he said. "There's no reason Sonny Rollins and Leonard Cohen, for example, can't play music together. Or James Taylor and Michael Brecker. Or Wynton Marsalis and Willie Nelson." The last two duos *have* recorded together, and Sanborn's latest CD, released in 2008, stretches the limits of that eclecticism.

"Here and Gone" (Decca U.S.) contains three tracks closely identified with Hank Crawford: "Stoney Lonesome," "What Will I Tell My Heart?," and "Please Send Me Someone to Love." In a way, said Sanborn, the CD is "like touching home plate. It felt like it was the right time to try to acknowledge my debt to him and to the music that really got me excited about becoming a musician in the first place." Crawford, who had suffered a stroke in 2000, died in January 2009 at the age of 74.

Other artists range from the jazz trumpeter Wallace Roney on "St. Louis Blues" to Eric Clapton performing "I Wanna Move to the Outskirts of Town." To Sanborn, the pairing of Roney and Clapton on the same album is "totally natural. Why not? As I step back and look at it after the fact, I say, 'Wow, there's a pretty wide diversity between Eric and Wallace.' But, in a way, there's not because they're both incredibly invested in the music that they're playing. When you can get somebody who has the ability to *inhabit* what they're playing, those are the kind of people you want to get involved with. That includes Derek Trucks (guitarist), Joss Stone (vocalist), and Sam Moore (drummer from Sam & Dave)," all of whom have guest appearances on the CD.

Jazz, Sanborn believes, is "a big tent. There is a lot of music that falls under the definition of what jazz is. I never quite understood people who wanted to pin one particular vein of the idiom against another—that *this* one is more artistically valid than *that*. In my opinion, all American popular music grew out of jazz, the element of swing being kind of a tenet of what defines the music. I think there's a certain spiritual aspect to it—the spirit of adventure, investigation, and experimentation, pushing the boundaries, harmonically, rhythmically and melodically, not being restricted by limitations one way or the other."

Up until the bebop era, Sanborn pointed out, "jazz was the mainstream, popular music of America. When it stopped being danced to, it started to become more marginalized. That's not to say it wasn't valuable as an art form, but on a mass cultural level, it had less significance. But the cutting edge of the innovation of music, more often than not, happens in the jazz world."

The late arranger Gil Evans, best known for his work with Miles Davis, had a major impact on Sanborn. "What Gil gave jazz and music in general was a vast, subtle palette orchestrally," Sanborn said. "He came on in the early days of jazz arranging, following very closely in the shadow of Fletcher Henderson and Duke Ellington. He did some very innovative orchestrations using some unusual instrumentations like tuba and bassoon in a traditional jazz setting. He expanded on that in the '40s and '50s when he worked with Miles Davis on those landmark albums like 'Porgy & Bess' (Sony: original release, 1958), 'Miles Ahead' (Sony: original release, 1957), and 'Sketches of Spain' (Sony: original release, 1959). Those albums expanded the range of what jazz was."

Evans, Sanborn continued, "was a tremendous influence on me. When I first moved to New York in 1973, I actually lived at Gil's house for about a year. I spent some time absorbing his aesthetic about how he approached the music. It was like going to graduate school.

He was a great human being as well as a great musician. 'St. Louis Blues' is a nod to Gil."

In November 2008, Sanborn had just returned from Europe and was planning a trip to Japan. Both trips were designed to expose the music from "Here and Gone." He hoped the CD would "bridge those seemingly wide chasms of style and taste and idioms. Music is a continuum. It's not like you need a passport."

CHAPTER 20

Jazz Ambassador: Billy Taylor

On a Friday in 1944, 23-year-old Billy Taylor arrived in New York City from Washington, D.C., hoping to start a career as a jazz pianist. "I dropped my bags and went to Minton's in Harlem," he recalled. "I had met some musicians in D.C. who were now working in New York, and I thought if luck was with me, I'd get a chance to work with some of these people."

Taylor waited until 3 AM before he had a chance to sit in at the piano at Minton's Playhouse, widely recognized as the birthplace of bebop. Luck *was* with him, however, because one of the musicians in attendance was the tenor saxophonist Ben Webster. "By the time I was invited up to play, what had been six guys on the bandstand was now 10 or 15 guys because people had gotten off work," Taylor said. "I looked up, and there's one of my idols, Ben Webster. He came and stood by the piano, kind of looking at what I was doing. He said, 'Come on down to the club where I'm playing because I'm looking for a piano player. Don't come on Saturday because it's too busy; come on Sunday when I'll have time to listen to you.' I went in on Sunday, played for him, and got the job. So, on my third day in town I was not only working, but I was working with Ben Webster at the Three Deuces on 52_{nd} Street. And we were playing opposite Art Tatum. The bill was the Ben Webster Quartet and the Art Tatum Trio."

The Three Deuces was the first club located east of Sixth Avenue on the famous block between Sixth and Fifth Avenues. "In that block, you'd see all of these big lights with everybody's name on it—all of the famous jazz people who were working in that area. It was like a history of the music right in front of you," Taylor said. Getting to listen to Art Tatum during his break was "a fantastic experience for me," and as a result, Taylor became one of Tatum's protégés. "I used to take him out and go places with him. I was kind of his eyes."

Taylor recalled one incident that had a lasting impact on him. "We were at an after-hours joint, and this guy came up and said, 'Art, I'd like to play your version of "Tiger Rag" for you,' and Art said, 'Okay.' The guy sounded good. He had transcribed everything and really did a good job of it. I was impressed, but Tatum couldn't have been more blasé about it. I said to him, 'This guy is one of the few guys I've heard who's close to what you're doing.' He said, 'Yeah, he knows *what* I do, but he doesn't know *why* I do it.' That stuck with me. The musicians who influenced me—Tatum, (drummer) Jo Jones, Willie 'The Lion' Smith, and Duke Ellington—were delighted that you took something that was theirs and used it, but you were supposed to make something of your own of it. They wanted me to learn whatever I could from them and take it to another level, and that's what I've tried to do. Over the years, my style has become basically bebop but with many other things added. My style is really very personal; my touch is really quite different from Art's. The kinds of things I can do with a ballad are more related to Eddie South and Ben Webster than they are to Art as a pianist. The idea of the music I play is a compilation of all of the things that make up my style."

At age 87, Taylor is one of jazz's elder statesmen. He had just completed a week of working with young jazz musicians as part of a summer jazz improvisation workshop for high school and college students held at William Paterson University in Wayne, New Jersey, and he capped off the week with what has become a tradition: a concert with his trio (bassist Chip Jackson and drummer Winard Harper) in William Paterson University's Shea Center for the Performing Arts. He's retired in the sense that "I'm only doing things that I can get to by train. I don't want to fly. I've been around the world a couple of times, and I'm delighted I had the opportunity to go to the places I did, but I just physically and mentally can't handle that type of travel anymore."

Taylor was born in Greenville, North Carolina, but his family moved to the Washington, D.C., area when he was still an infant. "I come from a musical family," he said. "Everybody played church music and classical music and popular music, but my Uncle Bob was the reason I play jazz piano. He knew many of the jazz musicians, and he really zeroed in on jazz for me."

Throughout his career Taylor has played with practically everyone, from Coleman Hawkins to Dizzy Gillespie, but just as important as his playing and composing has been to him, so, too, has his role as an advocate for the music. In the 1960s, while working full-time at night with his trio, he hosted a radio show on New York station, WLIB. Getting into radio, and, later, TV "helped me a great deal with saying what I wanted to say musically as well as being able to bring the music to a large amount of people," Taylor said. "I was very proud of the fact that I was on WLIB in New York. It really gave me an opportunity to be able to articulate the things that I believed in and (acted as) a pedestal to kind of shout to other people, 'Hey, this is what we're about, this is what we're trying to do.' First on radio and then on television, I presented people who I believed in, people I liked. I was able to communicate what Tatum was about, what Ellington was about, and what some lesser known people who deserved that same kind of attention were about."

One pianist who Taylor feels hasn't gotten his due is the 90-year-old Hank Jones. "Hank Jones is one of the greatest pianists around, and people just kind of take him for granted," said Taylor. "He took the same thing I took from Art Tatum and did something totally different with it." Another favorite is Jimmy Jones, who was Sarah Vaughn's accompanist for many years. "Jimmy Jones was a wonderful arranger and a wonderful composer, as well as an exceptional pianist, and his name is nowhere in the history books. He was really the kind of person who was listened to by a lot of people because of how he played."

While at WLIB, Taylor helped found the Jazzmobile, which brought free jazz concerts to the inner city. "On the radio, I was saying a lot of things about the lack of jazz in the school system. I shot my mouth off so much that I got put on a couple of committees to help with education. A group was formed called the Harlem Cultural Council. We were so upset that music had been taken out of the school system, and we wanted to do something about it," he said. "One of the members of the committee had been to the World's Fair and pointed out that people were walking around listening to some free music. There was this little cart that had musicians on it. We went to a beer company. They gave us a float, and we did the first concert in Harlem; the first year, 1964, we had enough money for about 10 concerts."

Today, Jazzmobile presents concerts in New York City, Washington, D.C., Maryland, Virginia, New Jersey, Westchester County, New York, and in several cities in upstate New York. The concerts are funded by the New York State Council on the Arts, the New York City Department of Cultural Affairs, New York State Senator David A. Pater, Assemblyman Keith Wright, and several corporate sponsors.

Taylor, who received a doctorate in music education from the University of Massachusetts in 1975, served as musical director and bandleader for the David Frost Show on television from 1969 to 1972. He hosted a weekly radio program called "Jazz Alive!" on National Public Radio in the late 1970s and early 1980s, and then moved back to television in 1980, profiling jazz musicians on "CBS Sunday Morning" for several years. In 1994 he became artistic advisor for jazz at the Kennedy Center for the Performing Arts, and in the summer of 2008 he was busy planning and programming Kennedy Center Jazz for the 2008–2009 season. "The thing I'm trying to do is to really focus on the many people who are either from Washington, D.C., or who lived in Washington or who came into focus in D.C.," he said. "We just want to make Washington a little prouder than it has been in the past of its jazz heritage. For instance, my friend. Ramsey Lewis, got his first big hit ("The In Crowd") at the Bohemian Caverns in Washington, D.C."

Taylor also pointed to the impact guitarist Charlie Byrd had on the D.C. jazz scene. "In a town that is divided racially, Charlie Byrd (who was white) was right in the black community playing gigs. He was the owner of a nightclub in Washington, and he had wonderful people playing there. People have forgotten that and other things that have happened from time to time," he explained. "We've got Duke Ellington, but we've got a whole lot of other folks, too." Byrd, who died in 1999 at the age of 74, founded the jazz club, Blues Alley. He was perhaps best known for having helped popularize the bossa nova with tenor saxophonist Stan Getz.

Just as Taylor was a protégé of Art Tatum, he is today a mentor for a 19-year-old pianist named Christian Sands. Sands is so good, Taylor said, that "Last season, I took him to the Kennedy Center with me. I let him close my set. I played with the trio, and then I got off the stage and let him do the last thing. I'm really proud of him. This year, I'm going to ask him to play my 'Suite for Jazz Piano and Orchestra.' It's one of my most difficult pieces; he's just learning it." In 2006, Taylor introduced Sands during a set at Kennedy Center's KC's Jazz Club. Mike Joyce, writing in the *Washington Post*, on September 25, 2006, described the 17-year-old as being "preternaturally gifted, as a rendering of Herbie Hancock's 'Maiden Voyage' swiftly demonstrated. Sands is even now capable of playing with veterans such as Jackson and Harper with quick-witted assurance."

On his own Web site, (www.christiansandsmusic.com), Sands lamented the declining popularity of some of the older jazz styles. "It's unfortunate," he wrote, "that the older styles, like stride, are starting to drift away." Taylor said he tries to get younger musicians "to learn as much about the history of the music as they can. That's where the line is drawn. They have to know the history, relate to the history, work through the history, and realize they are part of the continuum."

While the possibility of sitting in at places such as Minton's Playhouse no longer exists, Taylor said there *are* still opportunities for younger jazz pianists to learn from their elders. "I'm delighted by how many good teachers there are among jazz musicians," he said. "We're trying to bring in younger people. Dave Brubeck has things he's doing; Ramsey Lewis has things he's doing. We're trying to do the kind of thing that was done for us. That kind of camaraderie still exists to some extent—not to the extent we would like it to be, but more than one would think."

If there is one thing for which Billy Taylor would like to be remembered, it is helping people recognize that "jazz is America's classical music and that we have done the world a service by creating this music." On a personal level, "I've written a lot of music that I hope is going to be continued to be played in different contexts, such things as 'If You Really Are Concerned, Then Show It' and my signature, 'I Wish I Knew How It Feels To Be Free.'"

But what Taylor enjoys the most is "when someone comes up to me and says, 'Man I saw you at the Hickory House, and I've been listening to you ever since.' That's wonderful. People like that really felt something that I shared with them. If I could touch somebody like that, wow!"

Index

"A Flower Is a Lonesome Thing," 127
"Ain't Misbehavin', " 15–17
Airmen of Note, 183
Alden, Howard: on Joe Venuti, 29–30; on Joe Williams, 46–48; on Frank Wess, 46–48; on Sean Penn, 46–48
Alexander, Willard, 133–134, 174
Allen, Woody, 163, 167
American Tap Dance Foundation, 6
Anastasio, Paul, on Joe Venuti, 33, 35–36
Apollo Bar, 132
Arbors Records, 34, 167
Armstrong, Louis, 2, 8, 54, 141–142, 143
Armstrong, Louis All-Stars, 143–145, 147–148, 152
"A Simple Thank You," 125–126
Astaire, Fred, 51, 54
"A Train," 121

Bach, Johann Sebastian, 104
Baker, Chet, 156, 161
Balaban, Red, 148–149
Barnet, Charlie, 70–71
Baron, Art, on Norris Turney, Duke's Men, 121–122
Baroque counterpoint, 160
Barrett, Dan, 31
Barron, Kenny, 97–99
Baruch College, 83–84

Basie, Count: 18–19; as remembered by Joe Williams, Frank Wess, Buck Clayton, and Thad Jones, 37–41; Butch Miles, 42–43; T. S. Galloway, 43–45; 46, 50; Earle Warren, 66–68; 91
Basin Street East, 148
Bavan, Yolande, 134
Bebop, 34, 95–96, 99, 101, 148, 191
Beefsteak Charlie's, 84
Beiderbecke, Bix, 2, 8, 24, 137
Bennett, Tony, 7
Berry, Chu, 118
Berigan, Bunny, 149, 150
Bickford Theatre, 34, 86, 151
"Big, Sweet 'n Blues," 120
Bigard, Barney, 142
Billboard, 173
Billy Berg's, 142–143
Birdland, 104, 147, 176
"Birdland," 139
Blanton, Jimmy, 126
Blue Note (East St. Louis, IL), 189
'Blue Rondo ala Turk," 113
Blues Alley, 196
Bolden, Rick, 189
Book Nook, 1
Borderline Jazz Band, 151
Bossa Nova, 99, 101
Bridgewater, Cecil, on Dizzy Gillespie, 101–102

Brown, Cleo, 114
Brubeck, Dave: 60th birthday, "Take Five," Paul Desmond, 111–113; current projects and recordings, 113–114; future of jazz, 115; 197
Bryson, Jeanie: on Dizzy Gillespie, 97–98; jazz singing, 98
Butterfield, Paul, 189
Byrd, Charlie, 196

Café Society, 90
Callaway, Ann Hampton, 128–129
Calloway, Cab, 52; 76–77; 81, 83, 86
Capone, Al, 79–81
Carmichael, Hoagy: early life, 1–2; career highlights, 3; movie career, 4; death, 5; remembered by Hoagy Bix, 5–7; Bill Charlap, 7–9; Bob Wilber, 9–10;
Carmichael, Hoagy Bix, on Hoagy Carmichael, 5–7
Carnegie Hall, 1
Carney, Harry, 123
Carroll, Barbara, on Art Tatum, 61–63
Cary, Dick, 142
Catlett, Big Sid, 142
Cavett, Dick, 23
Centenary College, 31
"Centerpiece," 137
Charlap, Bill: on Hoagy Carmichael, 7–9; on Gerry Mulligan, 158–159; 167; on Dick Hyman, 168
Charles, Ray, 3, 187–188
Chattaway, Jay, 173
"Checkered Hat," 120
Chiaroscuro Records, 25
Chicago, University of, 146
Chicago Cotton Club, 79
Chicago Tribune, 128
Chilliwack, British Columbia, 151
"Chinese Blues," 146
Cincinnati's Cotton Club, 118
Clapton, Eric, 190–191
Clayton, Buck, on Count Basie, 39, 41
Clemente, Rio, on mixing classical and jazz, 106–107
Cleveland, Grover, Middle School, 75

Club Plantation, 142
Coalhouse Walker, 182
Cocomama, 125
Coleman, Bill, 96
Collective improvisation, 148
Columbia 30th, 85
Columbus Youth Orchestra, 21
Condon, Eddie, 148
Condon's, Eddie, 10, 20, 32, 84–85, 149
Conover, Willis, 60
Contemporary Productions, 177, 179
Cookery, The 90, 93
Coppola, Johnny, 125
"Cotton Club" (movie), 12
Cowell, Stanley: early influences, 181–182; "Ragtime," 182; education, 183; career, 184; educator, composer, 185–186
Cranshaw, Bob, 99
Crosby, Bing, 25, 145
Crawford, Hank, 187, 190
Cricket, 4
Cuscuna, Michael, 55

Dance, Stanley, 89
Davern, Kenny, 10, 170–171
Davis, Miles, 155
Debussy, Claude, 30
Decca Records, 4
"Delaware River Suite," 109–110
DeRosa, Rich, on Gerry Mulligan, 160–162
Desmond, Paul, 112–113
Dickenson, Vic, 84–85
DiBlasio, Denis, on Maynard Ferguson, 177–179
Diehl, Aaron, influenced by Fats Waller, Todd Stoll, Wynton Marsalis, Hank Jones 20–21; Art Tatum, 63–64
Dixieland, 2, 55, 171
"DIZZY: The Man and the Music," 100
Downbeat Readers Poll, 100
"Dreamland," 169
Dryden, Ken, 109
Duke's Men, 120–122

Index

Ebony Magazine, 127
"Echoes of Spring," 121
Eigsti, Taylor, 114
Eldridge, Roy, 85
Ellington, Duke, 12, 62–63, 117, 119–120, 122–127, 129, 194–195
Ellington, Duke, Foundation, 124
Ellington, Duke, Legacy Band, 124–125
Ellington, Duke, Society, 122
Ellington, Edward Kennedy III, 124
Ellington, Mercer, 119, 122–124
Embers, The 52, 54–55, 61–62
Emerson's, 75
"Essentially Ellington" competition, 10
Evans, Bill, 167
Evans, Gil, 187, 191–192
"Everyday I Have the Blues," 40
"Evolution of the Blues," 135
"Explorations," 139

"Fantasy," 108–109
Far and Away, 75
"Fats Lives," 19
Ferguson, Maynard: rock-fusion success, 173–175; death, 175; Don Sebesky, 175–176; Randy Sandke, 176–177; Denis DiBlasio, 177–178; Steve Schankman, 179
Ferguson, Maynard, Institute of Jazz Studies, 178
52nd Street, 52, 73
Fig Tree, 94
Finckel, Edward, 28
Fischer, Bill and Helen, 35
Folds, Chuck, on Fats Waller, 15–16
"Four Brothers," 133
Friars Inn, 2
Fryer, Jim, 151

Galloway, T. S.: on Count Basie, 43–45; current activities, 45
Garfunkel, Art, 167
Garner, Erroll, 59, 167
Gaslight Square, 189
Gensel, Rev. John, 75, 123
Getz, Stan, 97

Gibson, Dick, 10, 24
Gillespie, Dizzy: bebop, 95–96; Western Hemisphere unification, 96; European migration, 96; death, 96; Jeanie Bryson, 97–99; John Lee, 99–100; Cecil Bridgewater, 101–102
Gillespie, Dizzy, Alumni All-Stars, 100
"Gillespie, Dizzy, Songbook," 98
Giordano, Vince, 171
"Girl Talk," 129
Glaser, Joe, 143
Gleason, Jackie, 82–83
"Gonna Fly Now," 173
Goodman, Benny: remembered by Bob Wilber, 12–13; Derek Smith, 87; Ed Polcer, 149–150
Goodman, Benny, Centennial, 12
Gordon, Dexter, 125
Gordon, Wycliffe, 124
Granz, Norman, 60, 72
Greenberger, David, 105
Greer, Sonny, 15
Guinan's Playground, 25
Gully Low Jazz Band, 146

Haase, John Edward, 6
Haig, The, 155
Hall, Barrie Lee, 121
Hamilton, Chico, 156
Hammer, Jan, 166
Hammond, John, on Helen Humes, 90, 92–93
Hampton, Lionel, 69, 149–150
Hanna, Roland, on Art Tatum, 57–58, 60
Harlem Cultural Council, 195
Harper, Winard, 194, 197
Hawkins, Coleman, 72, 118, 137–138
Hawkins, Willie, 58
Heath Brothers, 182, 184
"Hello Dolly," 145
Henderson, Luther, on Fats Waller, 15–16
Hendricks, Jon: early years, 131–133; Lambert, Hendricks & Ross, 133–135; 1960s–1980s, 135–136; LH&R Redux, 136–137;

University of Toledo, 137–138; David Leonhardt, 138–139; Janis Siegel, 139–140
Hentoff, Nat, 33
"Here and Gone," 190, 192
Herman, Diana, 27
Hickory House, 61–62, 197
"High Society," 145
Hines, Earl "Fatha," 152, 160
Hines, Gregory, 7, 100
Hines, Pamela Koslow, 7
Hinton, Milt: with Cab Calloway, 76–77, 81–82; early life, 77–80; with Eddie South, 80–81; Jackie Gleason, 82; "The Judge," 83; death, 83; Warren Vache, 84–85; Derek Smith, 85–87
Hinton, Mona, 76–77, 84, 86
"History of Jazz," 167
Hodges, Johnny, 119–120, 127
Holiday, Judy, 160
Honeywell, Rice, 152
Horn, Alisa, 107–109, 160
Horn, Dr. Howard, 107
Horn, Shirley, 7, 9
Houston Symphony, 108
Humes, Helen: on Earle Warren, 65; comeback, 89–90, 92–93; early life, 91; with Count Basie, 91–92; singing style, 92; Earle Warren, 91–93; death, 93; Norman Simmons, 93; David Leonhardt, 94
Hyman, Dick: on Fats Waller, 16–17; Stan Kurtis, 27–28; on Art Tatum, 57, 59–61; on George Shearing, 105–106; Woody Allen, 163–164; 1980s, 164–166; 2008, 166–167; influences, 167; Randy Sandke, 167–168; Bill Charlap, 168; Dan Levinson, 168–171

"I Can't Get Started," 150
"If You Really Are Concerned, Then Show It," 197
"I Get Along Without You Very Well," 7
Indiana, University of, 1, 5–6
"Indian Summer," 113
Inventions Trio, 107–110, 160
Iowa, University of, 189
"I Waited For You," 102
"I Wish I Knew How It Feels to Be Free," 197

Jackson, Chip, 194, 197
Jamahl, Ahmad, 19
"Jazz Alive," 196
Jazz at Lincoln Center, 12, 68, 123
Jazz for Moderns, 134
Jazz in July, 167
Jazz in the Wood, 178
Jazzmobile, 101, 195
Jazz Standard, 136
Jim & Andy's, 84
Johnson, George, 2
Johnson, J. J., 186
Johnson, James P., 16, 18
Jones, Hank, 21, 58–59; on Art Tatum, 195
Jones, Jimmy, 195
Jones, Jo, 194
Jones, Jonah: musical philosophy, 51; early life, 52; 52nd Street, 52; Cab Calloway, 52–53; The Embers, 53; "On the Street Where You Live," 53–54; Fred Astaire, 54; death, 55; Warren Vache, 55–56
Jones, Kendrick, 7
Jones, Randy, 113
Jones, Thad: on Count Basie, 38–40; death, 41; Marvin Stamm, 48
Jones, Thad-Mel Lewis Band, 48–50
Joplin, Scott, 15–16
Josephson, Barney, on Helen Humes, 90, 93
Joyce, Mike, 196
"Jubilee," 8
"Judge, The," 83
"Jumpin' at the Woodside," 137
JVC Jazz Festival, 167

Kaminsky, Max, 146
Kennedy Center for the Performing Arts, 196
Kenton, Stan, 173, 175–177

Index

Kerr, Brooks, on Fats Waller, 17–18
Keystone Korner, 125
Kilgore, Becky, 31
King, Albert, 189
"King Porter Stomp," 150
Kirk, Andy, 70–71
Kirkwood High School, 188
Krupa, Gene, 13
Kurtis, Stan, on Joe Venuti, 27–29
Kyle, Billy, 114

Lambert, Dave, 133, 135, 140
Lambert, Hendricks & Ross, 131, 134–136, 139
Lang, Eddie, 23, 26. *See also* Salvatore Massaro
Lee, John, on Dizzy Gillespie, 99–100
Left Bank, 29–30
Leonhardt, David: on Helen Humes, 94; on Jon Hendricks, 138–139
"Let It Come to You," 114
Levinson, Dan, 150; on Dick Hyman, 168–171
Lewis, John, 58
Lewis, Ramsey, 196–197
LH&R Redux, 136
Lienhard, Noreen Grey: on Howard McGhee, 74–75; on Joe Morello, 75–76
London Philharmonic, 103
"Lonesome Boulevard," 162
"Louis Armstrong Plays W. C. Handy," 149
Louisville, 89, 91–92, 94, 138
"Let It Come to You," 114
"Lucky to Be Me," 114
"Lullaby of Birdland," 104
Lytle, Douglas, 113
Lyttleton, Humphrey, 123

Makowicz, Adam, on Art Tatum, 57, 59–60
Manhattan Transfer, 139–140
Manilow, Barry, 159
Malone, Russell, 128
Marable, Fate, 142
Marsalis, Wynton, 3, 12, 21, 123–124
Marty's, 46

Maslin, Janet, 164
Massachusetts, University of, 196
Mason Gross School of the Arts, 185
Massaro, Salvatore, 23, 26. *See also* Eddie Lang
Masso, George, 5
Maxwell, Jimmy, 127
Mayhew, Virginia, on Duke Ellington Legacy Band, 124–125, 126
Mays, Bill: Inventions Trio, 107–110; Gerry Mulligan, 159–160
McFerrin, Bobby, 138–139
McGhee, Howard, early life, 69; Lionel Hampton, 69; Andy Kirk, 70–71; Charlie Barnet, 70–71; Coleman Hawkins, Jazz at the Philharmonic, 72; drugs, alcohol, 52nd Street, 73; death, 74; Noreen Grey Lienhard, 75–76
McPartland, Marian: on Art Tatum, 61; Hickory House, 62; Duke Ellington, 62–63; "Piano Jazz," 63
McRae, Carmen, 98, 127
Melody Maker Magazine, 135
Metuchen High School, 98
Michael's Pub, 25–27, 30
Michigan, University of, 109–110, 183
Miles, Butch, on Count Basie, 41–43
Militello, Bobby, 113
Miller, Dick, 169
Mingus, Charles, 186
Minton's Playhouse, 193, 197
Modern Jazz Quartet, 110
Monmouth-evergreen, 9
"Mooch, The," 11
"Mood Indigo," 12
"Moon Mist," 127
Moore, Al, 142
Moore, Michael, 113
Morath, Max, 168
Morello, Joe, 75–76, 112
Mosaic Records, 55
"Mozart Jazz," 21
Mulligan, Gerry: mixing genres, 108; big band, 155; pianoless quartet, 155–156; 1980s, 156; television, American popular song, 157; death, 158; Bill Charlap, 158–159;

Bill Mays, 159–160; Rich DeRosa, 160–162
Murphy, Mark, 128
"Muskrat Ramble," 143

Nashville, 157
National Jazz Museum in Harlem, 127
"Nearness of You," 7, 9
Nelson, Willie, 3, 190
New Jersey City University, 161
New Jersey Jazz Society, 13, 149
Newman, David "Fathead," 139
New Orleans, 144
Newport Jazz Festival, 1, 113, 155
Newsweek Magazine, 4, 54
Nichols, Red, 3
"9:20 Special," 68
92nd Street Y, 106, 165, 167, 170
North Carolina Jazz Festival, 31
North Central College, 45
Northwestern University, 108–110, 189
Norvo, Red, 149–150, 156

Oberlin College, 183
Okeh Records, 91
Oliver, King, 2, 146
Oliver, Shelly, 139
Olivia's Patio, 61,
O'Neal, Hank, on Joe Venuti, 25–27
"The One and Only," 175
"On the Street Where You Live," 53–54
Onyx, The, 52
"Ooo Baba Leba," 92
O'Quinn, Keith, 159
Oregon Festival of American Music, 168
Original Dixieland Jazz Band, 168, 170
Orlov Choir, 114
Ostwald, David: on Louis Armstrong, 145–148; Gully Low Jazz Band, 147
Overton, Hall, 28

Parish, Mitchell, 1
Parker, Charlie, 96, 132–133
Penn, Sean, 47–48

"People to People," 114
Peplowski, Ken, 31, 150
Peterson, Oscar, 87, 129
Peyroux, Madeleine, 169
Philadelphia Museum of Art, 185
Philbin, Peter, 173
"Piano Jazz," 63
"Pictures at an Exhibition," 185
Pillars, Jeter, 118
Pizzarelli, Bucky: on Joe Venuti, 23–24, 26–27; influence on Jonathan Russell, 31–32; influence on Aaron Weinstein, 34
Polcer, Ed: influence on Jonathan Russell, 32; Louis Armstrong, 148–149; Benny Goodman, 149–150; Charlie Shavers, 150
"Prairie Home Companion," 30
Prince Georges Symphony Orchestra, 185
Providence Jazz Festival, 136
Public Broadcasting Service, 95, 114

Rachmaninoff, Sergei, 108–109, 137
"Radio Days," 164
Ragtime, 15–16, 182
Randalls Island Jazz Festival, 134
RCA, 17
Red Blazer Too, 147
Reed, Nancy, 124
Reeves, Dianne, 139
Reich, Howard, 128
Rich, Buddy, 43
Rimsky-Korsakov, 137
"Rite of Spring," 103
Riverboat Shufflers, 169
Rivkin, Gregory, on Louis Armstrong, 152–153
"Road Stories," 178
Rock fusion, 174
Rock 'n roll, 190
"Rocky," 173, 176
Rollins, Howard, 182
Roach, Max, 100–102, 184
Roney, Wallace, 190–191
Rosengarden, Bobby, 86
Ross, Annie, 133, 135
Rovinsky, Anton, 166

Rowan University, 177
Rowles, Jimmy, 24, 26
Rubin, Vanessa, 128–129
"Runnin' Ragged," 28–29
Russell, Jonathan: on Joe Venuti, 31; Bucky Pizzarelli, 31–32; Andy Stein, 32; Ed Polcer, 32
Russia, 114
Russian National Orchestra, 113
Ryan's, Jimmy, 20, 146

"St. Louis Blues," 192
Saint Peter's Church, 74, 123
Samba, 99, 101
Sanborn, David: influence of Hank Crawford, 187–188; early life, 188–189; Warner Brothers years, 190; "Here and Gone," 190–191; influence of Gil Evans, 191–192
Sandke, Randy: on Dick Hyman, 167–168; Maynard Ferguson, 176–177
Sands, Christian, 196–197
Sargent, Ed, 177
"Saxophone Dreams," 108–109
"Scent of a Woman," 29
Schaap, Phil, on Earle Warren, 68
Schankman, Steve, on Maynard Ferguson, 177, 179
Schuller, Gunther, 121, 186
Scott, Cynthia, 128
Sebesky, Don: mixing classical and jazz, 103, 110; Maynard Ferguson, 175–176
Shane, Mark: on Fats Waller, 18–20; Art Tatum, 64
Shavers, Charlie, 51, 56, 150
Shaw, Artie, 3, 12
Shaw, Arvell: with Duke's Men, 121; Louis Armstrong years, 141–145
Shearing, Ellie, 105
Shearing, George: mixing classical and jazz, 103–104; height of popularity, 104; serious fall, 105; Dick Hyman, 105–106
Shields, Larry, 170
Siegel, Janis, on Jon Hendricks, 139–140
Simmons, Norman: on Helen Humes, 93; Duke Ellington Legacy Band, 124; Duke Ellington, 126–127; vocalists, 127–129; Oscar Peterson, 129
Sims, Zoot, on Joe Venuti, 23, 26
Sinatra, Frank, 13
"Sing a Song of Basie," 133
Singleton, Zutty, 81
Skonberg, Bria, on Louis Armstrong, 151–152
"Sleepy Time Down South," 148
Smith, Derek: on Milt Hinton, 85–86; Oscar Peterson, 87; Benny Goodman, 87
Smith, Stuff, 28, 52
Smith, Willie, 118–119
Smith, Willie "the Lion," 16, 194
"So Hard to Forget," 34
"Song for Strayhorn," 162
"Sophisticated Ladies," 123
"Sophisticated Lady," 123
Soprano Summit, 11
South, Eddie, 80–81, 194
Southern California, University of, 183
Stamm, Marvin: influence of Thad Jones-Mel Lewis band, 48–50; trumpet heroes, 49–50; Inventions Trio, 107–110, 160
"Stardust" (the song), 1, 5, 9
"Stardust" (Bill Charlap CD), 7–8
Staton, Dakota, 127
Stein, Andy: on Joe Venuti, 29–30; Jonathan Russell, 32
Stewart, Buddy, 133
Stewart, Slam, 58
Stoll, Todd, 21
Stravinsky, Igor, 103
Strayhorn, Billy, 124, 127
Stribling, Simon, 151
Stride, 16, 18
"Sugar Babies," 165
"Suite for Jazz Piano and Orchestra," 196
Sullivan, Maxine, 10
Sumner High School, 142
Sunset Teen Town, 188
Sweet Basil's, 122, 124

Swing, 16, 191
"Swing That Music," 146

"Take Five," 111
"Talkin' 'Bout Love," 184
"Tango Project, The," 29
Tap City, 6
Tap dancing, 6–7
Tate, Buddy, 137–138
Tatum, Art: influence of Fats Waller, 18–19; influence on other pianists, 57–62; Dick Hyman, 165, 167; Stanley Cowell, 181; Billy Taylor, 193–195
Taylor, Billy: influence of Fats Waller and Art Tatum, early years, 193; major influences, 194; teaching, current trio, 194; radio and TV, 195–196; Jazzmobile, 195; Kennedy Center for the Performing Arts, 196; protégé, 196–197; legacy, 197
Taylor, Creed, 133
Teagarden, Jack, 142, 144
Telarc, 113
Temperley, Joe: on Earle Warren, 68; Duke's Men, 121; Duke Ellington, 122; Norris Turney, 123; Jazz at Lincoln Center, 123–124
Terra Nova, 97
Teschemacher, Frank, 170
"Thank You Uncle Edward," 124
Third stream movement, 186
Three Deuces, 60, 193
"Time Out," 111
"To Have and Have Not," 4
Toledo, Ohio, 131–132, 181
Toledo Symphony, 137, 185–186
Toledo, University of, 132, 137
Toledo Youth Symphony, 182
"Tonight Show, The," 86–87
Torme, Mel, 157
Touhill Performing Arts Center, 177
Townsend, A. B., 118
Trumbauer, Frankie, 137–138
Turney, Norris: early years, 117–119; Ellington years, 119–120; Newport Jazz All-Stars, 120; Duke's Men, 120–123; death, 120; Art Baron, 121–122; Joe Temperley, 123

Vache, Warren: on Jonah Jones, 55–56; Milt Hinton, 84
Venuti, Joe: practical jokes, 23–25; early years, 23; Bing Crosby, 25; Michael's Pub, 25–27; 1960s comeback, 26; Stan Kurtis, 27–29; Andy Stein, 29–30; Jonathan Russell, 31; Aaron Weinstein, 33, 35; Paul Anastasio, 35–36
Village Vanguard, 48
Violin capo, 33
"Vocalese," 139–140

"Walk on the Water," 155–156
Waller, Fats: influence on other pianists, 15–21; Chuck Folds, 15–16; "Ain't Misbehavin,'" 15–18; Luther Henderson, 15–16, 18; Dick Hyman, 16–17; Billy Taylor, 16–17; Brooks Kerr, 17–18; Count Basie, 18; Mark Shane, 18–20; Aaron Diehl, 20–21; Art Tatum, 57–58
Warren, Earle, passing for white, 65–67; early life, 66; Basie years, 66–67; death, 67; Phil Schaap, 68; Joe Temperley, 68; Helen Humes, 65, 91, 93
Washington, D.C., 196
Washington Post, 129
Webster, Ben: influence on Virginia Mayhew, 125; with Norman Simmons, 127; discovery of Billy Taylor, 193–194
Weinstein, Aaron: on Joe Venuti; 33–35, Bucky Pizzarelli, 35
Weiss, Eve: on Jonathan Russell, 31–32
Wendell Phillips High School, 79
Wess, Frank: on Count Basie, 37, 39–40; with Butch Miles, 41; with Howard Alden, 46–47
West, George, 183
West End Café, 65
Whiteman, Paul, 24

Whitlock, Bob, 156
Wichita State University, 183
Wiest, Gil, on Joe Venuti, 25–26, 30
Wilber, Bob: on Hoagy Carmichael, 9–10; Soprano Summit, 10–12; Benny Goodman, 12–13
Wilder, Alec, 5
William Paterson University, 160, 194
Williams, Joe: on Count Basie, 37–38, 40; death, 41; with Howard Alden, 46
Wilmington, Ohio, 117

Wilson, Philip, 189
Wilson, Teddy: influence on Mark Shane, 18–19; Joe Venuti prank, 24–25; influence on Dick Hyman, 163, 166–167
Wisconsin, University of Symphony Orchestra, 103
WLIB, 195

Young, Lester, 137–138
Youngman, Henny, 24
"Zelig," 163

About the Author

SANFORD JOSEPHSON is Director of Marketing and Public Relations for the Matheny Medical and Educational Center, a special hospital and educational facility for children and adults with medically complex developmental disabilities located in Peapack, New Jersey. He is a member of the New Jersey Jazz Society and Jazz Journalists Association and is also on the Board of Directors of the Healthcare Planning & Marketing Society of New Jersey and the New Jersey Advertising Club. He holds a Bachelor of Journalism degree from the University of Missouri and lives in West Orange, New Jersey, with his wife, Linda; son, Dan; and dog, Onyx. His other son, Alex, lives in New York City.

L
394
.J67
2009